MIKE BARTLETT

Mike Bartlett is a multi-award-winning playwright and screenwriter.

His plays include *Scandaltown* (Lyric Hammersmith, London); *The 47th* (The Old Vic, London/Sonia Friedman Productions/Annapurna Theatre); *Mrs Delgado* (Arts at the Old Fire Station, Oxford/Theatre Royal Bath/Oxford Playhouse), *Snowflake* (Arts at the Old Fire Station/Kiln Theatre, London); *Albion* (Almeida Theatre, London, also filmed for BBC Four); *Wild* (Hampstead Theatre, London); *Game* (Almeida); *King Charles III* (Almeida/West End/Broadway; Critics' Circle Award for Best New Play, Olivier Award for Best New Play, Tony Award nomination for Best Play); *An Intervention* (Paines Plough/Watford Palace Theatre); *Bull* (Sheffield Theatres/Young Vic Theatre, London/Off-Broadway; TMA Best New Play Award, Olivier Award for Outstanding Achievement in an Affiliate Theatre); *Medea* (Glasgow Citizens/Headlong/Watford Palace); *Chariots of Fire* (based on the film; Hampstead/West End); *13* (National Theatre, London); *Love, Love, Love* (Paines Plough/Plymouth Drum/Royal Court Theatre, London; TMA Best New Play Award); *Earthquakes in London* (Headlong/National Theatre); *Cock* (Royal Court/Off-Broadway, Olivier Award for Outstanding Achievement in an Affiliate Theatre; revived in the West End); *Artefacts* (nabokov/Bush Theatre, London); *Contractions* and *My Child* (Royal Court).

Bartlett has received BAFTA nominations for his television series *The Town* (ITV) and *Doctor Foster* (Drama Republic/BBC), for which he won Outstanding Newcomer for British Television Writing at the British Screenwriters' Awards 2016. His screen adaptation of his play *King Charles III* aired on BBC Two in 2017, and his other television series include *Life* (BBC One), *Sticks and Stones* and *Trauma* (both Tall Story Pictures for ITV), and *Press* (Lookout Point for BBC One). Bartlett has also written several plays for radio, winning the Writers' Guild Tinniswood and Imison Prizes for *Not Talking*.

**Other Playwright Collections
from Nick Hern Books**

Jez Butterworth

Alexi Kaye Campbell

Caryl Churchill

Ayub Khan Din

David Edgar

Kevin Elyot

Ella Hickson

Robert Holman

Stephen Jeffreys

Lucy Kirkwood

Liz Lochhead

Kenneth Lonergan

Conor McPherson

Mark O'Rowe

Jack Thorne

debbie tucker green

Enda Walsh

Steve Waters

Nicholas Wright

Mike Bartlett

PLAYS: TWO

Earthquakes in London
Love, Love, Love
The Enemy
13
Medea

Introduced by the author

NICK HERN BOOKS
London
www.nickhernbooks.co.uk

A Nick Hern Book

Mike Bartlett Plays: Two first published in Great Britain as a paperback original in 2022 by Nick Hern Books Limited, The Glasshouse, 49a Goldhawk Road, London W12 8QP

All plays were first published in single editions by Methuen Drama, an imprint of Bloomsbury Publishing Plc, and are reproduced with permission, with the exception of *The Enemy* which was first published by Nick Hern Books Ltd in the collection *Decade*

Extracts in *Earthquakes in London*: 'Deep Water' written by B. Gibbons/G. Barrow/A. Utley. Published by Chrysalis Music Ltd © 2008. Used by permission. All rights reserved; 'Rebellion (Lies)' words and music by Howard Bilerman, Win Butler, Régine Chassagne, Tim Kingsbury and Richard R. Parry © 2005, reproduced by permission of EMI Music Publishing Ltd, London W8 5SW

Cover image: iStock.com/tiero

Typeset by Nick Hern Books, London
Printed in Great Britain by Mimeo Ltd, Huntingdon, Cambridgeshire PE29 6XX

ISBN 978 1 83904 057 3

Contents

Introduction
Mike Bartlett

I've resisted writing introductions to plays. Like many writers, I felt that I didn't want to explain or add anything beyond that which could be found in the texts themselves. However, while reading during the recent Covid-19 lockdown, I realised that what I did find interesting was accounts of how writers *found* their plays – where the ideas had come from. So that's what I'll try to recount here, if it's of interest. If it is *not* of interest, which is a distinct possibility, then I fully suggest skipping this introduction and carrying straight on to the plays. They will hopefully speak for themselves, and if they don't, then probably no introduction will help anyway.

* * *

Between 2007 and 2009 I'd had my first three plays professionally produced: *My Child*, *Artefacts* and *Contractions*. These were all short, with a few central characters, and very condensed in their form. However, over this period, I had also written a number of other plays, which were different in two ways: firstly, they were longer, with many characters and a greater scale, and secondly, they were, quite rightly, rejected. Perhaps if I describe them briefly, you might see why. One was called *A Thin Place Between Heaven and Earth*, about Prince William visiting the Scottish island of Iona after university before embarking on his royal destiny. Another, *Fortress*, a three-act, confusing piece of work about a British soldier returning from war suffering from PTSD and with an unreliable memory (leading sadly to an equally unreliable plot). There were a couple of others, neither any better. I clearly had a desire to write bigger ideas on a larger scale but had not yet found a way of making a play like that coherent. Looking back I think I was writing on instinct alone, without enough planning, and while this creative energy could sustain smaller ideas, larger concepts seemed to fall apart across the greater duration of the play, the ideas and interest failing to hold.

However, in 2009 Ben Power, then Associate Director of Headlong Theatre, approached me to consider writing a play for them. Along with Rupert Goold, the Artistic Director, Headlong had established a reputation for new plays and revivals that felt contemporary, large-scale and asked intelligent, relevant questions of the audience. They had just produced Lucy Prebble's astonishing play *Enron*, which I'd loved. In our first meeting, Ben said they wanted me to write a play where I did all the things I thought I wasn't allowed to do: a large cast, with a big idea, on a grand scale. He asked if I had any ideas. As often when asked this in meetings, the truthful answer was no. But I knew that I wanted to write about climate change next, in some form, and I had at least thought of a title for it: *Earthquakes in London*. I didn't know anything else at that point, but they decided it was enough to commission me and I went off to make a start. I decided that perhaps the solution to writing it successfully would be to plan it carefully, and also to take every new idea I had for the next six months, and throw it into the plan. To just assume it was part of this larger whole.

Therefore, as I read about James Lovelock, I thought about an old man isolated in Scotland, towards the end of his life. I had an image of a character walking through London, a well-meaning but compromised politician in a moment of crisis, a young disempowered activist. I visited the shop Liberty for the first time and had a crisis of my own, related to the prices – that went in. As well as an older woman in the park, being nostalgic. All these small ideas were brought together through the emerging plan, and eventually I delivered a very long and unwieldy play to Headlong. Ben and Rupert loved the ambition at least, and we got to work redrafting. Around that time, Nick Hytner, Artistic Director of the National Theatre, saw my play *Cock* at the Royal Court Theatre, and asked to read the next thing I was working on. I sent him *Earthquakes* and with the speed of response playwrights only dream of, he called me three days later, said he loved it and wanted the National to produce it. Which they did, in the Cottesloe Theatre (now the Dorfman).

Looking at an early draft now, it's rough, but crucially, I had found the spirit and the metaphor of the play: the idea of a Weimar-style cabaret just before the end of days. Of living and dancing, shouting and making love *now* because our time is limited. And through all the gloom inevitable in the subject matter there are embers of hope: in the growing consciousness and love of the sisters for each other. In the humour and compassion throughout. And ultimately in the young girl who decides at the very end to walk to London, with a message that the world needs to hear – that she demands a future. One of the aspects that Ben and Rupert pushed on, and which I think about a lot with larger plays now, is that one should focus less on what you want the play to *say*, and more about finding the right questions to ask. For *Earthquakes*, these were questions of legacy, responsibility and freedom, in the face of super-charged capitalism and an advancing and devastating climate emergency.

I also wanted the form of the play to reflect the excess of the culture. I wrote in a stage direction, it should be 'too much', and in the astonishing production Rupert gave it, designed by Miriam Buether, it really was. A catwalk flowed through the auditorium. Audience members could stand around it, or sit at barstools right up to it. At either end were two small end-on stages. Scenes flowed and overlapped, with big musical numbers, light, mess, chaos, costume, physicality and joy. Rupert, as a director – in a very charming way – pushes on every aspect of the production to be better. And that was true of the script. It was reshaped, added to, cut down and rewritten throughout the whole process. A very different experience to the careful respect for the 'text' that I had experienced at the Royal Court, and it wouldn't help every play, but this huge patchwork needed wrestling into shape, and the whole thing eventually began to cohere into one story. The phenomenal playwright Tony Kushner once wrote in an essay about some plays being like lasagne – everything thrown in and bursting, on the brink of collapse, but just about holding their shape. This felt like that.

* * *

Around the same time I was writing *Earthquakes*, I was also under commission to Paines Plough, a new-writing touring theatre company run by James Grieve and George Perrin, who with their previous company – nabokov – had produced *Artefacts* (my first professional commission). They had commissioned a follow-up play from me with the Drum in Plymouth. As this was going to be a touring show they had sheepishly asked that it have a small cast and minimal production requirements. I reassured them that the request was completely reasonable. A writer was a grown-up professional, and should be able to tailor a play to the circumstances of the production. I went on to claim that these restrictions could even inspire creativity. However, despite the talk, once again I had no ideas and the commission was now overdue. I had a spare week and I had to write something.

So each day I went to the café near my flat in Kilburn and wrote all day. Then I brought it home where my girlfriend generously read it. On the Monday I can't remember what I wrote but she said it was pretty bad. On the Tuesday I wrote a dialogue about students in Plymouth talking, contrasted with their parents having a conversation about them. This was also deemed, correctly, not great, but there was a theme emerging, about baby boomer parents sitting in big houses with lots of money, and their children, unable to buy, or even rent, a house and struggling. On the Wednesday I thought about where those parents had started. What were their opportunities and dreams, and how had those been disappointed, or corrupted? So I began to write about when those parents met, in the heady sixties. By the end of the Wednesday I had written a large chunk of the first act, with Henry and Kenneth waiting for Sandra, and this time, fortunately, my girlfriend liked it and wanted to know what happened next. Unfortunately, when it was eventually finished, it had a cast of five, was over two hours long and needed three completely different sets. Despite this complete failure to adhere to the brief, James Grieve, who was to both produce and direct it, read it overnight, declared he didn't know quite how they would do it but he loved it and knew that they *would* do it. (This was a characteristic reaction from James. His work with George Perrin commissioning and producing a whole generation of playwrights and artists is incredible – but that deserves a book in itself.) Over the next two years the play toured the country twice, before transferring to the Royal Court. I loved how, in performance, particularly in the final act, the play would split the audience between the boomers and their children. When Rose asked her parents to buy her a house, the older members of the audience laughed at this as a self-satirising joke; their children, on the other hand, saw it as a completely sincere, outraged cry for justice that the whole play built towards.

* * *

For my generation, in Britain, 9/11 had been a pivotal and formative moment. We had grown up in an unusually stable decade, since 1989 and the fall of the Berlin Wall. Philosophers had declared history dead, New Labour had appeared to discover a way to have social justice and a thriving economy, and as technological development began to accelerate, with the internet and mobile phones, we naively and incautiously had every reason to believe that the world would continue to improve. For those privileged enough to benefit from all this, progress began almost to be taken for granted. Then the planes crashed into the towers. The first many of us knew about it was when we received a text message, as I did, that simply read 'Turn on the TV'. For me, once that news was on, everything else was cancelled, and I sat on the sofa that day and late into the night with some friends (I was in student accommodation in Leeds), all of us wondering if more planes would crash into other buildings the next day; if this was the start of a Third World War.

Ten years later, Headlong were creating a collaborative project, *Decade*, to mark the tenth anniversary of 9/11. They approached a number of writers to create short plays, which they would then curate into an evening of work. I had been evasive, unwilling to commit until I had a good idea, but they needed to know soon if I would be contributing. My current excuse to avoid writing it, in May 2011, was that I was in Mexico, for the opening of a production of my play *Cock*. But the truth was, away from my daily routine, I had time to write, I just couldn't think of a useful contribution that would somehow deal with the enormity of the event, or indeed, channel the feelings of tragedy on the day. Having pretty much given up, I checked my phone, and 9/11 was in the news again. Osama bin Laden had, after ten years, been tracked down and killed by American Special Forces. I began thinking about who the actual man was, that fired the fatal shot. How his name would almost certainly be withheld, but how it would utterly change his life, and one day probably be revealed.

Then I remembered a form for an unfinished play I had experimented with years before, where each line was only one or two syllables long. It made for an edgy, staccato rhythm, indicating characters that were a mix of very confident, and yet mistrustful of each other. Mixing this content and form I wrote the play, now called *The Enemy*, and sent it off. Rupert, and the project's co-director, Robert Icke, liked it, and the almost athletic challenge it set for the actors. The final production was fluid and moving, a real mix of voices and opinions, and as emotional as it was intellectual. And if perhaps it failed to completely capture the effect of 9/11 on our culture, that was an accurate reflection of our continued trauma and confusion about it.

* * *

In 2011, I had been asked to become writer-in-residence at the National Theatre. It was a unique opportunity to be part of the work of the building, and in response I wanted to try to write something that could go on in the same year – that could speak to the moment. Therefore, together with Ben Power, who was now an associate director at the National, we devised a plan where an autumn slot would be kept free in the Olivier until the summer. If at that point I had written something of worth, then we'd do it. If not, they would do a revival instead. My starting point was religion. I'm not religious myself, but it's been a big part of my life. My grandfather was a United Reformed Church minister and a conscientious objector in the Second World War, my mother is a lay-preacher, and I took an A level in Religious Studies. Despite never being a believer, I have always been fascinated by its centrality to culture, politics and identity. By 2011 this subject had, probably charged by 9/11, become a major point of public discussion. Sam Harris, Christopher Hitchens, Richard Dawkins and Daniel Dennett had a number of debates on the subject. Hitchens had written a bestselling book *God Is Not Great*. At the same time, there felt like a growing dissatisfaction amongst younger adults. Disappointed by the government, especially the Conservative/Liberal Democrat coalition, they were protesting again, beginning to demand a voice, in a way that had not been seen perhaps since the sixties. I attempted to write about this in a magical-realist mode, as a movement of young people drawn to London through following a central figure, an everyman called John. I wanted to explore the power of this, but also its danger. Who gets to play God? The play was called *13* and reading it now I notice I got a number of things right – there was indeed an energetic desire of a new generation to question the assumptions of their parents and grandparents, to fight for social justice and to defy the, by then commonplace, doctrine that the youth were apathetic and lazy. But I got the battleground wrong. In the play it was physical public protest and religion. It became clear only a few years after *13* was produced that a new generation's revolution would in fact be about social media, identity and equality.

The production was staged in the Olivier Theatre, directed by Thea Sharrock and with an astounding design by Tom Scutt. As with *Earthquakes*, I wrote and rewrote almost continuously, taking notes all the time. I wanted the form to be like a meeting – a religious gathering – for which the curved amphitheatre of the Olivier seemed appropriate. But this time something didn't quite cohere. Whether the play needed more work in terms of form, whether it was the theatre or the production, or some combination, I'm not sure. The individual parts of the play – performances, design and some of the scenes – landed fantastically, but as a whole the 'lasagne' proved a little too close to collapse.

While the play just about worked with audiences, critically it was a failure. I was lucky that I had other projects to move on to, but at that point my biggest profile work had been a failure, and it certainly knocked my confidence. It has never been professionally revived, but what has been amazing to see has been the number and quality of drama-school productions of the play; it is quite possibly my most performed play in terms of amateur productions. Something in the play speaks to the generation it was written about, and they perform it with passion and authenticity. And that's a lesson that I remember now – that plays (and in fact television) can travel and grow, and that although a lot of the attention is on the opening night of the first production, that may not end up being where the work finds the most meaning. If they have some value culturally, the core ideas can sustain and grow over time.

* * *

...which links very well to *Medea*. This play arose because I wanted to direct something again. I had originally wanted to become a director after university and had assisted on a few productions. But I was a keen but rather insecure presence at the time, and those are not ideal qualities in a director. Instead I found myself writing and had been happy doing so ever since. But while working on *Earthquakes in London*, Rupert Goold had spotted that I was drawn to all the aspects of production and suggested I read some of the Greek classics. Medea stood out for me – a central character that demanded to be heard, but who one could not entirely pin down. Of all the classic plays I read, it felt the most contemporary and pressing. Once I had started to work on it, I read about women who had been betrayed, who were then driven to extreme actions, taking matters into their own hands in pursuit of a justice they were lacking. My approach was to try to be very faithful to Euripides in terms of intention and form, but to translate it in terms of time and setting, to see what I discovered. The element that came to define the character was Medea's denial to be simply the victim. She refused to be pitied or left behind. Instead, alone, she demanded justice for her children, and also for herself.

Once I had a draft we began to move towards production, where I would be directing my own work for the first time. Rachael Stirling came in to read; seemingly effortlessly she found the meeting point of the classic and the contemporary. She was witty, scathing and deeply moving. The design, by Ruari Murchison, was a cross-section of a new-build house. The production opened at the Citizens Theatre in Glasgow, a perfect setting with its history of making classic plays both avant-garde and accessible. It then toured, and as it was performed, we found two things. Firstly, that when school groups came, young women in particular would love it, especially the character of Medea herself. Afterwards they would wait in groups in the foyer for Rachael to appear and then descend on her, keen to show their appreciation but also to carry on the conversation the play had started.

The other thing we noticed was that we couldn't get the end right – with the murder of the child. We reconceived it when we toured to

Watford and it was better, but still it felt like an anticlimax. The horrific gesture just didn't feel right. In that final action Medea somehow became pathetic rather than glorious, her 'justice' psychopathic rather than meaningful. She became deeply unusual rather than an everywoman. Perhaps this was because that's the one element of the play that *is* very unusual. Women everywhere are betrayed and dismissed, but they hardly ever kill their children. Perhaps the audience sensed that. *Medea* came third in the original play competition that it was part of in Ancient Greece. The first and second place plays are lost unfortunately, but I wonder now if this has always been the problem? After a thrilling and truthful unfolding of the drama, the ending was (uncharacteristically for Euripides) unbelievable, and the reason? Not the deus ex machina or the flying chariot in the sky, but because at the last moment she had become a misogynist trope – simply, the mad woman. I was learning the very difficult balance with adaptation: one must be faithful, but critical too.

Despite the troublesome finale, the play did well. It never transferred to London as perhaps we hoped, but in the audience when it came to Watford were Roanna Benn and Jude Liknaitzky, who worked for a television production company called Drama Republic. A discussion of the play led us to wonder what a television drama version might be. Two years later we were making *Doctor Foster*, a BBC One drama series about another woman betrayed by her husband. This followed the outline of *Medea* relatively closely, but now I had learnt my lesson. Instead of killing her son, she protects him, and the series ended with her, not unscathed, but in triumph. The final episode was watched by ten million people. As I write now in 2022, the series has been broadcast in over twenty countries and remade in ten different versions across the world. So, again, the opening night in Glasgow in 2012 wasn't the complete meaning. It was only the beginning of an idea, or maybe a character, starting to find its audience.

A Note on Collaborators

Writing this introduction it's noticeable that the same names come up repeatedly. This is reflective of one of the most enjoyable things about theatre: collaboration, and one of its best aspects as a community: support. Some of this collaboration and support came from more senior established figures in the industry – over this period, for me: Rupert Goold and Nicholas Hytner. Other collaboration and support came from peers, who I'd known since we were starting out in our twenties: James Grieve, Thea Sharrock and

Ben Power. But the thing that has linked them has been a sustained belief in me as a writer, not just for the next play, but in the long run. I never had the feeling from any of them that the relationship with me was contingent on the success of the next play. And that's how one feels able to take risks. I felt that if I made a mistake, either artistically or politically, that they would stand behind what we had made together. The Royal Court Theatre used to have a policy – perhaps they still do – where for new writers they wanted to encourage, they would sit them down on the morning of the press night, and offer them the next commission – deliberately *before* the critics had given their verdict. This is a precise illustration of the support I'm talking about.

Looking back, all of the plays in this book were created in a time before the culture was revolutionised by social media specifically constructed to encourage division. Making work now, if we are to keep pushing on both form and content, the 'right to fail' is much more important than ever, and in theatre the most important aspect of this is the right to fail *together*. We need to support each other (and that means me, as a writer, supporting the director as well) on seemingly ridiculous, unfashionable and genuinely countercultural projects, in the hope that they might spark something new, or at least of value, to the audience.

EARTHQUAKES IN LONDON

Acknowledgements

This play could not have been written without Elyse Dodgson, Jonathan Donahoe, Clare Lizzimore, Rachel Wagstaff, Duncan Macmillan, the cast and production team, and particularly Miriam Buether, Rupert Goold and Ben Power.

Earthquakes in London was first performed in the Cottesloe auditorium of the National Theatre, London, on 4 August 2010, in a co-production with Headlong Theatre. The cast was as follows:

MARINA	Lucy May Barker
TOM	Gary Carr
YOUNG ROBERT	Brian Ferguson
GRACE / RECEPTIONIST /	
JOGGER	Polly Frame
SIMON / ROY	Tom Godwin
COLIN	Tom Goodman-Hill
CARTER	Michael Gould
PETER	Bryony Hannah
BUSINESSMAN / DANIEL /	
STUDENT / DR HARRIS /	
BARMAN	Clive Hayward
MRS ANDREWS	Anne Lacey
SUPERMARKET WORKER /	
YOUNG MAN / TIM	Syrus Lowe
FREYA	Anna Madeley
ROBERT	Bill Paterson
JASMINE	Jessica Raine
CASEY / OLD WOMAN / SALLY /	
LIBERTY	Maggie Service
STEVE	Geoffrey Streatfeild
SARAH	Lia Williams

All other parts played by members of the company

This version of *Earthquakes in London* was first performed at Theatre Royal Plymouth on 22 September 2011, in a Headlong Theatre and National Theatre co-production. The cast was as follows:

SIMON / ROY / WWII OFFICER /	
POLAR BEAR / PASSERBY 1	Ben Addis
UNDERSTUDY /	
DANCE CAPTAIN	Sam Archer
PETER / MOTHER	Helen Cripps
TOM	Kurt Egyiawan

4

COLIN	Seán Gleeson
MARINA / MOTHER / UNDERSTUDY	Siubhan Harrison
STEVE	John Hollingworth
MRS ANDREWS	Maggie McCourt
SARAH	Tracy-Ann Oberman
JASMINE	Lucy Phelps
SUPERMARKET WORKER / CASEY / OLD WOMAN / LIBERTY / MOTHER	Nicola Sangster
CARTER / DANIEL / POLICE OFFICER / DR HARRIS	Gyuri Sarossy
ROBERT	Paul Shelley
GRACE / RECEPTIONIST / MOTHER / JOGGER	Natalie Thomas
YOUNG ROBERT / BUSINESS MAN / SCAMMER / BAR MAN / DR TIM / PASSERBY 2	Joseph Thompson
FREYA	Leah Whitaker

All other parts played by members of the company

Director	Rupert Goold
Set Designer	Miriam Buether
Costume Designer	Katrina Lindsay
Lighting Designer	Howard Harrison
Music	Alex Baranowski
Projection Designer	Jon Driscoll
Choreographer	Scott Ambler
Sound Designer	Gregory Clarke
Company Voice Work	Jeannette Nelson

Project developed for Headlong by Ben Power

The creative team for the 2011 UK tour included
Director: Caroline Steinbeis; Associate Set Designer: Lucy Sierra;
Lighting Designer: Tim Mitchell; Associate Projection Designer:
Emily Harding; Associate Projection Designer: Paul Kenah;
Associate Choreographer: Steve Kirkham

Characters

ROBERT
GRACE
FREYA
STEVE
TOM
JASMINE
SARAH
SIMON
COLIN
SUPERMARKET WORKER
CASEY
PETER
CARTER
BUSINESSMAN
MANY STUDENTS
MRS ANDREWS
DANIEL
ROY
MANY SWIMMERS
FIFTEEN MOTHERS WITH
    PUSHCHAIRS
OLD WOMAN
SECOND WORLD WAR
    OFFICER
YOUNG MAN
BARMAN
MARYNA
RECEPTIONIST
TIM
WAITER
SMOKING MAN
COMMUTERS
STREET PERFORMERS
TOURISTS
MARCHING BAND
NEWSPAPER SELLER
USHERS

LIBERTY
BUSKER
POLAR BEAR
EMILY
JOGGER
PASSERBY 1
PASSERBY 2
OTHER PASSERSBY
POLICE OFFICER
NARRATOR
YOUNG ROBERT
DR HARRIS
NURSE

6

Note on the Text

The play is presented using as much set, props and costume as possible. The stage should overflow with scenery, sound, backdrops, lighting, projection, etc. Everything is represented. It is too much. The play is about excess, and we should feel that.

Scenes crash into each other impolitely. They overflow, overlap. The production should always seem at risk of descending into chaos but never actually do so.

(/) means the next speech begins at that point.

(–) means the next line interrupts.

(…) at the end of a speech means it trails off. On its own it indicates a pressure, expectation or desire to speak.

A line with no full stop at the end indicates that the next speech follows on immediately.

A speech with no written dialogue indicates a character deliberately remaining silent.

Blank space between speeches in the dialogue indicates a silence equal to the length of the space.

ACT ONE

Prologue

1968.

Cambridge.

Black and white.

ROBERT CRANNOCK *is on a date with* GRACE, *who is wearing a floral dress. They eat.* ROBERT *is awkward.*

'In the Year 2525' by Zager and Evans is playing quietly in the background.

ROBERT	I'm sorry if the letter was too forward.
GRACE	I liked the letter.
ROBERT	I got carried away, I'm sorry.
GRACE	No.
ROBERT	I didn't mean to sound strange.
GRACE	It wasn't strange. I liked it. Love letters in my pigeonhole. Romantic.
	What do you do Robert? I mean I know you're a postgraduate, but what exactly do you... do.
ROBERT	I'm doing a doctorate
GRACE	In?
ROBERT	Atmospheric conditions on other planets.
GRACE	Other planets? Like aliens?
ROBERT	Some of the work is to do with finding life yes.
GRACE	Like *Star Trek*?
ROBERT	Well... NASA are interested, so –
GRACE	You're joking?
ROBERT	No.

GRACE   NASA?

ROBERT   Yes.

GRACE   Wow.

ROBERT   Yes.

GRACE   Wow.

ROBERT   …

GRACE   So how do you know? If there's life?

ROBERT   Well, all life gives off excretions of some kind. Gases, minerals.

GRACE   We all give off gases?

ROBERT   Yes.

GRACE   Even girls?

ROBERT   And all these gases –

GRACE   Have you / researched this?

ROBERT   These excretions, from all of these creatures, they go up into the atmosphere, and you can imagine globally they would make quite a difference to its composition. So it follows that if we could accurately measure the composition of gases in the atmosphere of a planet like Mars, we could tell whether there was life.

GRACE   And?

ROBERT   What?

GRACE   Is there?

ROBERT   We don't know.

GRACE   Oh.

ROBERT   We haven't done it yet. Not enough funding.

GRACE   Right.

ROBERT   But as I say, NASA are interested.

             She looks at him.

GRACE   So all the time, every bit of life, animals, humans, everything, change the environment.

ROBERT   Yes. You are right now. The room is entirely different
              because you're in it.

GRACE   You think?

ROBERT   Doesn't matter what I think. The atmosphere in this
              room is completely dependent on how much you
              move, whether you talk, if you've got a cold, how hot
              you are.

GRACE   How hot I am?

ROBERT   Yes. Imagine if we all came in with a fever, the room
              would get much hotter, and then we'd get even hotter
              as a result, our fever would get worse and the room
              would become hotter in turn and so on and so on,
              upwards and upwards.

GRACE   Hotter and hotter.

ROBERT   Exactly.

              Sorry. Wittering on. Supposed to be a date. I like your
              dress.

GRACE   No, Robert, you've raised a very important question.

ROBERT   Really?

GRACE   Yes. How hot do you think I am?

ROBERT   How hot?

GRACE   How. Hot.

ROBERT   Well…

              Oh.

              You mean…

GRACE   It's 1968. It's the summer. We're young. We can do
              what we want.

              ROBERT *puts his hand on her forehead. She smiles.*

ROBERT   Above average.

              She smiles, and puts her hand on his head.

GRACE   Boiling.

              So what happens now?

They look at each other.

'In the Year 2525' plays – gets louder. Cross-fade scene and music into –

Proper Coffee

2010

A kettle boils.

FREYA*'s face isolated.* FREYA *is singing along to a cover of 'In the Year 2525' by Venice Beat feat. Tess Timony. She loves it.*

She sings some more.

We see FREYA. *She is pregnant, wearing a man's shirt and making coffee in her kitchen. She has headphones on and dances. A television is on as well.*

Everything is done in rhythm – coffee, kettle… sugar… eats a spoonful herself.

We see STEVE *in the shower. He hears her singing – bemused.*

STEVE   Freya?

            FREYA *keeps on singing.*

            Freya!

            FREYA *sings a bit more then takes a headphone out. The music is quieter.*

FREYA   What?

STEVE   What are you / singing?

FREYA   I'm making coffee.

STEVE   What?

FREYA   Coffee! Do you want some?

STEVE   Proper coffee?

FREYA   It's always proper coffee.

STEVE   What?

FREYA   It's always proper coffee, / no one drinks *instant*.

STEVE   What? I can't hear you! I'm in the shower! I can't hear you!

               FREYA *dances. The music becomes background in Starbucks.*

               TOM *enters and offers a coffee to* JASMINE.

TOM   Full-fat latte, two brown sugars, cream on top.

JASMINE   Do I know you?

TOM   Thought I'd do the honours. Did I get it right?

JASMINE   Don't know yet what does Rohypnol taste of?

               She drinks a bit.

TOM   It was Marxist Criticism. We used to get our coffees at the same time. I liked the look of you, remembered your order. I'm Tom.

JASMINE   Yeah.

TOM   You're Jasmine. I heard you dropped out.

JASMINE   I had an argument with my lecturer.

TOM   What about?

JASMINE   Charles Dickens. Do you smoke?

TOM   I can.

JASMINE   Good boy.

               SARAH *appears, talking to* SIMON, *her assistant.*

SARAH   There aren't any plants.

JASMINE   Let's take this outside.

SARAH   Department of climate change, massive office and nothing's green. It's ridiculous.

SIMON   It's on the list. And you need to put something in for Casey. She's leaving.

SARAH   Who's Casey?

SIMON   By the wallchart? Under the window?

SARAH   Why's she going? Pregnant?

SIMON   Redundant.

SARAH   Oh.

SIMON   She's the chaff we talked about.

SARAH   Right. Yes. Right.

SIMON   Smaller government. That's your policy.

SARAH   Not *my* policy Simon.

SIMON   I'm afraid so, minister. What sort of plants do you
           want? You mean flowers?

SARAH   Here's ten for Casey. No not flowers. Flowers are dead.
           We want some life round here. Get a cheese plant.
           They still have those?

           FREYA *continues to make the coffee. Watches
           television at the same time.*

           COLIN *is in a supermarket and approaches a young
           assistant.*

COLIN   Excuse me.

SARAH   They had them in the eighties.

COLIN   I'm looking for a guava.

S. WORKER A what?

COLIN   A guava.

S. WORKER What's that?

COLIN   It's a vegetable.

S. WORKER Right.

COLIN   Possibly a fruit.

S. WORKER Vegetables and shit are over there.

COLIN   I'm sorry?

S. WORKER Vegetables and fruit and all that are over there.

COLIN   I know but I've looked and I can't find it.

S. WORKER   Probably don't have it then.

COLIN   Probably.

S. WORKER   Yeah.

COLIN   Can you check?

S. WORKER   Chhh.

> SUPERMARKET WORKER *goes off to check. Still the music in the background.* JASMINE *and* TOM *are smoking outside.*

JASMINE   He's sat there opposite me, I said I'm not being funny but if you want two thousand words by Monday you can whistle, I have to *work* weekends, different for you *Gary*, fucking baby boomers, get your grant, got your degree then don't pay for your kids. So he says 'Do you have financial difficulties Jasmine?' and I'm like 'Gary. We all have financial difficulties, read the fucking papers.' Then he suddenly goes red, shouts that I'm 'thick as corrugated shit' whatever that means and says I only got in here because of who my sister is, so I lost it completely, threw a bookshelf at him.

TOM   A bookshelf?

JASMINE   It was *Bleak House* that got him in the eye, hardback so he had to go to hospital. They said I was a menace, attacking my lecturer with a weapon, I said something about the power of the written word and that was it. Out.

TOM   You don't look like a menace.

JASMINE   I am, Tom.

> SUPERMARKET WORKER *comes back.*

S. WORKER   Is this it?

JASMINE   I'm a natural fucking disaster.

COLIN   How should I know? I don't know what a guava is. You tell me.

S. WORKER   Yeah. This is it.

COLIN   You're sure?

S. WORKER   Yes.

COLIN   Positive? Because this is important. I want you to
               understand that if I get home and this isn't a guava I'm
               in big trouble. So it follows that if I get home and this
               isn't a guava *you're* in big trouble, yes?

               He reads her badge.

               …Sue. You're in big trouble if this isn't a guava Sue.
               So.

               You're sure?

S. WORKER Candice said it was and she's good with fruit.

COLIN   Right, thanks.

               STEVE *enters with his suitcase, just as* FREYA,
               dancing, throws his coffee across the kitchen. STEVE
               jumps out the way. FREYA *takes her headphones off.*

FREYA   Didn't mean to do that. Oops.

STEVE   Oops.

               STEVE *smiles and grabs a cloth instantly to mop it up.*

FREYA   I can make another.

STEVE   No, I have to go really, sorry…

FREYA   Don't be sorry.

STEVE   Sorry I'm going at all.

FREYA   Don't be – we need work, money, especially now, in
               the current climate, the way things are, that's what you
               say.

STEVE   And it's only three days so –

FREYA   Exactly. It's only three days so –

STEVE   And you'll call me if anything –

FREYA   Yes I'll call you if anything but nothing will nothing
               does nothing happens you know how it is round here
               these days.

STEVE   I meant the baby.

FREYA   Oh right the baby, well of course / the *baby*

STEVE   You've got the number of / the hospital.

FREYA   There was a programme on TV they're detecting
             something in the ground.

STEVE   / Freya?

FREYA   They think something might – What? Yes I've got the
             number of the hospital. It's on the cupboard where you
             put it.

STEVE   On the fridge.

FREYA   On the fridge exactly. Are you sure you don't want any
             of this coffee? It's fair trade, kind of fruity, I like it.

STEVE   I have to go – but you'll be alright?

FREYA   The building might collapse while you're away.

STEVE   Freya –

FREYA   This is what I was trying to tell you. They said there's
             going to be an earthquake.

STEVE   There's not.

FREYA   There is.

STEVE   Not here.

FREYA   Right here, yes, they've detected tremors. It was on
             television. Do you fancy my sister?

STEVE   What?

FREYA   Not Sarah, obviously. Obviously not her. The other
             one. Jasmine.

STEVE   No – Freya where does this / come from?

FREYA   Why not? She's pretty.

STEVE   She's nineteen.

FREYA   Exactly. Thin, good-looking, bet she's good in bed. Of
             course you like her, you've had that thought. I used to
             look like that when we first met, I found some
             photographs, but what happened? Look at me now, fat
             and red like a massive blood clot or something. No
             wonder you don't want sex with me any more. You
             should give her a call I'm serious I really am.

             They look at each other. He moves closer, hugs her.

STEVE   I don't think you're a massive blood clot.

FREYA   Or something, I'm definitely something.

STEVE   I wanted sex with you last night as it happens.

FREYA   I can't I can't not with this, it's like it's watching.

STEVE   I love you.

             He kisses her tummy.

             You too. I'll call when I get in.

FREYA   I'm a bit lost at the moment, Steve, really. Don't go.

             A moment.

STEVE   Just three days. That's all. It's not as bad as you think.
             Never is.

FREYA   Oh. Okay. Good.

             *He kisses her again and leaves. As the door shuts,
             FREYA jumps and the walls shake a little. She's
             scared. As TOM and JASMINE talk, FREYA looks
             around her, then produces a packet of cigarettes and
             lights one.*

TOM   So your sister's famous?

JASMINE   My older sister is. Not in a good way. She's a
             politician. I didn't get in here because of my sister, I
             got in *despite* her, they *hate* her here.

TOM   What does she do?

JASMINE   When my mum died, my dad was a mess, so my sister
             looked after us but she was awful at it, really bad,
             because she's got absolutely no heart. Totally cold.
             She's made of metal, like the Terminator or something.
             But worse. She's like Terminator 3.

             SARAH is giving a speech for her team.

             Yeah, she's Terminator 3.

SARAH   Hello! Hi. We're so sorry to be seeing... Casey... go,
             leave. Yes. And although of course I absolutely believe
             our new... policy of smaller government is the right
             one at this difficult time, it doesn't mean it's not a...

sadness... when it impacts on someone personally. Casey's been fantastic as part of the ministerial team, a real laugh, ever since I've been here I've noticed that she's so... *funny*. Anyway, Casey, we've had a whip-round and got you this.

SARAH *gives a gift bag to* CASEY. CASEY *looks inside*.

CASEY   A coffee machine.

SARAH   Yes.

CASEY   I've been here five years.

SARAH   Well it's quite a good one I –

CASEY   I don't drink coffee.

SARAH   You don't –

CASEY   Herbal tea.

SARAH   Oh.

CASEY   It's always been herbal tea.

SARAH   Right... well... someone hasn't done their research.

CASEY   Research? Didn't anybody *know*? Jesus. You have no idea. We don't need *less government*. Everything's getting worse, and you're cutting the support. It's what the Tories would do crisis or not, but I voted Lib Dem. I voted for you. And what good did it do?

               She looks around at everyone and gives the machine back.

               Put it on eBay. I'm leaving the country.

               SARAH *steps down, speaks to her aide*.

SARAH   Good idea. Get the car.

SIMON   You can't, you have a meeting in your office in three minutes.

SARAH   My stomach's rumbling.

SIMON   Here. Egg salad. Tesco Express. You can eat it on the way back.

*He gives her a horrible-looking sandwich. She just
stands for a moment. Exhausted.* FREYA *watches
scenes from a documentary about the planet. Tectonic
plates. Storms and hurricanes.*

Are you…?

Another moment.

Should I…

She looks up and snaps out of it.

SARAH   What? Egg? Perfect.

            SARAH *crams the sandwich into her mouth as she
            leaves.*

            There's a knock on FREYA's *door, she goes to answer it.*

            TOM *and* JASMINE *are going back inside.*

JASMINE   My sister's coming along tonight actually.

TOM   To what?

JASMINE   To what I do now. To my job. It's a bit political too.
            You could come along if you want. You'll be shocked.
            First time I've done it. It's *very* political Tom. Very in-
            your-face kind of political. You might not be able to
            cope. It might be all too – *political* for you. I've got a
            costume. So what do you think? Want to risk it?

            TOM *smiles.*

TOM   Yeah.

            FREYA *opens the door. It's* PETER, *a teenage boy
            with glasses in a grey hoodie.*

PETER   Alright miss. You busy?

FREYA   Peter. / What are you –

PETER   Is that whisky? You shouldn't be drinking if you're
            pregnant, we saw it on a video in Biology, Mr Greg
            showed it us yeah and it said if you drink your baby
            ends up disabled or something maybe it dies in you
            and they have to pull it out with tweezers. Can I come
            in? I'm not doing very good. I want your advice.

FREYA   How did you know where I live?

PETER   Went on the internet, put your name in, it's not difficult. Big bump you've got now. I need to talk. Can I come in?

FREYA   I might get into trouble.

PETER   Nah you can't be a paedophile cos you're a woman and the hood's not cos I want to cut you it's cos it's raining, come on miss it's fucking biblical out here pardon my mouth used to talk didn't we? I liked it when we talked but you only come into school two days a week and not even that now. You're not busy clearly, you're watching TV. Is your husband in?

FREYA   He's gone away.

PETER   His car's outside.

FREYA   He got a taxi to the airport.

PETER   Yeah not supposed to fly any more though are you? How long's he gone for then?

FREYA   Just a couple of days.

PETER   Bet you could do with the company then.

FREYA   No.

PETER   Bet you could though.

FREYA   Peter, you should go back to school.

PETER   No one visits you do they?

FREYA   ...

PETER   That's cos pregnant women are a bit of a pain. Sweaty and fat, stuck in the house, moaning and moaning, I don't think that miss, but most people do that's why they don't visit. But I'm here.

               I got you a flower.

               He holds out a flower. She looks at him.

FREYA   Thank you.

               She takes the flower. He enters.

SARAH *is having a meeting with* CARTER *in her office. She offers him a biscuit.*

CARTER   Thank you. It's wonderful to meet you at last. Been a year. Thought I'd done something wrong.

SARAH   I've been very busy.

CARTER   Well, better late than never. How are we doing?

SARAH   In two days' time, after concluding my review, I recommend to the PM.

CARTER   So I hear.

SARAH   And I thought you might want a heads-up, to give you time to formulate a public response.

CARTER   A heads-up. Lovely. A response to what?

SARAH   We're nice people, Mr Carter.

CARTER   I'm sure you are. Everyone's *nice* these days aren't they? Even me. I bought my son Adam a bike, for his birthday. Very expensive. He loved it. And what have you nice people got to offer us?

SARAH   I thought you might want to come on board with the decision now, rather than wasting time and effort fighting it.

CARTER   The decision.

SARAH   Yes.

           Another biscuit?

           He looks at her.

CARTER   Adam's learning quickly, he's six, he looked at his bike, and he said 'what's the bad news Dad?' He said you only buy me presents like this when there's bad news. He was right. His mother had run over the cat. This coalition government, whatever it is, you're supposed to be business friendly.

SARAH   We're very business / friendly, yes.

CARTER   So what do you mean, what are we talking?

SARAH   The Heathrow decision played very well for us, the public didn't want that third runway, they were pleased we got in, and stopped it, so now I'll be recommending a complete halt to expansion.

CARTER   Where?

SARAH   Everywhere.

CARTER *is surprised.*

CARTER   Look, Heathrow? Fine, I understand your position, you had to pull back, but it was assumed at the time, it was very strongly hoped, in fact, that in return, there would be balance.

SARAH   There isn't the need.

CARTER   We let Heathrow go, but we get Birmingham, Edinburgh, London City instead – Belfast – that was understood.

SARAH   It can't be justified environmentally.

CARTER   A few miles of concrete here and there, a couple of sheds, it's not the end of the world. Have you talked to your colleagues, because I can't see this being very popular.

SARAH   A definitive halt to expansion will make a huge impact.

CARTER   Only as a symbol.

SARAH   A symbol exactly. We have to be seen to be doing all we can to lower carbon emissions. We want to set an example.

CARTER *looks at her.*

CARTER   This is your big idea.

SARAH   If you like.

CARTER   You're a symbol yourself really aren't you Sarah? Can I call you Sarah? Bet you never thought you'd be in power at all, but hung parliament, green credentials and a famous father –

SARAH   My position in this government has nothing to do with my father.

CARTER   Everyone thinks it does.

SARAH   Then everyone is wrong.

CARTER   Touched a nerve.

SARAH   Not at all.

CARTER   You're upset.

SARAH   Do I look upset?

CARTER   The way you rub your fingers together like that yes.

She's surprised for a second, but look back at him.

SARAH   We're not short of airports. In two days I have a
            meeting and I will put the case very firmly. The Prime
            Minister will make a decision, and that will be it. We'll
            announce next week.

CARTER   You look tired.

SARAH   I work hard.

CARTER   I don't think it's work.

            CARTER takes a biscuit.

            Before tomorrow, I'll change your mind.

SARAH   Really?

            He passes the biscuits across.

CARTER   Yes.

            Biscuit?

            FREYA and PETER.

PETER   I like your posters, you into Hitchcock?

FREYA   They're my husband's.

PETER   And *Grand Theft A*uto. You play that a lot do you?

FREYA   That's his too.

PETER   I find it a bit violent myself. I don't think driving round
            killing people should be in computer games. There's
            one where you can rape a girl. That's a bit weird they
            allow that considering everything that's gone on.
            Coldplay album? Everyone's got a Coldplay album
            these days, saw them on TV at Glastonbury they were
            rather good. What's yours then?

FREYA   The books. I –

PETER   What are you reading at the moment?

FREYA   Late Victorian poetry. Peter –

PETER   That sounds really incredibly boring. Can I sit down? /
           Are you going to give me a whisky? What's this?

FREYA   Of course you can sit down. I don't know about a
           whisky –

PETER   Jees, you've been smoking as well, your baby's gonna
           be a fucking 'tato with what you're doing.

FREYA   Peter, what do / you want?!

PETER   What's the programme?

FREYA   They say there's going to be an earthquake.

PETER   Here?

FREYA   My husband laughed as well but it's what they –

PETER   No they're right, it's true. There's going to be a
           massive tremor, the day after tomorrow, a huge seismic
           event, right in the capital. Things'll seem very different
           after that.

           She looks at him. Shocked – how could he know?

           My problem is I don't have any friends. Atomisation.
           It's very common in society today. Increasingly people
           use internet dating to make a connection and find
           companionship but I'm only fourteen so I prefer porn.
           I am allowed a whisky actually. It is legal. In the home.
           If you're fourteen. So.

FREYA   I'm not going to give you whisky.

PETER   I think you should though. Then we can talk properly.

           She considers.

FREYA   Why not?

           FREYA *goes to get* PETER *a drink.* PETER *sits down
           in the chair and relaxes as a* BUSINESSMAN *on a
           plane, next to* STEVE, *does the same.*

BUSINESSMAN   Remember when you could smoke?

STEVE   What?

BUSINESSMAN   Smoke. On planes.

STEVE   I see the ashtrays in the toilets. But I don't ever remember…

BUSINESSMAN   Fifteen years ago, you could go to the smoking section and smoke, didn't do any harm, no more planes went down, less than now, it was long before, you know… *terrorism* – maybe it's linked. Frustrated Arabs. All they want is a fag. Cos they can't drink can they? Could be linked. Joking of course. You going to Scotland on business is it?

STEVE   No.

BUSINESSMAN   Holiday then?

STEVE   It's personal.

BUSINESSMAN   Oh right, well. Keep your own.

Fair enough.

Up to you.

STEVE   I told my wife it's business.

BUSINESSMAN   Oh.

STEVE   But it isn't.

BUSINESSMAN   Ah.

Yes.

Well.

I know all about that.

STEVE   What?

BUSINESSMAN   That.

STEVE   No.

BUSINESSMAN   Sometimes I'm in LA, and I always let her know in advance, I say I won't, say it's not good for me, but I drop a cheeky email, turn up and we have the time of our lives. Keeps my marriage healthy. Keeps me trim she does. Carly.

STEVE   Carly?

BUSINESSMAN   Twenty-seven. Blonde. Tits. You know. Tits. Twenty-seven. LA. Sun. Tits. Blonde. Jesus. Says it all.

Why she goes for me I don't know, well I do, flash the money a bit, but life's short isn't it so you do what you have to, and my wife knows, sure she's done the same, my view is, if it keeps you trotting on, keeps you happy and the kids don't know then what's the harm? No you go for it mate. Full speed.

STEVE   It's not…

BUSINESSMAN   Sorry?

STEVE   It's not an affair.

BUSINESSMAN   Oh. But you let me go on about…

STEVE   I didn't feel I could stop you.

BUSINESSMAN   Always do this. Always end up talking to strangers on planes. Must be nervous I suppose.

STEVE   You fly a lot?

BUSINESSMAN   It's bad for you.

STEVE   Bad for you?

BUSINESSMAN   Of course, the more you fly, the greater chance you'll be in a crash. It's not natural.

If God had meant us to fly, he'd have his own airline.

Rumbling. Turbulence or possibly the sound of thunder. The lights flash.

'There She Goes, My Beautiful World' by Nick Cave & The Bad Seeds plays.

JASMINE *comes on dressed in branches and leaves.*

She holds a sign which says 'The wilful destruction of the rainforest'.

She dances.

She slowly peels off leaves and branches.

Eventually she is left with leaves in the vital places, à la Adam and Eve.

She picks up a sign:

'Originally, there were six million square miles of tropical rainforest'

Another sign:

'Only a third is left'

She raises her eyebrows.

There are cheers from the crowd.

Flirty eyes.

She picks up another sign.

It says: 'Don't leave the world naked'

As she goes, leaves fall from the ceiling.

FREYA *brings* PETER *his whisky then lights a cigarette.*

PETER   Hmm. I'm enjoying this. This is good, really good whisky. Did you buy it?

FREYA   Peter, if there's going to be an earthquake why aren't people scared?

PETER   I was in an earthquake once in Tokyo. Me and my parents were doing karaoke in this room –

FREYA   Can you answer / my question please.

PETER   – and the floor started moving and the walls tilted, shook a bit but not like you imagine, everything just went... drunk. Do you ever feel like that miss, stuck in this flat like you are, that the walls are moving and everything's becoming dangerous?

FREYA   All the time.

           FREYA *drinks the whisky.*

           But what can I do?

           TOM *and* JASMINE *are in a bar.*

TOM   Never seen a stripper before.

JASMINE   It wasn't stripping.

TOM   This is a strip club.

JASMINE   It's burlesque.

TOM   There's a man waving.

            COLIN *appears and waves. He's still carrying a carrier bag with the shopping.*

JASMINE   It's my sister's husband.

TOM   You invited your sister's husband?

JASMINE   I invited my sister. She said she'd come so I got *political*, thought she'd like it, but she texted at the last minute, said Colin was coming instead. Colin's been around since I was a kid, he was a banker, lost his job, now he's got time on his hands. Warning: He can be a bit –

COLIN   Brought my shopping!

JASMINE   I can see that.

COLIN   Bit weird. Well done!

JASMINE   You liked it?

COLIN   You can really dance.

JASMINE   Yeah.

COLIN   Haven't seen you perform since school.

TOM   And hasn't she grown?

COLIN   Well... I... I suppose so.

JASMINE   This is Tom.

COLIN   Oh right. Hello. Are you her latest...

TOM   Latest?

JASMINE   Thanks Colin.

TOM   Her *latest*?

COLIN   Squeeze.

JASMINE   Oh god.

TOM   We've only just met.

COLIN   Well the night's young.

JASMINE   For fuck's sake.

An awkward pause.

COLIN   I thought you made a very good point actually
             Jasmine.

TOM   There was a *point*?

JASMINE   The signs?

TOM   I wasn't really looking at the signs.

COLIN   The destruction of the rainforest.

TOM   So that's why you were dressed as a bush.

JASMINE   A tree.

TOM   Certainly looked like a bush from where I was sitting.

             Awkward.

COLIN   Do you want a drink either of you?

JASMINE   No thanks Colin.

TOM   Nah.

COLIN   Right.

             Well. Great to... see you. Jasmine.

             I should probably be going... got some milk needs the
             fridge, asap, don't want it to...

             Smell, but really...

             Well done.

             Good work!

JASMINE   Good to see you.

COLIN   Right. Bye.

             Pause. He goes.

JASMINE   God.

TOM   Actually I did read the signs.

JASMINE   Really.

TOM   Yeah, I'm quite into the environment. My family from
             before, they're Eritrean? and they –

JASMINE   Er sorry to interrupt you but I've had enough of the
            environment, hear about it all the fucking time, I only
            did it for my sister and she didn't even turn up. I'll do
            a Nazi one next week probably. They love Nazis. Have
            you got any pills? You look like the sort of person that
            carries drugs around in their pocket.

TOM   A sort of black person you mean?

JASMINE   A sort of careless person I mean, who leaves their coat
            lying around.

            She holds them up.

            Found them earlier.

            She opens the bag.

            FREYA *and* PETER.

FREYA   Shall I be mother?

PETER   I'm spinning.

FREYA   I know what you mean. I don't see anyone for days,
            the walls start shaking, so I think about going out but
            it's all shouting and dirt, so I stay in, but then... I've
            started singing, ever since I got back. When I sing I
            forget she's there.

PETER   Got back from where? Can I have a cigarette?

FREYA   I don't know what to do.

PETER   I didn't see anyone for three days once and got really
            paranoid my head was too big for my body, but it's not,
            is it? Is it? Is it? Cos earlier Gary Franks said I looked
            weird, chased me out of school said I was special
            needs.

FREYA   You are special needs.

PETER   Not in a bad way, not like those deaf kids you spend
            your time with.

FREYA   Don't say that.

PETER   I can do an impression of a deaf person.

FREYA   No.

PETER   I can, look, it's funny.

FREYA   Don't.

             PETER *moves closer to* FREYA – *threatening.*

PETER   If you don't give me a cigarette I'll do an impression
             of a deaf person.

FREYA   No!

             Don't

             Here.

             She throws him the cigarettes, PETER *grabs them and*
             stops. A throbbing beat has begun. FREYA*'s in pain.*

PETER   I know cigarettes are supposed to be bad for you but
             apparently if you give up within five years you're
             pretty much back to normal and I'm very young so I
             think I'll be fine miss.

FREYA   In my head.

PETER   Do you think that's right?

             Miss?

             Do you think I'm right about that?

             Miss?

             Miss?!

             The sound of a plane in the distance.

             A computer screen is projected.

             Someone is writing.

WRITING   'I feel that I would be right for the position of senior
             accounts manager as I am both strong...

             He deletes.

             strong both as a team player and a leader.

             Lights up on COLIN, *who is typing.*

             ...I have demonstrated this on many occasions, leading
             my team through many years of excellent service over
             the last ten years. Ten. Years...'

The cursor goes to Google. It types.

Student Girls Party Pictures.

As images appear the stage becomes full of students dancing in mini-skirts, boys with their tops off, grinding up against each other. Dance music gets slowly louder. In the middle are JASMINE *and* TOM. COLIN *stands up, watching, wanting to be involved.*

FREYA *is now faced away from* PETER, *leaning against a wall, a throbbing beat in her head.*

PETER *is trying to light the cigarette.*

PETER   As you know, I don't really like being outside, around lots of other people, but do you remember what you said miss? I'd stabbed Luke Reynolds with a compass, and got detention, and you said I couldn't just sit around feeling sorry for myself, I had to get off my arse and fucking do something. Find the good things.

FREYA   I don't think I used those words.

PETER   You did use those words. You definitely said fucking do something. I found the honesty quite bracing. You're one of the only people in my life who tells me the truth.

FREYA   So you think I should get up and –

PETER   I don't know, but what with the shaking

FREYA   I was imagining it, the walls can't –

PETER   I didn't mean the walls.

FREYA   Oh.

PETER   Your hands miss. Look.

Her hand is shaking.

You should pack a bag and get out and see what's going on. Find the good things. Before it's too late.

They look at each other. He lights the cigarette, smiles and relaxes.

FREYA *leaves. Determined.*

COLIN *watches them dancing. Enjoys it. He then changes the track on iTunes to Coldplay – 'Viva La Vida'. The students cheer – enjoying the cheese.*

SARAH *enters.*

SARAH   What's this?

COLIN   Coldplay

SARAH   You bought a Coldplay album?

COLIN   In Tesco on the way home yeah.

SARAH   That's the sort of thing boring middle-aged women do.

COLIN   Right.

SARAH   You don't look like a boring middle-aged woman.

COLIN   You do.

SARAH*'s tired of the bickering.*

SARAH   Found anything yet?

SARAH *goes into the kitchen where the shopping is laid out.* COLIN, *very quietly, sings at the computer.*

COLIN *shouts through to the kitchen.*

COLIN   You see this is the problem, that's always the first thing you ask, you get in and you don't kiss me, touch me, even look at me –

SARAH   What's this?

SARAH *is standing in the doorway holding a fruit.*

COLIN   A guava.

SARAH   No.

COLIN   Right.

SARAH   Get the ingredients. That's all I asked. It's not a guava Colin, it's a plum. Find a job. That's the problem. Not me. Find a fucking job. I'll make a sandwich.

SARAH *goes.* COLIN *keeps on singing to himself, restrained and shy, watching the students dance.*

STEVE *appears, trying to hide from the wind, and starts knocking on a door.* TOM *dances with*

JASMINE, they kiss passionately. COLIN watches. SARAH makes a sandwich. PETER goes to the CDs and looks at them.

SARAH goes to bed. The door is opened by MRS ANDREWS.

MRS ANDREWS   Yes?

STEVE   I'm here to see Mr Crannock.

MRS ANDREWS   Mr Crannock is in bed.

STEVE   I'm Steve Sullivan.
His daughter's husband?

MRS ANDREWS sighs.

MRS ANDREWS   Is he expecting you?

STEVE   No.

MRS ANDREWS   ...

STEVE   Please. It's very cold.

She lets him in. JASMINE and TOM dance. PETER chooses a CD and puts it on – the same Coldplay song. Listens. Mouths along. He likes it.

At the next chorus PETER sings loudly like a choirboy. COLIN still very quietly.

FREYA appears with a bag, hat and coat, ready to go out.

FREYA   You can put the heating on if you like. The switch is in the hall,

PETER   What are you doing?

FREYA   There's food in the fridge.

PETER   I didn't mean you should go now. It's raining cats and dogs out there, and you're pregnant, you probably shouldn't even stand up for too long, it might fall out or something.

FREYA   You can stay here. You won't steal anything will you?

PETER   Can I watch your DVDs?

FREYA   Yes.

PETER   Even the eighteens?

FREYA   If you want.

PETER   Can I drink your whisky and vodka?

FREYA   Whatever you like. You've got the place to yourself for a couple of days. Okay?

PETER   Okay.

FREYA   Right.

          Okay...

PETER   Are you going to be alright miss?

FREYA   She's kicking. Stop it!

          The good things.

          I can't stay here.

          FREYA opens the door and leaves.

          PETER stands up and sings.

          The students join in, singing the backing vocals.

          PETER sings, the students dance, and COLIN sits by his computer motionless and sad.

          Everyone sings as FREYA walks off into the night. Lights fade.

          Music in the dark. Music fades.

          End of Act One.

ACT TWO

Prologue

1973.

Technicolour.

ROBERT *and two businessmen,* DANIEL *and* ROY. ROY *is smoking.*

ROY	Good to see you. Have a seat.
ROBERT	Thanks.
ROY	How's the baby?
ROBERT	Oh, you –?
ROY	Daniel mentioned there was a baby. A baby girl.
ROBERT	Right, yes.
DANIEL	Wonderful.
ROY	Wonderful. And your wife?
ROBERT	Very happy obviously, well we both are.
ROY	Very happy. You both are.
DANIEL	Perfect.
ROY	Perfect. So. Robert. You're wondering why you're here? When does the main UK airline call in a Cambridge boffin like you? Well, our bods predict that in thirty years' time there'll be thousands of planes in the sky, flying people all over the place, which makes us happy of course, because there's a lot of money to be made.
ROBERT	Yes.
ROY	But there are increasing concerns.
DANIEL	Questions.
ROY	Sorry?

DANIEL	Questions, I think Roy.
ROY	Questions, exactly, about what the effect will be of all this air travel? With the emissions. Into the atmosphere.
ROBERT	Right.
ROY	People are starting to get worried.
DANIEL	Curious.
ROY	People are starting to become *curious* about what burning all that fuel might do. To the world.
DANIEL	The environment.
ROY	The *environment*. So we thought we'd get an expert in who could do a study.
	Look into your crystal ball and tell us what's going to happen. So what do you think? Is it possible?
ROBERT	Well. We'd... we'd need to model the world on a scale no one's done before. And... well... I don't want to be rude, but obviously you're hoping for a negative answer here aren't you?
DANIEL	No no.
ROY	A what?
DANIEL	He means do we want him to get us the result which says these fumes are doing no harm at all? Should he fix it?
ROY	Ah. No. Robert, you do your science and you tell us what you find.
	We won't interfere at all.
ROBERT	No interference.
DANIEL	None.
ROBERT	Right.
ROY	And this is only the first phase. If this project seems promising, we're authorised to commission further work, over the next ten years.
ROBERT	Really?

ROY   Absolutely. Because your results might not just be
           useful for us, but many similar organisations. The
           motor industry, oil companies. They would all be very
           interested in promising results.

ROBERT   What do you mean promising?

ROY   Results that seem to be useful.

DANIEL   Meaningful.

ROY   Right. *Meaningful.* I need a coffee.

ROBERT   Well I'm sure it's possible to achieve a certain clarity,
           but this is a very new subject, there's no real way of
           knowing how quantifiable in real terms the...

ROY   This would be the fee.

ROBERT   Right.

           He reads it.

           That's... Oh. Yes. That's good. I'm sure we could
           make a start with that.

ROY   No. Robert.

           That's not the budget.

           The project will have a separate budget.

           That's your fee.

           That's for you. To keep.

DANIEL   And remember there's potential for a good deal more
           of this to come. I would imagine someone like you, in
           your position, academic, young family. This could
           make a real difference.

ROBERT   Yes.

ROY   Why don't you take it away and have a good old think?

All the Mothers

The present.

Hampstead Heath – early morning. Birdsong.

FREYA *is sat by the pond.*

A number of male swimmers are in the ponds, swimming. They have similar swimming hats and swimming costumes. One by one they come and stand in the fresh morning air. Birds fly past, a clear blue sky.

FREYA *watches them for a while.*

One of the swimmers starts to play ukulele.

FREYA *starts singing along to 'Deep Water' by Portishead. The first swimmer is surprised, but interested. Three other swimmers stand in a line and act as backing singers.*

FREYA   I'm drifting in deep waters
                Alone with my self-doubting again
                I try not to struggle this time
                For I will weather the storm

                SARAH *gets to her desk, piled with papers. It's first thing, but she's exhausted – she sits down and makes a start.*

                JASMINE *sits on the end of the bed, waits, upset.*

                I gotta remember
                (Gotta remember)
                Don't fight it
                (Don't fight it)
                Even if I
                (Even if I
                Don't like it
                (Don't like it)
                Somehow turn me around
                (Somehow turn me around)

                No matter how far I drift
                Deep waters
                (Deep waters)
                Won't scare me tonight

                SARAH *picks up the phone.* FREYA*'s phone rings. The swimmers look annoyed with* FREYA.

TOM appears, and JASMINE goes off with him. The swimmers go off.

She answers.

SARAH   I missed your call.

FREYA   I thought we could meet up?

SARAH   I can hear birds.

FREYA   I'm on the heath.

SARAH   Hampstead Heath?

FREYA   Yeah, by the ponds. I packed a bag, left early.

SARAH   You don't live anywhere near Hampstead Heath.

FREYA   Very early. Apparently there's a view where you can see the whole city.

SARAH   Parliament Hill.

FREYA   I think I'm looking for that. So are we going to meet then?

SARAH   I could do Thursday?

FREYA   I meant today really.

SARAH   I'm busy Freya.

FREYA   You're always busy Freya, but Steve's not here and I couldn't get hold of Jasmine, / so I thought we could –

SARAH   Don't ask Jasmine, you called Jasmine?

FREYA   You have got time, I know you have.

               A beautiful perfect woman dressed in black with black sunglasses, pushing a pram, goes past.

SARAH   Get here, to the department, for one o'clock. We'll have twenty minutes. Well, ten. Come to the desk and tell them who you are.

FREYA   Thanks.

SARAH   Right.

               SARAH hangs up. The MOTHER accidentally drops a leaflet from the pram. FREYA picks it up and reads it.

FREYA   A picnic, on Parliament Hill.

               Perfect.

               Excuse me.

               FREYA *follows the woman, off through the Heath.*

               ROBERT *'s House.*

               STEVE *is asleep on the sofa.* MRS ANDREWS
               clatters in, open the curtains.

MRS ANDREWS   Are you not awake yet?

               STEVE *wakes up.*

               How did you sleep?

STEVE   How do you think?

               STEVE *stands up in just his boxer shorts, woozy.*

               The sofa's too short, so I tried the floor, but there was a
               draught.

MRS ANDREWS   Mr Sullivan...

STEVE   What?

MRS ANDREWS   You're not at your best.

STEVE   Oh.

               He puts his jeans on. Then a T-shirt.

               Isn't there a spare room?

MRS ANDREWS   There's my room.

STEVE   I'm sorry?

MRS ANDREWS   If you'd called ahead, we could've made
               arrangements.

STEVE   What do you mean?

MRS ANDREWS   When your wife visited, I stayed at my sister's.

STEVE   Oh – you... Freya called ahead?

MRS ANDREWS   Do you two not talk about these things? Now, Mr
               Crannock has got up and gone out. He starts very early,
               and won't be disturbed. You've never met I understand?

STEVE   No.

MRS ANDREWS   No, well if he trusts you you'll get a drink, if he likes you, he'll talk all night. He'll be back to the house later this afternoon, as will I.

STEVE   What am I supposed to do until then? You've got no television, I didn't bring my computer, there's no reception on my phone.

MRS ANDREWS   You'll have to occupy yourself I suppose.

STEVE   With what?

          MRS ANDREWS *looks at him.*

MRS ANDREWS   There's a radio.

          MRS ANDREWS *goes.*

          FREYA *sees an* OLD WOMAN *laying flowers at a war memorial. The* OLD WOMAN *wears a coat and headscarf.*

FREYA   Excuse me.

OLD WOMAN   Alright dear?

FREYA   I like your flowers.

OLD WOMAN   Thank you dear.

          The OLD WOMAN *smiles. They both look at the memorial.*

          Was it... your husband?

OLD WOMAN   Dunkirk.

FREYA   And you still miss him?

OLD WOMAN   I miss what went with him. How it was, when we were together.

FREYA   Did you have children?

OLD WOMAN   It was a different country then. England was made of wood and metal. Not plastic, like this. You know what I'm saying?

FREYA   No I –

OLD WOMAN   It had teacakes, cricket whites, cut grass. Yes? Blitz spirit, rooms full of smoke.

FREYA   Okay. Yeah I suppose it / must've been

OLD WOMAN   Short trousers, dinner jackets, tea dances.

FREYA   I always wanted to go to a –

OLD WOMAN   Devonshire cream, Coventry steel, the home guard, the muffin man, the post man, larders in the kitchen, fires in the living room, the damp smell of gravel in outdoor toilets. You don't know what I'm talking about.

FREYA   No.

OLD WOMAN   That was our England. All gone now of course. Things move so fast. The cars, the internet. Yes we had children, but I never see them. Always got something better to do.

             So instead, I come to the heath.

             And wait.

FREYA   What for?

OLD WOMAN   The silver lining. Soon it'll all be over.

             They look at the memorial.

             SIMON *enters* SARAH's *office.*

SIMON   Your sister's at the front desk.

SARAH   Now?

SIMON   Now.

SARAH   I said one o'clock.

             SIMON *hands* SARAH *an envelope.*

             What's this?

SIMON   Not sure. It just arrived. What about your sister?

SARAH   Send her up, and get me a Starbucks.

SIMON   Skinny?

SARAH   No. Fat. Really fucking... fat.

             SIMON *goes.* FREYA *is with the* OLD WOMAN.

FREYA   I'm looking I'm really looking for something good,
             happening now, but you're saying things are only
             getting worse.

OLD WOMAN   Religious intolerance, economic collapse,
             tsunamis, riots… it's the perfect conditions.

FREYA   I don't understand.

OLD WOMAN   Is it a boy?

FREYA   A girl.

OLD WOMAN   A little girl. Well. I hope she can fight.

             *A young man in a Second World War uniform comes
             on. He takes the* OLD WOMAN*'s arm and kisses her.*

FREYA   What?

OLD WOMAN   There's a gathering storm.

             *He takes off her headscarf and she stands upright – a
             young couple from the 1940s.*

FREYA   How do you know?

OLD WOMAN   Old people can predict the weather…

             The man opens an umbrella and it starts to rain.

             You see?

FREYA   She can fight. I've felt her kicking.

OLD WOMAN   Haven't you got anyone to take you home?

FREYA   No. He's…

             Gone.

             The OLD WOMAN *goes with her husband, just as a*
             MOTHER *comes past with her pram.* FREYA *goes off
             after her.*

             JASMINE *enters* SARAH*'s office with* TOM.

JASMINE   I've got a problem.

SARAH   Where's Freya?

JASMINE   Where she normally is, probably – at home, eating
             crisps.

SARAH   Who's this?

JASMINE   He's the problem.

SARAH   Does he have a name?

JASMINE   Tom.

SARAH *takes them in for a second.*

SARAH   Okay. I'm going to look over my letters but I am listening.

JASMINE   Last night, I was at a party.

SARAH   Thought you were dancing last night.

JASMINE   After that. It was a porn star party, we all dressed as porn stars you know

SARAH   Not really.

JASMINE   And I went back with Tom. We fucked and stuff, and he was taking pictures on his phone I thought for fun yeah?

SARAH   Yep.

JASMINE   And then today this morning when I'm a bit morning-ey, just woken up, he tells me that his family in Africa are being affected by climate change and that you aren't doing anything so his family are going to die. Apparently you're making this big statement about 'airport expansion'.

SARAH   Next week, that's right.

JASMINE   So he says why don't we go and see your sister and get a commitment.

SARAH   And you said.

JASMINE   There's no way I could change her mind she doesn't listen to a word I say.

SARAH   Absolutely right.

JASMINE   But then he said he's only gone with me, he's only done any of it, so that he could blackmail you. He's part of some group or whatever. He says if he doesn't get an assurance, he'll send the pictures to the paper.

SARAH   What were they of?

JASMINE	The pictures? Drinking, puking. Us in his room fucking.
SARAH	Nothing illegal?
JASMINE	Nothing in the pictures.
SARAH	Does he speak?
TOM	This is happening, right now, to people like me, to my family. And if you don't believe me…

He gets papers out of his bag.

Letters, photographs, measurements. Rainfall, crop growth, all from my family in Eritrea. Now, I realise you probably don't even know where Eritrea is but –

SARAH	Borders in the west, in the south, and in the south-east…
TOM	Yeah okay, yeah, exactly, and they're struggling to –
SARAH	The population's an estimated five million? The capital is – I assume you're going to tell me about the current and tangible effects of climate change on the agriculture, on the villages, your family.
TOM	You're aware of all that.
SARAH	That's sort of my job.
TOM	Then it's worse. You know what's going on and you still allow runways and flight paths. You don't listen, we've raised petitions, spoken to our MPs, all you say is you 'appreciate our view', you 'encourage the debate' – but nothing happens.
SARAH	You don't know what we're going to announce.
TOM	I can guess.
SARAH	You can guess absolutely you can have a wild stab in the dark but you don't *know*.

I want you to understand a couple of things Tom. Firstly my sister's a student. She has sex. So what? You think the public are going to be interested? *I'm* not interested.

Secondly, in this country you elect your government, and then we consult and make decisions based on what is right for the people. We take into account different factors – environmental, economic, social. It's complicated because we have to consider everything. Transport means investment. Investment means greater employment. Greater employment means less poverty, which presumably you're in favour of? That's why you have people like me, to make a *judgement*. So what are you doing, Tom? Blackmail? Of a democratically elected member of parliament?

TOM *slams his papers on her desk.*

TOM   It's a protest.

SARAH   Good. There. You've protested. It's over. Now delete the photos, get out of my office, stop wasting my time.

TOM   Are you going to read all this?

SARAH   I'm certainly going to file it.

TOM   You can't dismiss me.

SARAH   This isn't the student union Tom. We're the fucking government. Go away.

TOM *turns to go.* JASMINE *turns as well.*

Not you.

TOM *stares at* SARAH *for a moment. Then goes.*

JASMINE   I only came here for your sake.

SARAH   You didn't want your arse in the *Daily Mail*.

JASMINE   Wouldn't be the first time.

SARAH   What?

JASMINE   When I run out of toilet paper the *Daily Mail*'s just what I need.

SARAH   You have absolutely no idea how hard I'm working, do you? How many meetings I have, the paperwork –

JASMINE   Yeah, Colin said you're always here.

SARAH   It's public office Jasmine. It's the most important thing in my life, I can't –

JASMINE   He'll leave you.

SARAH   What?

JASMINE   Colin. Surprised he hasn't already.

SARAH

JASMINE

SARAH   You have no idea.

JASMINE   I know what men want. And I bet you're not giving it
            to him. Fucking ice woman, frosty the snowbitch think
            you're all big and clever power tights and shoulder
            pads, fucking Thatcher look at you. I'd have been
            better off with Dad probably.

SARAH   Be careful Jasmine.

JASMINE   He can't have been worse than you.

SARAH   You've never met him.

JASMINE   You've never let me.

SARAH   Let you? You're nineteen. He's a shit Jasmine, if you
            don't believe me, yes please give him a call instead. Or
            you could talk to some friends about all your problems
            – you never do that either do you? For some reason
            you never have friends to turn to. You ever wonder
            why you're always being fucked over like this?

JASMINE   I'm not being –

SARAH   Again and again I think you are, clearly you are, you
            ever thought why?

JASMINE   You're jealous.

SARAH   Jasmine, when you want to know, just ask. I've got a
            whole thing ready to go, I know exactly what your
            problem is.

JASMINE   …

SARAH   You want to hear it?

            JASMINE is upset. SIMON enters, interrupting.

SIMON   One fat coffee.

            *JASMINE goes. SIMON gives the coffee to SARAH,
            as SARAH makes a phone call.*

SARAH   Call John Carter. Tell him I got the letter, and I want to meet, this afternoon.

SIMON   You don't have time.

SARAH   I'll make time.

             SIMON *goes.* FREYA *is on Parliament Hill looking for mothers. She answers the call.*

FREYA   Do you know where Parliament Hill is?

SARAH   I'm sorry?

FREYA   There's this big event, this afternoon. Why don't you come here?

SARAH   Freya –

FREYA   A picnic. There's stalls, and a band. The sun's out. I'm going to buy some sandwiches. Ice cream.

SARAH   Can you listen. I've had to move things around, I can't meet you any more.

FREYA   You said you'd make time.

SARAH   I know but things change and you're alright aren't you? Your… picnic.

             A YOUNG MAN*, dirty and sweaty, runs up to* FREYA *grabs her arm.*

YOUNG MAN   Please! Please. Please. Please.

SARAH   Everything's just gone a bit mad here.

YOUNG MAN   My kid. My kid's in trouble.

FREYA   Yeah, everything's gone a bit mad here too.

SARAH   Got to go.

             She hangs up.

YOUNG MAN   He's in hospital, I've just found out, I need the bus fare to get down the road, I don't have any… change… I'm sorry, I'm really in a hurry. Shit. Shit.

FREYA   How old is he?

YOUNG MAN   What?

FREYA   Your kid.

YOUNG MAN   Seven. He fell over at school I think, I –

FREYA   And you dropped everything and ran.

YOUNG MAN   Yeah –

She reaches in her pocket – pulls out a fiver.

FREYA   It's all I've got. I was going to get lunch.

Here.

She gives it to him.

YOUNG MAN   Bless you love. Bless you.

The YOUNG MAN *runs off, ecstatic.*

FREYA   Good luck!

The sky gets darker. FREYA *feels a sharp kick.*

Ow!

Clutches her stomach.

JASMINE *is in the street, unhappy, in the rain.* TOM *is following her.*

JASMINE   It was basically rape.

TOM   What?

JASMINE   What you did. Bit like rape or something.

TOM   No it wasn't, you had a good time. I didn't plan it like –

JASMINE   So you took the pictures because –

TOM   You took the pictures. You suggested it. I was just hoping to persuade you to talk to your sister, but then when you wouldn't and I had the pictures on my phone –

JASMINE   No / no no

TOM   I realised I could do something.

JASMINE   Have you ever even been there?

TOM   What?

JASMINE   To… You know.

TOM   Eritrea.

JASMINE   Yeah. You ever actually been there?

TOM   I want to but I'd have to fly so –

JASMINE   Right so, your family? Shut up. Never met them. Are you sorry? What you did to me?

TOM   I tried three times to talk to you about it instead, but you just shouted me down, get another drink, walk away. So no I'm not sorry, you didn't leave me a choice.

            She pushes him away and storms off, leaving him in the street.

            MRS ANDREWS *is sorting through tablecloths.* STEVE *talks to her. The clock strikes four o'clock.*

STEVE   How much longer is he going to be?

MRS ANDREWS   He'll be home soon.

STEVE   I could help if you like? With that?

MRS ANDREWS   Go and stand over there.

            STEVE *does as he's told.*

STEVE   You were here when my wife visited.

MRS ANDREWS   In the day, yes.

STEVE   What was she like?

MRS ANDREWS   I don't know. She was polite, she was like a young lady. I hope you know better than me.

            Beat.

STEVE   They talked.

MRS ANDREWS   All night I believe.

STEVE   What about?

MRS ANDREWS   You think I was in there listening? I stayed at my sister's.

            Pause.

STEVE   You know he hasn't seen his children in years.

MRS ANDREWS   Aye.

STEVE   You know why?

MRS ANDREWS   I stay out of his business. You'd best talk to him.
                If you're sensible, and you might be, you might not be,
                I don't know, but if you are, you'll not cross him.

STEVE   Why not?

                MRS ANDREWS takes a towel and begins unfolding it.

MRS ANDREWS   Because, Mr Sullivan, while I'll admit you don't
                look stupid, whilst I'll concede you seem to have some
                kind of brain, you're no genius.

STEVE   And he is?

MRS ANDREWS   Yes.

STEVE   A genius?

MRS ANDREWS   Aye.

STEVE   What does that even mean?

                *The door bursts open and ROBERT enters. A seventy-
                year-old man, in a raincoat, and holding a small wind
                turbine.*

ROBERT   A person of extraordinary intellect and talent.

                A person who has great influence over another. Take
                this.

                He gives the turbine to STEVE.

                A wise man. A shaman. A prophet.

                *MRS ANDREWS shuts the door and gives him the
                towel on cue.*

MRS ANDREWS   Mr Crannock.

STEVE   I'm sorry to just –

ROBERT   Shh. I've had the data, had that for a while, but now
                you're here in person, now I'm looking at you... you
                don't work too hard, that's clear, a sense of humour but
                nothing with edge. You used to be a sportsman.
                Cricket?

STEVE   Football.

ROBERT   Football. Ha! But that's been dropped. Your shirt's a
              bit tight round the sides, you've put on weight recently.
              You like things to be simple. Fish fingers and chips.
              Don't like posh food. You're that sort of man. Yes?
              Chicken nuggets and pizza. Ketchup. Beans.
              Children's food. You haven't cut your fingernails
              properly, tells me you're self-employed. Yes? Good.

              So? Me?

              Come on *Steve*. Who am I? Am I what you expected?

STEVE   You're lonely. But I knew that already.

ROBERT   Oooh. Killer. But no actually, not so lonely. Mrs
              Andrews keeps me company. She's a blessing.
              Problem is. She loves me.

MRS ANDREWS

ROBERT   Those *eyes*. I tell her, Mrs Andrews, it's not you, it's
              your *age*. It's prohibitive. I know why you're here.

STEVE   Good.

ROBERT   And I'm not interested, could've told you over the
              phone. Now this…

              ROBERT *pours himself a drink.*

              Is a very fine single malt. Should I be drinking at my
              age, at this time in the afternoon, you're thinking?
              You're not a whisky drinker are you Steve?

STEVE   Not really.

ROBERT   Not really? You are or you're not. Where did you
              sleep?

STEVE   On the sofa.

ROBERT   We don't have a spare bed do we?

MRS ANDREWS   No.

ROBERT   Flirting! Look at her. There isn't a bed, there you have
              it, straight from the horse's mouth – no offence Mrs A
              – and you didn't call ahead, so it looks like you're on
              the sofa again tonight.

STEVE   If we can just talk now I can get going, I don't –

ROBERT   I work hard, you can see this I work all day I've got
                things to do. I'm very busy.

STEVE   I've come all the way here –

ROBERT   So make the most of it there's hotels – scenery. A loch
                nearby, a castle.

STEVE   I'm here because of Freya.

ROBERT   I know Steve, *I know* why you're here.

STEVE   She said this about you.

ROBERT   What?

STEVE   That you get angry quickly.

ROBERT   She told me about you too.

STEVE   Did she?

ROBERT   About the problems.

STEVE   What problems?

ROBERT   Exactly.

                Have you made up your mind?

STEVE   What about?

ROBERT   Are you a drinker of whisky?

STEVE   Alright.

ROBERT   You are?

STEVE   Yeah, I'll have one.

ROBERT   Good.

STEVE

ROBERT   Good boy. Better.

                Doing better.

                He pours one. Gives it to STEVE.

                There.

                They drink.

STEVE   It's good.

ROBERT   Mine is. You've got the cheap stuff.

              It is late and overcast now. Dark. Windy.

              JASMINE *arrives at a bar. A* BARMAN *comes over.*

JASMINE   I want the strongest drink.

BARMAN   I'm sorry?

JASMINE   The most alcoholic drink you sell.

BARMAN   Look, it's only five.

JASMINE   Are you a clock?

BARMAN   What?

JASMINE   Cos you look like a barman, you work in a bar, but
              you're telling me the time. It's quite simple, I want to
              get as drunk as I can, as quickly as possible, so –

BARMAN   Absinthe.

JASMINE   Two please.

BARMAN   One for you and one for...

JASMINE   The sheer hell of it. Come on...

              She reads his name badge.

              Paul.
              Paul! This is urgent.
              I need to get off my face...

              JASMINE *hits the bar suddenly.*

              Come on!

              The BARMAN *pours* JASMINE *her shots.* FREYA
              follows the two MOTHERS *to a picnic, listening to
              'Happiness' by Goldfrapp. The sky is clouding over,
              getting darker.*

              Meanwhile, CARTER *is waiting in the street.* SARAH
              approaches him, windswept, and unhappy.

SARAH   I'm late I know. Long day. Where are we going?

CARTER   Don't you have an umbrella?

SARAH   Clearly not.

CARTER   This way.

They go off, under his umbrella.

The group of MOTHERS *in black with black prams
and sunglasses appear again. They dance and sing,
holding their wrapped-up babies, showing them to
each other, drinking their coffee and ignoring* FREYA.

They sing and dance to 'Happiness' by Goldfrapp.

FREYA *watches them, and tries to take part.*

After a while FREYA *takes a headphone out and
speaks to them.*

FREYA   Excuse me?

MOTHERS   Yes?

FREYA   I'm here for the picnic.

            The MOTHERS *look her up and down. Smile in a fake
            way.*

MOTHERS   Not being funny but –

FREYA   Okay.

MOTHERS   Yeah.

FREYA   My baby's kicking.

MOTHERS   How sweet!

FREYA   Not in a good way.

MOTHERS   Ahhhh.

FREYA   Do you worry about the future?

MOTHERS   Not really.

FREYA   What might happen?

MOTHERS   No.

FREYA   What might happen to your children?

MOTHERS   Henry's very bright, he's already reading.
            He'll go into hedge funds
            Or a surgeon.
            Something like that.

FREYA   How was the birth?

MOTHERS   Natural.

FREYA   How do you manage with it all?

MOTHERS   Easily.

FREYA   None of you got down about it?

           None of you felt your child was a…

MOTHERS   A?

FREYA   A mistake?

MOTHERS   No. God. No.

FREYA   And what about people who are poorer than you?

MOTHERS   We do what we can.

FREYA   Yes but –

MOTHERS   Charity work. Every Thursday. Primrose Hill. We
           carbon-offset holidays.

           You know.

FREYA   But that's not enough, and if it's not enough, then
           what's the point.

           Aaaahhh!

           *She clutches her belly again. They look at her for a
           moment, more serious now, almost threatening. They
           stand, wielding their children, almost like weapons.*

           (*Over singing.*) Call me an ambulance.

           Please.

           Please!

           The singing continues.

           Then they slowly encircle her.
           She is scared but has nowhere to go.

           The women throw the babies up in the air.
           *They explode into black powder, like soot or dust, that
           covers everyone, and is blown about by the wind.*

           The music continues as the women disappear, FREYA
           falls to the floor, and the lights fade.

           End of Act Two.

ACT THREE

Prologue

1973.

ROY, DANIEL *and* ROBERT.

ROY *and* DANIEL *are looking through a few sheets of paper.* ROY *is smoking.*

ROBERT	It's just a preliminary document. To give you some idea of the way it's going.
ROY	We understand what it is.
ROBERT	So you know where it's headed. I thought it would be good to get your... views.
	At this stage.
ROY	You think this is what will be in the final report.
ROBERT	The way it's going yes.
ROY	You can't imagine that they'll be any... surprises.
DANIEL	New factors.
ROY	New factors yes, still to come.
ROBERT	I can't see how there would be no.
ROY	Right. Can't see how there would be.
DANIEL	Hmm.
ROY	Because the thing is, these aren't really the results we were expecting.
DANIEL	They're not meaningful.
ROY	Meaningful.
	Exactly.
	What do they tell us?

ROBERT   Quite a lot actually. If you do this sort of work it's
            clear that releasing huge quantities of carbon dioxide
            into the atmosphere at such a high altitude will cause
            heat to be reflected rather than released, potentially
            causing rising temperatures and –

ROY   No.
            Robert.
            Hang on.
            With respect.
            All that you've just said, that tells you a lot.
            It tells *us* very little.
            We wondered if there was any way you could make
            them *meaningful* to us.

ROBERT

ROY   If there was a way the report could focus on something
            that we can understand. Because if there was. A clearer
            focus.

            This could be the start of a very fruitful relationship.

ROBERT   Yes but this is –

ROY   As we spoke about.

ROBERT   Right.

ROY   Perhaps it's a question of how you present it.
            Perhaps it's as simple as that?

ROBERT

DANIEL   Or maybe you need some more resources.
            To see things clearly.
            Is that what we're talking about?
            Are we talking about resources?
            Or should we discuss the fee?

ROBERT   It's not about money…

DANIEL   Of course.

            DANIEL *writes on a piece of paper.*

            He passes it across. ROBERT *reads it.*

            I think you should keep going. There's six months
            before the final report. That's a long time. Anything
            could happen.

Mad Bitch

The evening. Dark.

FREYA *is at the reception of a hospital. She meets* MARYNA, *a Polish cleaner, who is playing 'I Am Not a Robot' by Marina and the Diamonds on a tinny radio.*

FREYA   You have to help me.

MARYNA   Nie potrafie mowie po angielsku. [I don't understand English.]

FREYA   It's hurting. It's really – Ow!

                A RECEPTIONIST *comes over.*

MARYNA   Jestem tulko sprazatacza, / idz ee znajdz lekarza. [I'm just the cleaner, go / and talk to a doctor.]

FREYA   This is a hospital you have / to help me.

RECEPTIONIST   Alright...

MARYNA   She says it hurts.

RECEPTIONIST   I can see that.

                MARYNA looks FREYA *in the eyes.*

MARYNA   Po burzy zawsze slonce przychodzi. [After the storm, the sun always comes.]

RECEPTIONIST   Thank you Maryna, I'll deal with it.

                MARYNA picks up her mop and watches.

                Now what's your name?

FREYA   I'm not telling you my name.

RECEPTIONIST   You can't be treated until we / have some information –

FREYA   I'm pregnant. You have to treat me.

RECEPTIONIST   Let's just start with a / name, can you give me a

FREYA   I pay my taxes, the whole point is you treat me so treat me I don't want to talk to you, where's the doctor?

RECEPTIONIST   You will see a doctor, I'm just trying to get some
                details. How / long have you been –

FREYA   I'm not telling you anything, I don't like you, I'm in
               pain. It's kicking so hard. Ow!

RECEPTIONIST   How many weeks?

FREYA

RECEPTIONIST   How many weeks?

FREYA   Let me in!

               A young doctor, TIM, *comes in.*

TIM   Is there a problem?

MARYNA   I think you should let her in.

               JASMINE *is knocking on* COLIN*'s front door.*

COLIN   Alright!

               As the receptionist takes FREYA *into the hospital,*
               MARYNA *watches, then walks away.*

               *A baby is crying somewhere. The rhythmic sound of a
               heartbeat.*

               COLIN *answers the door.*

JASMINE   I'm wet as fuck.

COLIN   It's not a good time.

JASMINE   Can I come in or what?

COLIN   What?

JASMINE   Funny.

               She walks past him into the house.

COLIN   She's not back till late.

JASMINE   Never is these days. She's got a reception till nine, then
               a late meeting, checked with her secretary, went over,
               had an argument today, so I know.

COLIN   You went to her work?

JASMINE   I'm not interested in her anyway that's not why I'm
               here.

She looks at the house.

I hated it when you moved. That was my house. I loved that place. But this is so... *House and Garden.* Yeah... none of my mates are around got exams or whatever so I thought you'll be on your own and you could probably do with a laugh so I brought a bottle of tequila. And a spliff or two, or three.

COLIN   I don't really smoke illegal drugs, it's sort of frowned on for –

JASMINE   You should.

COLIN   For husbands of government ministers.

JASMINE   You should, given everything that's happened to you.

COLIN   A drug habit? Right.

JASMINE   You lost your job.

COLIN   I'll find something else.

JASMINE   To take?

COLIN   A job.

JASMINE   You probably wanted kids but she's past it now.

COLIN   Not really.

JASMINE   No she is, well past it, trust me.

COLIN   I mean we don't want kids.

JASMINE   The house must feel empty, with you here, on your own all day.

She lights a cigarette.

COLIN   You can't smoke inside, you know that.

JASMINE   She isn't here.

So. Why can't you get a job? Too old is it?

COLIN   In their terms, and I've never been one of the city boys really. Never done that stuff.

JASMINE   What stuff?

COLIN   Cars, booze, coke.

JASMINE   Strippers.

COLIN   Exactly. Strippers. God.

            A moment.

            And you're right, it's not been the easiest of months for
            her either, so she tends to take it out on… well…

JASMINE   You.

COLIN   People.

JASMINE   You. It's all got a bit bleak recently, hasn't it?

COLIN   Why are you here?

JASMINE   I'm your fairy godmother.

            She offers him a cigarette.

COLIN   I don't smoke.

JASMINE   If you're gonna have a mid-life crisis, better have a
            fucking good one. It won't kill you.

            He takes one. She lights it.

            She pours two shots of tequila.

            Bad things are happening. Let's stick our heads in the
            sand.

            They drink.

            SARAH *is in a restaurant with* CARTER.

CARTER   For me, a restaurant is never about who will be here,
            but who certainly won't. And there are a lot of people
            who certainly won't be here. The wine's excellent, the
            meat isn't local which in London is a good thing, the
            service is eight out of ten. The cheese. Well, the cheese
            is something to write home about. Dear mother I have
            just tasted the most delightful cambozola –

            She gives him the sheets of paper.

            Oh.

            Straight to business. Thank you.

SARAH   Why don't you tell me what they are?

CARTER   Well. They are... results. Of some tests. Photocopies of
            the originals I think. It's a preliminary report by Robert
            Crannock... your father yes?

SARAH   Why did you send them?

CARTER   Me?

            No I didn't send them. I don't know anything about
            them.

            The waiter comes over and pours some wine. SARAH
            drinks straight away.

SARAH   Alright well, why *might* someone...

CARTER   Why *might* someone have sent them?

SARAH   Exactly, yes, let's *imagine*.

CARTER   Well these are signed by your father, the results of a
            project he did for the largest airline in the UK, oh hang
            on that's my company isn't it? Yes I remember this, a
            project over twenty years to investigate whether
            emissions from aircraft would have any lasting impact
            on the environment. Now this report seems to suggest
            that clearly, yes. Yes.

            A huge impact.

            These emissions would prove disastrous, for the world.

SARAH   Right. That's what he thinks.

CARTER   But that wasn't his conclusion Sarah. Not at the time.

            For twenty years, his public reports said the opposite.
            That burning fuel, and carbon emissions, would have
            little or *no effect*. It was one of the main factors in the
            expansion of the industry. So the question we... sorry.
            Not me. The question you have to ask yourself is why
            would he do that? For twenty years.

            When he knew the truth. Why would he lie?

            Of course, everyone makes mistakes, we don't mind it
            took him twenty years to work it out, but if it were
            revealed that he knew *all the time*... in green circles he's
            a god... if this came out, his reputation would collapse.

And you're his daughter. Perhaps it would rub off on you.

I presume he was paid. I wonder how much?

SARAH *smiles*.

SARAH   Yes.

CARTER   Yes?

SARAH   You're right. The public should know. I'll give the report to the press in the morning.

CARTER   You will.

SARAH   Absolutely. And thank you, because this is a lovely restaurant, the wine is delicious, and especially for this, because I think my father deserves whatever he gets.

CARTER   Really?

SARAH   You should've done your research. I hate him. I'm more than happy to disown him publicly. Any excuse.

        So sorry, John – no more runways.

        She drinks from the wine.

CARTER   I like the way you hold the glass. By the stem. It's impressive. You're wasted.

SARAH   Not yet.

CARTER   In politics, I meant.

        CARTER *takes the papers off her.*

        You'll forgive the attempt? This sort of thing normally works on politicians. They get scared. Because most politicians are geeks, as you know Sarah. That's why they're so ugly.

        The waiter arrives again.

        But you.

        You're not ugly at all. You're… striking. Intelligent. So what are you doing?

        What do you want?

SARAH   What do I want?

CARTER   To eat.

SARAH   Oh.

CARTER   I've done my best. It didn't work.

           So, let's relax now, eat, drink.

           Enjoy ourselves. Make a night of it.

           Let's talk like men do.

           The sound of a baby in the womb.

           TIM *is standing with* FREYA.

TIM   We've run all the tests. I'm pleased to say, it's perfectly
           healthy.

FREYA   I've been smoking. And drinking. I fell over in the bath.

TIM   She's fine.

FREYA   Other mothers aren't like this.

TIM   Women often go through many feelings, but when you
           give birth –

FREYA   You should get rid of it. The baby. Before it's too late.
           Ow!

TIM   It's not possible.

FREYA   You do it all the time.

TIM   Not in these circumstances. She's too advanced.

FREYA   If I was a cave woman, I could do it myself. Punch
           myself in the stomach.

           Or wait till it was born and hide it or bury it or
           something. Maybe I will. I thought this was civilised.
           I thought I had rights.

TIM   We are civilised. You do have rights. But at this stage,
           so does your daughter. Is someone picking you up?

FREYA   I'm on my own. There isn't anyone. I'm staying here.
           I need to stay here.

TIM   We don't have room.

FREYA   Sign a piece of paper and it's done – what?

TIM   What's really the matter?

FREYA   I keep on telling you, there's something wrong.

TIM   Not with the baby?

FREYA   I was out all day, I saw so many people and none of them cared. Are you a good doctor?

TIM   Are you a good patient?

FREYA   Good patients would tell you their names.

TIM   I'm Tim.

FREYA   Hello.

TIM   Hello Freya.

FREYA   Oh, you know.

TIM   Found your wallet in your bag. Now all we need is an address.

FREYA   Good hands.

TIM   Thanks.

FREYA   I bet you keep your girlfriend happy.

TIM   Boyfriend actually.

FREYA   Boyfriend right, I bet you wouldn't leave him by himself if he was having a baby.

TIM   Hard to say.

FREYA   I'm not very happy at the moment. Brave face, but I'm struggling. You should let me stay.

TIM   Freya I can't unless you're in for a... Do you want to see her?

FREYA   Who?

TIM   Your daughter.

FREYA   No.

TIM   If you see her, you can stay the night. That's the deal.

    TIM *smiles*.

FREYA   You're just like my husband.

TIM   In what way?

FREYA   He's always smiling too, like nothing's wrong.

           She winces with pain.

           STEVE *looks, very seriously, at* ROBERT.

STEVE   It's a nice house.

ROBERT   Jealous.

STEVE   Not really.

ROBERT   Small flat you've got. She finds it claustrophobic.

STEVE   Is that what she said?

ROBERT   What do you think? Is she happy? With the house? Is
           she happy? With you?

           These are the questions.
           Point is, you don't know.
           What do you do Steve?

STEVE   I'm sure she mentioned it.

ROBERT   Of course, but – I want you to be proud of it, Steve. I
           want you to declare it.

STEVE   I'm a writer.

ROBERT   You're a writer. Good. Of?

STEVE   Books. Sort of trivia books.

ROBERT   Sort of trivia books. That's right. What sort of trivia
           books?

STEVE   For the Christmas market mainly, they're like
           stocking-fillers.

ROBERT   And what do they like, fill the stocking with. What are
           they called?

STEVE   The latest one was *Fifty Shit Things About Britain*.

ROBERT   *Fifty Shit Things About Britain*. Wow. Steve. Wow.
           That's what you think? That Britain's shit.

STEVE   Yeah, nothing to be proud of really.

ROBERT   Well I don't know, there's always your book.

STEVE   We're working on a sequel actually, for this year.

ROBERT   *Another Fifty Shit Things About Britain*?

STEVE   *Fifty Shitter Things About Britain.*

              They sell very well.

              The first bought the flat.

              This one's for Emily.

ROBERT   Emily?

STEVE   …

ROBERT   Tell me some of your shit things.

STEVE   Look, this isn't the point, I'm not here to chat –

ROBERT   Why not? Are you staying? Tonight?

STEVE   You said a hotel.

ROBERT   There isn't one, and it's terrible anyway. Stay here.

STEVE   No.

ROBERT   Why not? Scared?

STEVE   It doesn't feel right.

ROBERT   What does that mean, 'doesn't feel right'?

STEVE   To stay under your roof.

ROBERT   You don't know me.

STEVE   I know what you did to them.

ROBERT   What I *did* to them. I didn't *do* anything. I said things. I told them the truth. *Did something*, sounds like you're implying I hit them.

STEVE   No.

ROBERT   Or fucked them something like that. You're not implying something like that are you?

STEVE   Of course not.

ROBERT   Then watch your fucking language.

Choose better words.

Stay. And we'll talk. We'll find the time. Later on. Yes?

STEVE   Okay.

ROBERT   Good. Now, tell me why Britain's so shit.

JASMINE and COLIN have wine and are quite stoned.

JASMINE   I feel so fucking aimless Colin, I want to go where I want, do what I like, spend money, I want to shout all the time. Cos it's bullshit, just everyone, isn't it? Pushing emails around, shall we meet? Shall we have a pre-meet? How about Thursday? I'm busy Thursday, well how about we meet to work out when's good, let's pencil that in, fucking about on Facebook, events, messages, profiles, pretending to have friends, and I don't mind but none of it's *achieving* anything, it's one big 'general meeting', just chatter, and when it all fucks up, which it will, just statistically, historically, when it all goes pear-shaped, they'll be full of regrets. 'I should've slept with him, I should've gone there, done that while I had the chance.' And I never want regrets Colin so while I still can I'm gonna fuck some shit up.

COLIN   I've never done that.

JASMINE   What?

COLIN   Fucking... shit... or...

JASMINE   Oh Colin.

COLIN   I've found for the sake of dignity it's better to stay away from the... shit.

JASMINE   We have to sort you out.

COLIN lets out a long strange depressing sigh.

SARAH and CARTER in a bar – more relaxed now.

Cocktails and a night-time view over London.

SARAH   I have a fundamental belief in the role of government. I'm very clear about that.

CARTER   Sarah, it's wonderful your clarity.

SARAH   And we're very different you and me.

CARTER   Different in many ways, I'm not denying that, I'm
             simply saying that with your skills, contacts, your
             background, you don't know how much you're worth.

SARAH   I'm not interested in money.

CARTER   A thousand a day, possibly more.

SARAH   It's not what motivates me.

CARTER   I know I know, okay, but the improved quality of life
             that's something else. I spend my evenings with my
             children. Do you spend your evenings with your
             children?

SARAH   I don't have any children.

CARTER   You don't have any children alright, do you see much
             of your husband?

SARAH   Enough.

CARTER   Enough?

             He smiles – you see?

SARAH   We're going through a… thing at the moment it's
             not… oh.

CARTER   This is what I mean.

SARAH   Fuck. What am I doing? I'm telling you about my
             marriage why am I telling you about that? Jesus. Shut
             up Sarah.

CARTER   We're just talking.

             SARAH *drinks her mojito.*

             But alright so quality of life, that's not a factor either,
             because there are important things you care about. I
             understand. Targets, limits, carbon trading, an
             international agreement. How's all that going by the
             way? Cos these days I don't hear so much about it.

SARAH   There's a lot of momentum to get something done.

CARTER   Momentum.

SARAH   Yes I know I know alright.

SARAH *grabs a waiter.*

Can I get another mojito?

He goes.

CARTER   Come on Sarah, you like things to *happen*. You know
          really that the solution will lie in utilising the market.
          Technology and innovation.

SARAH   Carbon-ingesting algae you mean?

CARTER   Carbon –

SARAH   An orbiting umbrella.

CARTER   Sarah, you're being / naughty.

SARAH   No no, my favourite – turning the Moon into a huge
          solar panel.

CARTER   That's kind of how innovation *works*. It's *new*? If
          people will pay, the world will change, fast. The
          internet existed for ten years, no one had it, but as soon
          as it could do adverts it went in every home.

SARAH   The environment is longer term, less quantifiable,
          without government incentivising industry there won't
          / be any commercial activity.

CARTER   Sarah, *Sarah*! You could be doing so much more than
          incentivising. This is what I'm saying. There aren't
          many people around like you. If you were in business
          you could solve environmental issues right now, you
          could save lives and build economies and you could do
          it quickly. And then after work you'd go home to your
          big house, your happy husband, and do what you like.
          Concerts, painting, cooking.

SARAH   I used to like cooking.

CARTER   What's your husband's name?

SARAH   Colin.

CARTER   Colin? Right. Colin?

          They both smile.

          Right.

SARAH   He's an amazing man.

CARTER	I'm sure he is.
SARAH	But when I come in these days he just looks at me.
CARTER	Because you're killing yourself with this half-arsed government when you're capable of so much more. He knows it. I know it.
SARAH	Well…
	We'll have to wait and see.
CARTER	Wait for what?
SARAH	The next election, see where we are.
CARTER	That could be three years.
SARAH	Slowly slowly –
CARTER	Why wait?
SARAH	You mean…
CARTER	Come to us in the new year.
SARAH	I thought we were talking theoretically.
CARTER	No.
SARAH	You want me to work for you.
CARTER	Well actually Sarah, if you came across, I would be working for you.

She looks at him.

Proper salary, resources, investment, whatever you want. An expense account. Leading the field. Clean up the industry, from the inside. You tell us what to do.

SARAH	This is an offer?
CARTER	A great big offer. You get what you want.
SARAH	Yes.
CARTER	And so do we.

They look at each other.

SARAH	You're a clever boy.

She drinks. This is the deal.

CARTER   The things you could do Sarah. So much bigger than
            planes and runways.

            ROBERT, STEVE *and* MRS ANDREWS *are having
            dinner.*

ROBERT   Did you fly here Steve?

STEVE   I didn't have much choice.

            ROBERT *looks at him.*

ROBERT   You haven't read my books have you?

STEVE   I had a look today, while I was waiting.

ROBERT   You had a *look*?

STEVE   A skim, yes.

ROBERT   They aren't difficult, even Mrs Andrews managed
            them.

STEVE   Your books aren't why I'm here.

ROBERT   Mrs Andrews, let me explain. Steve is worried about his
            wife. Now I haven't spoken to any of my daughters for
            twenty years. They don't like me, they're doing their
            own things – My eldest is the environment secretary.
            My youngest is at university. And Freya. What she does
            I don't know. She's pregnant, does that count?

STEVE   She's a teaching assistant.

ROBERT   Yes, she helps deaf children or something, but quite
            strangely one evening, Steve got home and found his
            wife had gone. Where? Well he eventually discovered
            that she had got on a train and come up to Scotland, to
            talk to her dad. And yes. We spoke. You gave her fruit
            cake.

MRS ANDREWS   Aye.

ROBERT   Very appropriate in retrospect, because after she got
            home, she wouldn't tell her husband what we spoke
            about. He knew where she'd been, but Freya refused to
            talk. She wouldn't even say why she went in the first
            place. I presume she's become unhappy. Confused.

STEVE   She hardly leaves the flat any more, she cries at night.

ROBERT   Right, so then even more strangely, Steve decides to
            fake a business trip and come and talk to me himself.
            Not realising of course that if he needs to do that then
            there's much bigger issues at stake.

STEVE   Like what?

ROBERT   Like not what I said to her.

STEVE   Okay.

ROBERT   But why she won't talk to you. Why you're sneaking
            up here without telling her.

STEVE   I need to know what's happening.

ROBERT   I'm in two minds as to what to say, Mrs Andrews.
            Steve's come all this way. But do I betray the trust of
            my daughter, and get involved or do I keep my mouth
            shut, for once?

            They look at each other.

            The problem is Steve, that it is, in fact, all about my
            books. If you want an answer, you'll have to
            understand some science. You'll have to listen. And it
            won't be humorous. It's very interesting, but there
            aren't any *laughs*. Can you deal with that?

STEVE   Go on.

ROBERT   Everything in the planet is codependent. It exists in ever-
            changing, ever-evolving balance much like a gigantic
            organism itself. Did you get that far with the books?

STEVE   Yes / I did.

ROBERT   Species live and die and evolve and the planet evolves
            too through cycles of hot and cold and responding to
            the demands of life, and life responds to the demands
            of the planet. But the problem is –

MRS ANDREWS   Global warming.

ROBERT   You see, there's a keen brain under all that – Global
            warming, yes. You know how that works. Of course
            you do. You've seen *Blue Peter*. And people draw their
            graphs, they show the rise in temperature, they show a
            small but steady rise, they say it can be limited, you
            know by how much?

STEVE   A couple of degrees?

ROBERT   Two degrees yes, as long as we recycle, do you recycle
            Steve?

STEVE   Yes.

ROBERT   And insulate our homes, I expect you've done that too.

STEVE   Looked into it –

ROBERT   Of course you have I'm sure you've got a bag-for-life,
            and all that makes you feel better I know but it's a
            complete waste of time because the global climate has
            never been interested in two-degree anything. If we
            look at geological records of historical climate change,
            the onset of the last ice age for instance, we see there is
            no steady climb, no year-by-year increase. There is in
            fact a relatively stable climate system, and then
            something happens, the system is stretched and in a
            moment, it collapses and changes, in hundreds not
            thousands of years. You understand?

STEVE   …

ROBERT   Let's imagine this house is a planet. What regulates the
            climate?

STEVE   The thermostat?

ROBERT   Mrs Andrews. When the house is too hot she opens
            windows, when it's too cold she switches on the
            heating. She brings in new material to eat or drink, and
            she removes the waste when I'm done. She cleans the
            air and the ground and she regulates my life, don't
            you? We are symbiotic, she would not exist without
            me. I couldn't live without her.

STEVE   Right.

ROBERT   But she's very unhappy at the moment Steve. Because
            when the population is doubled like this, her systems
            are stretched. The house gets hotter, quicker, food and
            drink are consumed at twice the rate, the floor is twice
            as dirty. She's under pressure, but is there a steady
            increase in her anger? Can you detect a slow rise in her
            temperament? No. She's stable, she's holding it
            together. But there will come a day, if you stay too
            long Steve, when the system's been stretched too far,

and she'll snap. Suddenly she'll take away your sofa, she'll hide the food, leave the heating on, steal your phone and spit in your drink, she'll do everything in her power to remove the problem. To remove you. And she'll succeed Steve, you'll be gone, because she's stronger than any of us.

We were part of system, a relationship, and we abused it. The world will be fine in the end, and it knows what it wants. It wants to get rid of us.

MRS ANDREWS   The end of humanity.

STEVE *looks at them.*

STEVE   Can we get back to Freya?

ROBERT   You don't believe me?

STEVE   I don't see how it's relevant.

ROBERT   The end of humanity not relevant?

STEVE   To what we're talking about, no.

ROBERT   Mrs Andrews. He doesn't believe me.

You think I'm a strange old man.

Pause.

ROBERT *stands up, goes to* STEVE, *grabs him.*

Up.

STEVE   What?

ROBERT   We're going.

STEVE   Where?

ROBERT   The end of humanity. We're going to see it.

JASMINE *and* COLIN *are smoking a spliff.*

JASMINE   I'm not wearing underwear.

I never do.

COLIN   Uncomfortable.

JASMINE   It makes life that bit more exciting. You should try it.

COLIN   I don't think it's the same with men.

COLIN *stares. Fixed. Empty. Nothing for a moment.*

JASMINE *looks at him. He's blank.*

JASMINE   Colin!

What's gonna change?

She pokes him.

Come on!!!

What's *happening*?!

She pokes him. Pokes him again.

Keeps on poking him.

Poke poke.

He looks at her.

Then he stands up.

What? What?

Have I pissed you off now?

Goes to the CD player. Picks a CD. Puts it on.

What are you doing?

'Rebellion (Lies)' by Arcade Fire plays.

What's this?

COLIN   Arcade Fire.

JASMINE   Okay, yeah I remember them.

COLIN is standing moving a bit.

COLIN   Freya gave it to me one Christmas.

Used to play it in the car.

COLIN starts to dance to it, very awkwardly. He knows the words, but is not used to moving his body.

JASMINE   Oh.

My.

God.

COLIN   You like it?

JASMINE   Er... I...

             JASMINE *is amazed.*

             COLIN *dances.*

             Yeah.

             COLIN *sings along, loudly now.*

COLIN   Sleeping is giving in,
             no matter what the time is.
             Sleeping is giving in,
             so lift those heavy eyelids.

             People say that you'll die
             faster than without water.
             But we know it's just a lie,
             scare your son, scare your daughter.

             As he goes he grows in confidence, he starts to let go.
             There is a kind of beauty to it.

             JASMINE *is laughing and smoking.*

             CARTER *pays for the drinks at the bar.*

CARTER   You look different Sarah.

SARAH   What?

CARTER   You look younger.

             SARAH *smiles.*

             COLIN *dances with things in the room. Bashes*
             around. Starts to go crazy. No ironic moves. He means
             it.

             He pulls JASMINE *up. Dances with her, sings to her.*
             She can't believe it.

COLIN   People say that your dreams
             are the only things that save ya.
             Come on baby in our dreams,
             we can live on misbehaviour.

             Every time you close your eyes
             Lies, lies!
             Every time you close your eyes
             Lies, lies!

                Every time you close your eyes
                Lies, lies!
                Every time you close your eyes
                Lies, lies!

                Every time you close your eyes.

JASMINE   You're mental!

COLIN   Every time you close your eyes.
                Every time you close your eyes.
                Every time you close your eyes.

                He lets himself go completely.

                FREYA *and* TIM. *The music playing underneath.*

FREYA   She's not kicking any more.
                She seems happy. I think she likes you.

                She smiles.

                Maybe she could be a doctor, do something good.

                He smiles.

TIM   Back in a minute.

                He goes out.

                CARTER *and* SARAH *are outside in the rain under
                an umbrella.*

COLIN   People try and hide the night.
                Underneath the covers.
                People try and hide the lie.
                Underneath the covers.

                Come and hug your lovers
                Underneath the covers.
                Come and hug your lovers
                Underneath the covers.

                Hide it from your brothers.
                Underneath the covers.
                Come and hug your lovers
                Underneath the covers.

CARTER   There's a fifty. For the cab.

SARAH   It won't be that much.

CARTER   Buy something for your husband.

             SARAH *smiles, gets in a cab and drives off through the city.*

             COLIN *continues to dance and mime along with the words.*

COLIN   People say that you'll die
             faster than without water,
             but we know it's just a lie,
             scare your son, scare your daughter,

             JASMINE *is going as mad as he is. They dance close*

             Scare your son, scare your daughter.
             Scare your son, scare your daughter.

             She kisses him suddenly.

             He stops her. Stands back.

             They look at each other as the music continues to play.

             JASMINE *sits. Relights the spliff.*

             COLIN *listens to the music a bit, then fades it down and switches it off.*

             We hear the sound of the storm outside.

             ROBERT *is walking with* STEVE *up to a tree.*

ROBERT   There's a nest in this tree. Redwings, beautiful patterning. They were the reason I moved here. I found the birds, bought the house nearby.

STEVE   I'm asking about / Freya.

ROBERT   The birds were endangered and climate change was the cause apparently. So I thought, they will be my barometer. Like the ravens in the Tower, when they leave, it's over. They said rising temperatures were driving them elsewhere. What do you think?

STEVE   Doesn't feel warm right now.

ROBERT   Well exactly, how could you know it was the air temperature? If you want to understand these things, you have to look at the entire system, the mountains, the animals, the air, the sea, it's infinitely complicated

Steve, but that's what I do, I sit in that shed and I try to see the future.

STEVE   Just you and your shed.

ROBERT   Every model suggests things are going to be worse than anyone imagines. I've seen something terrible,

STEVE   You're the only one who's noticed.

ROBERT   People say they want the truth – facts, and figures, but actually they want to be told it can be avoided, with minimum effort. When Neville Chamberlain came back from Hitler. He said he had a peace treaty, said he could *trust* this obviously evil man. Why did he believe it? Why did *we* believe it? Because we had to, or we'd be facing untold horrors. Always Steve, faith will come before truth. That's who we are.

STEVE   Freya's read your books, she knows what you think, so why did she come all the way up here?

ROBERT   They all know what I think. Best way to reduce the carbon footprint?

STEVE   What?

ROBERT   No foot. You want to be green?

STEVE   Okay –

ROBERT   Hold your breath. The planet can sustain about one billion people. We currently have six billion. So in the next hundred years it will balance the books. You understand?

STEVE   I don't –

ROBERT   Five billion people wiped from the face of the Earth in a single lifetime. Mass migration away from the equator, world wars, starvation...

STEVE   And Freya –

ROBERT   Freya came to ask my advice about children.

STEVE   And what did you say?

ROBERT   You have to understand –

STEVE   What did you *say*?

ROBERT   I told her that her child will regret she was ever born. Hate her mother for forcing her into a terrible world.

           I told her to do whatever it takes.

           I told her to kill it.

           STEVE *looks at him. Horrified.*

           TIM *is operating the ultrasound on* FREYA.

           We see a very blurred image. Of something. Faint sound of the womb.

TIM   There. Can you see?

FREYA   No.

TIM   Look.

FREYA   I can't see anything.

           STEVE *and* ROBERT.

STEVE   You told her to kill it.

ROBERT   Yes.

STEVE   Emily.

ROBERT   It's a / foetus.

STEVE   We're calling her Emily and I've no idea what's going to happen, but she's there, and growing, and she's my child too, not just Freya's, she's much more important than your theories... your fucking *birds*.

ROBERT   It's not just theory / it's

STEVE   You had no right. No right to say that to her.

ROBERT   It's the truth.

STEVE   You listen! To me.

ROBERT   The birds? You want to know about / the birds?

STEVE   For once, you listen. You had no right to say that to her. Do you understand?

ROBERT   Steve!

STEVE   No –

ROBERT   The birds had gone before I even moved in.

STEVE moves away, to avoid hitting him.

It's Weimar time, it's *Cabaret*, across the world. You feel it, we all do. We know there's nothing to be done, so we're dancing and drinking as fast as we can. The enemy is on its way, but it doesn't have guns and gas this time, it has wind and rain, storms and earthquakes.

STEVE   Just shut up. / Shut up.

ROBERT   This isn't theory. This is *death*, this is *loss* and *pain*. Freya's not the first to suffer, and she won't be the last.

STEVE   She's beautiful and clever, but she's not strong, she came up here for help. She wanted her dad to make her feel better.

ROBERT   Then she came to the wrong person.

STEVE   What did she do?
What did she do when you told her?

ROBERT   The world as it is, a disgrace.
The world as it will be, unbearable.

STEVE   I have to get back. I couldn't get through to her at home. She's gone somewhere.

ROBERT   You can't get back now.

STEVE   She might be killing my baby, so –

STEVE leaves.

ROBERT   She had to know the truth.
It's better it never lived.

TIM is still trying with the ultrasound.

FREYA   You aren't what you seem.

TIM   I'm sorry?

FREYA   I saw you. Through the glass. Talking to the nurse. Ow! It's started again.

TIM   I just need to find the…

FREYA   I teach deaf children at school. Part of my job.

TIM   Really?

FREYA   Means I lip-read.

TIM   Oh.

FREYA   Mad bitch.
           Waste of time.
           Then you both laughed.

TIM   It was a joke.

FREYA   No. It's what you think. And it doesn't matter except I
           thought you were the good thing, you were the last
           glimmer.

           And then you went out.

           Aghh!

           She hates you now.

           On the screen is a very clear image of a foetus.

TIM   I've had a long day. I'm sorry.
           But look.
           There she is.

           Things'll seem better.
           She'll make a difference, won't she?
           When she's here.

FREYA   Yes.

           She will.

           She will make a difference.

           The foetus is on the screen. Kicking.

           Its mouth moves and we hear a small voice.

FOETUS   Mummy?

FREYA   It spoke.

TIM   What?

FREYA   It moved its mouth.

TIM   It's just –

FREYA   No. I lip-read. It's speaking.

FOETUS   Mummy? Mummy?

Help.

Help me.

Sound of the womb getting louder and louder.

Sounds like an earthquake.

Mummy?

Shaking.

The foetus turns its head to face us and screams.
Blackout.

End of Act Three.

Interval.

ACT FOUR

Prologue

1991.

ROBERT *is watching television in the dark, drunk. A door opens onto a hall where bags are packed.* SARAH *comes in.*

SARAH   I've packed enough for a week, for all of us, but we'll have to come back for the rest at some point, if you're serious about all this. There's too much, there's all the baby things, the nappies, the sheets, the toys, the bottle, I mean I can't fit the cot in my car, we'll have to get a van or something, I don't know, if you're serious.

I don't know if you are serious but if you mean what you said, I'm going right now.

ROBERT   With you I tried.

SARAH   What?

ROBERT   Everyone had said if you have a child you'll change, you'll know what to do, everything will fall into place, and so I went into the hospital on the day you were born and there was your mum sat in the bed, and she gave you to me, to hold, and I looked at you, and I waited.

For that moment when I would feel like a father.

The moment everyone spoke about, when I would love you, completely, above anything else. But it wasn't happening.

I looked over at your mum and she smiled. It had happened for her.

I looked down at you.

Still nothing.

So I looked up at your mum and smiled back, and right then, I started pretending. A few years later we had Freya, and Jasmine, and every moment, all the time, I wasn't a father. I never felt it.

But now she's gone, now your mother's dead, there's no reason to pretend. She was the one I loved. Just her. Yes. I'm serious.

SARAH   What work?

ROBERT   What?

SARAH   You said you had work to do, that you needed to focus.

ROBERT   I've got to *stop pretending*.

          SARAH *looks at him. Very upset. Holding it in.*

SARAH   So every time you've hugged me and talked to me at bedtime, and drove me to university –

ROBERT   Yes.

SARAH   All the hours we talked, all that was –

ROBERT   You believed it at the time.
          That's what mattered.

          A baby is crying.

SARAH   I left Jasmine with Freya.

          Coldly, SARAH *goes over and kisses* ROBERT.

ROBERT   You look like your mother. That's what I can't deal with. You all look just like her.

          SARAH *exits, leaving the door open.*

          The baby cries.

          Don't have children.
          Don't ever bring me grandchildren.

          He turns back into the room, facing away from the door.

          We hear the ten-year-old FREYA*'s voice.*

FREYA   Daddy?

ROBERT   Go away.

FREYA   I found this dress. I think it was Mum's. Can I have it? I like the flowers.

ROBERT   Don't touch a thing.

FREYA   Daddy?

ROBERT   Leave me alone.

FREYA   Daddy?

ROBERT   No!

FREYA   I'm pregnant.

            ROBERT *turns. Facing him is thirty-year-old* FREYA,
            pregnant, holding the dress.

            What do I do?

            *Growing sound of white noise again, like a rumble,
            maybe like water, building up into…*

Thomas Hood

Early in the morning.

Light just on FREYA *in her hospital bed. She gets out of bed fully
dressed, and puts her bag on.*

She puts her headphones in and presses play, and sets out.

MARYNA, *the Polish cleaner from before, sees* FREYA *and starts
singing 'I Am Not a Robot'.*

FREYA *leaves the hospital with* MARYNA, *and passes a group of
men smoking outside.* FREYA *steals one.*

The man steals his cigarette back.

FREYA   Oh.

            FREYA *walks down the road into the city, with*
            MARYNA, *and picking up some other commuters
            behind her. They walk with her, singing.*

            As FREYA *starts to become happier, the commuters
            stop and lift her up and around, as she sings.*

            *They put her down and they run – into Covent Garden!
            Various street performers appear, including a robot
            performer, a juggler, a few tourists, and some kids.*

FREYA plays with them all, hopscotch, eating fruit from a stall, dancing with a waiter.

Everyone dances. A marching band appears, some people dressed as animals. People on TV in shop windows joining in. Everything moving. Signs, shops, the sun!

Huge lights, glitter from the ceiling, or a newspaper seller throws her free papers in the air. Ushers dancing and singing in the audience.

PETER appears, looking for FREYA. Everyone starts moving off, going about their normal boring business. MARYNA goes home.

The newspaper seller clears up her papers, slightly confused, and leaves.

FREYA starts to text on her phone.

FREYA is crying, and texting, she leans against a wall and sinks down to her knees. PETER taps her on the shoulder.

PETER   Hello miss.

FREYA   Oh / no.

PETER   Was that you singing?

FREYA   You're supposed to be at home.

PETER   I know but I got bored it's all box sets and nothing in your flat, led me to a complete feeling of apathy sat around like that, I see what you meant now, so I thought I'd come and find you, you don't mind do you? You look terrible. Not being rude but you look completely white. Like someone addicted to heroin. Or someone that's dead. What are you doing?

Dark clouds appear. White noise.

FREYA   Nothing. Leave me alone.

She gets up and walks off, still texting.

He waits for a moment, then follows her.

The white noise turns into radio in a cab office. STEVE is arguing with MRS ANDREWS.

MRS ANDREWS   Forty minutes

STEVE   No, I've been here all night, I'm not waiting any
                longer.

MRS ANDREWS   Well I'm sorry but they said the driver's on his
                way and a Ford Focus only goes so fast in this weather.

STEVE   Ford Focus? Jesus.

MRS ANDREWS   It's no bad thing you learn a lesson. You may be
                worried, you may want to get home but you can't beat
                nature. You can't hold back the tide.

STEVE   Well we can.

MRS ANDREWS   What?

STEVE   That's exactly what the Thames Barrier does. Stops the
                tide coming in. We build tunnels, we fly, we go to the
                Moon, of course you can beat nature –

                STEVE *receives a text message. He reads it.*

                We can do what we want, and right now I want my
                fucking taxi. So.

                He looks up.

                Forty minutes, you're sure?

                White noise.

                SARAH *has made breakfast in the kitchen.*

                COLIN *comes in.*

SARAH   Late night?

COLIN   Can you not?

SARAH   I made some tea.

                She puts it on the side.

COLIN   Shouldn't you have gone by now?

SARAH   I want to talk.

COLIN   I know I know, we made a mess, we'll tidy up. Don't
                worry, go.

SARAH   I've made a decision.

COLIN   A decision?

SARAH   I've had an offer.

COLIN   Right... you're...

SARAH   I'm going to resign. Take a new job.

COLIN   Look, I've got a headache.

SARAH   In the commercial sector. I'll start in the new year.
          I was. Wrong. Colin.
          I'm sorry.
          You come first.

          COLIN *smiles*.

          What? That's funny?

COLIN   You're going to work for a company?

SARAH   A multinational company, position on the board
          maybe. It pays well, the hours are better.

COLIN   You used to throw things.

SARAH   I... what?

COLIN   You used to throw things through windows.

SARAH   I'm sorry Colin you're not making sense.

COLIN   You'd bunk off work, go into town and shout your
          lungs out. Protesting against whatever it was, I'd come
          and pick you up round the corner.

SARAH   Well thankfully I've grown up so –

COLIN   Wearing those dresses, you used to get in the car, your
          face would be red with shouting, and your hair down,
          you'd have thrown something at some bank, or the
          police and you'd jump in the car and say drive – just
          drive, and we'd speed off, like a film, in my Volvo.

SARAH   You hated all that.

COLIN   At least we argued about things that mattered.

          Now you want to be on the board.

SARAH   I thought you'd be pleased. I thought you'd at least talk
          to me about it.

COLIN   Look.

SARAH   What?

COLIN   We hate each other.

SARAH   I don't hate you.

             They look at each other.

             It's Jasmine.

COLIN   No.

SARAH   She's been talking, making you like this, while I'm the one mopping up, dealing with her fucking...

COLIN   Just fun.

SARAH   Her *vomit*, I take her to the doctor, pay her rent, credit cards and –

COLIN   It's not Jasmine.

             A moment. SARAH *picks up the tea, offers it.*

SARAH   Are you going to drink your tea?

COLIN   You should go. You'll be late.

             JASMINE *comes down, in her nightdress, smoking a cigarette.*

JASMINE   Tea! Great.

             She takes it off SARAH *and drinks.*

SARAH   You can put that out Jasmine. You know not to smoke inside.

JASMINE   I'm not smoking.

SARAH   This is my house.

JASMINE   Yeah, it looks like you.

SARAH   What?

JASMINE   Dated. Subsidence, dry rot. Cracks beginning to show. In desperate need of redecoration.

SARAH   I've done everything for you and you're...

JASMINE   Do you know what comes before part B?

SARAH   What?

JASMINE   Part A!

SARAH   For Christ's –

JASMINE   Come on that was funny.

SARAH   You're like Dad. Just like him.

JASMINE   Wouldn't know would I?

SARAH   Colin can we have a conversation...

JASMINE   We should take you shopping today Colin, find you
            some new clothes, sort you out, what do you think?

            SARAH*'s phone gets a text message. She picks up the
            phone, looks at it, puts it in her pocket – looks at*
            COLIN.

COLIN   Good luck with your job.

            SARAH *goes, upset.*

JASMINE   We so got it on last night – alright, we didn't exactly
            get it on but you were a bit frisky for a minute or two –
            alright maybe you weren't a bit *frisky*, but your heart
            was going like bang bang bang, bang bang – alright
            maybe not bang bang bang but –

COLIN   I nearly told her I wanted a divorce.

JASMINE   Oh.

COLIN   Just now.

JASMINE   Because of us? Cos you're great Colin but I don't
            know if I want a proper relationship.

COLIN   Don't be stupid Jasmine.
            I'm serious.

JASMINE   ...

COLIN   So what do you think?

JASMINE   A divorce? Don't know.

            JASMINE*'s phone gets a text. She picks it up. Shrugs.*

            Things change.

A hint of white noise. JASMINE *reads her text.*

STEVE, *tired and unshaven, comes into the living room and picks up his bag.* ROBERT *is there.*

ROBERT   Did you call her?

STEVE   She's texted. She wants to meet.

ROBERT   Good, she wants to meet. Good.

STEVE   You're right she'll have a difficult life.

ROBERT   Freya?

STEVE   Emily. She'll not have the things we had, maybe.

ROBERT   That's right.

STEVE   The world could be terrible. It could be.

ROBERT   Yes.

STEVE   But she'll be clever, like her mum, so that's good, and she'll have a practical attitude which comes from me. An intuition.

ROBERT   This isn't the point Steve.

STEVE   I think it is. The point. I really think it is. Even if things do get difficult, really tough, like you said, the world'll be better with her in it. She'll add something special.

ROBERT   Don't you think all fathers think this?

STEVE   No, not all fathers. No.

ROBERT   …

STEVE   And anyway this isn't the future, she's already there, thinking, learning. Sucking her thumb, listening.

ROBERT   You like things simple. I understand. Fair enough. You don't want to think about it.

           ROBERT *laughs, sits down. The taxi beeps.*

           Do what you want. Not my problem any more.

           STEVE *picks up his bag, takes out a book and gives it to* ROBERT.

STEVE   My book.

ROBERT   Your book.

STEVE   There's something on page thirty-seven you'd
            recognise. It's about angry old men who think they're
            prophets and stand on street corners with signs,
            shouting at anyone who walks past.

ROBERT   Fascinating.

STEVE   They want the world to end when they do.

ROBERT   Really?

STEVE   And they smell.

ROBERT   What?

STEVE   Because they're on their own, they smell, a bit, of piss.

            Don't get up.

            He leaves. ROBERT *sits in the chair. White noise
            grows.*

            TOM*'s phone rings. He's in his underwear, just woken
            up.*

            SARAH *has arrived at work, and is trying to get
            through.*

SIMON   The PM says half an hour this morning but only if it's
            important.

SARAH   Say it's vital.

SIMON   Are you sure?

SARAH   Use that word when you tell him.

SIMON   / 'Vital'.

TOM   Hello?

SARAH   Tom. This is the secretary of state for energy and
            climate change we spoke yesterday, you came to visit.

TOM   How did you get my number?

SARAH   I've been thinking about what you said and I wondered
            if you'd be around for lunch.

TOM   Lunch?

SARAH	Yes. Today. Somewhere nice.
TOM	I've only just got up.
SARAH	That's fine. Get dressed. You've got a tie?
TOM	I'm a student.
SARAH	I'll send a car. He'll bring a tie. Half-twelve?
TOM	How do you know where I live?
SARAH	44 Lonsdale Road.
TOM	Yeah but –
SARAH	Perfect. Half-twelve. See you then.

She hangs up.

SIMON	Minister, what are you doing?
SARAH	I'm cooking.

FREYA *is walking down the street followed by* PETER, *walking behind her.*

PETER	Did you walk all the way here?
FREYA	Yes.
PETER	Like Dick Whittington?
FREYA	What?
PETER	It's a pantomime.
FREYA	I know what it is. / Jesus.
PETER	I saw *Dick Whittington* at the Hexagon in Reading.
FREYA	Peter –
PETER	It had Les Dennis in it. It was a bit embarrassing all round I thought. But anyway in that he walks to London and becomes mayor. Maybe you'll become mayor.
FREYA	I've had enough. I want to stop.
PETER	Or perhaps you're here because of the earthquake.

She stops.

It's supposed to happen today.

FREYA   I know, I know it's *supposed* to but –

PETER   Right so when it does you'll need a sidekick. Dick
             Whittington had a cat, I can be the cat?

             She turns away from him.

FREYA   I'm imagining you. The drink or the pills in hospital or
             some kind of paranoia, schizophrenia something like
             that, the blood rushing to my head.

PETER   There's a long history of earthquakes in the capital.
             One in 1580 killed two people and made everyone
             think that it was Judgment Day.

FREYA   Peter... / shut up.

PETER   Another one in 1931 originated in Yorkshire but made
             chimneys fall down in Clapham. The most recent was
             in 2008. They happen quite a lot.

FREYA   You should be interested in girls or something.

PETER   I am.

FREYA   I'm tired.

PETER   I am interested in girls or / something.

FREYA   Why isn't there ever anywhere to sit down!?

             She sits down on the ground.

             They say when you give birth, the pain is unbearable.
             That's why women forget. Your skin tears, there's
             blood and there's shit and you scream and it feels like
             you're going to die.

             She scratches at her stomach a bit.

PETER   You still got my flower?

             She has the flower stuck in her bag.

FREYA   I like it.

PETER   You should keep going miss.

FREYA   Why?

PETER   I think you're nearly there.

             That way.

FREYA *stands and carries on*. PETER *smiles and follows*.

Liberty, on Carnaby Street.

JASMINE *sits with a* LIBERTY WOMAN, *waiting for* COLIN.

JASMINE   I'm not going to steal anything.

LIBERTY

JASMINE   Do you have to wear all that make-up?

           You must be depressed working in a shop like this, standing here all the time, you look really depressed.

LIBERTY   This isn't just a shop.

JASMINE   What?

LIBERTY   This is Liberty.

JASMINE   But how much do you get paid?

LIBERTY   I'm sorry?

JASMINE   It's probably not much is it?

LIBERTY   What do you do?

           JASMINE *shouts through the changing room.*

JASMINE   Colin! You know how to get dressed right?

           No reply.

           You should break out, come with us, what's your name?

LIBERTY   Liberty.

JASMINE   That's the name of the shop I meant what's *your* name?

LIBERTY   It's my name as well.

JASMINE   Coincidence.

LIBERTY   Not really. I wanted to work here from when I was fourteen. I love this place, the people, the lighting. Most items cost well over two hundred pounds. I used to come here for hours and walk around and touch things. Then when I was eighteen I applied for the job. I put Liberty on the form, as my name. I thought it would get their attention. I was right. When I got the job, I applied to deed poll, so my bank details would match. I wear this amount of make-up so my skin tone goes exactly with the colour of the walls? And you'll notice my clothes coordinate with the posters, and the sign outside.

JASMINE   Well, *Liberty*, that's brilliant but we're drinking ouzo and you should blow this off, come and have a laugh with us.

LIBERTY   You and your dad?

JASMINE   He's not my dad. We're together, out on the town, we're going to have it, what do you think?

She looks at LIBERTY *and smiles.*

LIBERTY   No thanks.

JASMINE   Can't believe you're called Liberty. What was your old name?

LIBERTY   Nicola.

JASMINE   I like Nicola.

LIBERTY   Nicola's shit. Liberty's better. What's your name?

JASMINE   Jasmine.

LIBERTY   Who called you that? Your mum or something?

JASMINE   …

LIBERTY   Jasmine doesn't mean anything. Liberty's better.

It means freedom.

SARAH, TOM *and* CARTER *in a restaurant.*

CARTER   How are you feeling today?

SARAH   I'm feeling really good, thank you.

CARTER   Stronger constitution than the country you're running. Not many people can say that. Who's this?

SARAH   This is Tom.

TOM   Hi.

CARTER   Work experience?

SARAH   Tom's a friend.

CARTER   Hi Tom. Nice tie.

TOM   She said we were going somewhere posh.

CARTER   Posh? Here? No. This isn't posh.

SARAH   I met Tom yesterday. He has family in Eritrea. Do you know where that is?

CARTER   There are so many countries aren't there? Africa or something probably? We don't fly there, I know that.

TOM   The crops don't grow any more. The temperature is rising year on year. The people, my family, they're getting to the point where either they move or they die.

SARAH   Tom doesn't really approve of your plans.

CARTER   What are you doing Sarah?

TOM   You think your suit looks really good don't you?

CARTER   It's not about what I think, actually, Tom, it's a fact. This suit is really impressive.

SARAH   Tom tried to blackmail me. He thought at the time Heathrow wasn't enough he heard I was due to make an announcement and he demanded a complete halt to air-travel expansion. Now, I gave him hell because I don't like to be blackmailed. As you know. I told him I hadn't made up my mind.

CARTER   Which turned out to be true.

SARAH   But speaking to my husband this morning, he mentioned how I used to throw things at the windows of large corporations like yours. As you know we're going through a difficult time at the moment but he seemed to think I was more attractive back then, and I could see what he meant.

CARTER   Oh I get it, you're making a *point*, she's *using* you Tom. Well look, Africa's a pretty shit place to grow vegetables global warming or not, what with the sun and the desert and the *civil war*. Maybe your family should move, get away from it all on one of our nice big planes, or is that not the point you're making?

SARAH   I was reminded why I went into politics, Tom and I / aren't so different.

CARTER   I know a fantastic therapist, Sarah, if that's what this is really / about.

SARAH   So I gave Tom a call, asked him to join us.

CARTER   This thing with *teenagers* / it's *strange*

SARAH   Then I called the Prime Minister's office to bring forward the meeting.

CARTER   The Prime Minister?

SARAH   I sat down with him and put forward my case.

CARTER   You did.

SARAH   A total halt to expansion, guaranteed. No more runways, control, terminals, nothing, right across the country. I said he had to be firm, make a lasting decision. I told him a strong message on this would unite the government, and be popular with the country.

CARTER   And what did he say?

SARAH   He's very green. He's got a wind turbine on his roof. Next week, we announce. It's over.

           CARTER *smiles at them.*

           In Liberty.

           COLIN *comes out from the dressing room. He's wearing a very expensive suit, shirt and tie, with new shoes. He's had a haircut as well. He looks fantastic.*

JASMINE   Wow.

COLIN   Is it alright?

LIBERTY   How does it feel?

COLIN   Not sure. How much is it?

           LIBERTY *gets out a calculator.*

LIBERTY   Well, with the suit, the shoes, the tie, the shirt. The cufflinks, the vest, the care cover, you'll want that, the socks, the laces...

           Five thousand pounds and forty-four pence.

COLIN   Oh my god.

LIBERTY	Perhaps your girlfriend would like something of her own?
COLIN	She's not my girlfriend.
LIBERTY	She said she / was –
COLIN	Is that what you told her?
JASMINE	No.
COLIN	Jasmine!
JASMINE	Colin!
COLIN	She's my wife's sister.
LIBERTY	Oh just your… well… that explains it then.
JASMINE	What?
LIBERTY	Why she's trying so hard.

A moment.

Anyway what do you think?

Shall we put it through?

Is it something you think you could own?

SARAH, TOM *and* CARTER.

CARTER	Tom, do you have a computer?
TOM	Yeah.
CARTER	Phone?
TOM	Of course.
CARTER	You drive a car?
TOM	And get to the point?
CARTER	All of them developed for profit. It's how we progress. But Sarah thinks we've reached the first moment in human existence where we have to stop, and go backwards. She thinks this moment is entirely different to anything that's ever happened.
TOM	But the world *is* / different. It has limits.

CARTER   There will be more air travel Tom. Because people
          want it. People have the right. To be free, to make their
          own choices.

TOM   What's more important, a stag weekend in Amsterdam
          or the entire nation of Tuvalu sinking underwater? Six
          flights a year to a second home, or starving families in
          Eritrea?

CARTER   I admire the passion Tom, and clearly you're a bright
          boy with huge potential but is this really what you
          want to do? You could come with me in a minute, I'll
          show you round the office, I'll pay your university
          fees, and before long you'll be eating in restaurants
          like this, with beautiful people and respect and all the
          resources you need to protect the people you love. Or,
          you could end up serving in restaurants like this, on the
          edge, struggling financially, a slow crawl to last place.
          Sarah's just made the wrong decision, there are so
          many women like her, lonely, past it, no children but
          she needs a project, so now we're all her fucking
          children, stupid and careless and in need of protection,
          and that's fine, she's nothing, she'll be forgotten, but
          it's not too late for you Tom, what do you think?

SARAH   Tom's got what he wanted.

TOM   What?

SARAH   This is a good day for him.

TOM   This isn't / what I wanted.

SARAH   Like me, he just wants things to be fair.

CARTER   So you're not enjoying the restaurant Sarah? Or the bar
          last night? Your big house? / Nice holidays?

SARAH   I'm not denying people their lifestyle but –

TOM   Why / not?

SARAH   There has to be a balance between –

CARTER   You should've seen the salary we offered her. And we
          never ask twice so –

SARAH   I'd rather eat my own shit than work for you.

CARTER   Sort of thing you'd actually do. And anyway –

A bit of bread hits CARTER –

What.

TOM   Shut the fuck up.

– thrown by TOM, *who's standing up.* SARAH *smiles.*

SARAH   Good shot.

He throws another bit at SARAH.

Hey.

TOM   No.

We shouldn't be flying at all.

CARTER   Ah, now, you see?

SARAH   Tom.

TOM   No *expansion* still means thousands of flights every
            single day. You've all had your whole lives to sort out
            the planet, and you've done precisely nothing. Now,
            according to the best scientists, we've got about five
            years left before it's too late, so you'll forgive me if I
            don't wait for the next *election*, you'll understand if
            I'm *impatient*. Because while you continue to have
            conversations like this, in London restaurants, in
            government lobbies and Notting Hill gardens, while
            you show off your little wind turbines, and while
            you're talking and talking, you're still doing absolutely
            fuck-all. And meanwhile, the clock is ticking, the ice
            caps are melting, people are dying and it's my
            generation who'll pay the price, long after you're both
            dead, so I think this is the turning point. Right now.
            I'm going to sleep with more sisters of elected
            politicians, I'm going to handcuff myself to railings,
            I'm going to attack police, issue bomb threats. Until
            something is done, something *real*, I'm going to add to
            the long and noble tradition of direct action.

He takes a plate and smashes it on the floor.

There are children dying that shouldn't be dying.
Lifestyle? Fuck your *lifestyle*.

He kicks over a chair.

Cunts. All of you. Are you embarrassed? You should be.

TOM *leaves*. CARTER *smiles*. SARAH *drinks her wine*.

A busker appears and starts playing.

FREYA *is now walking with* PETER *by the Houses of Parliament.*

FREYA   My dad says, in a few years, they'll look back, on the ruins of London, when the city's underwater, and the old people will say, do you remember walking down Oxford Street? The view from St Paul's? By that time there'll be heatwaves, storms, even this earthquake might be caused by us they think. Something to do with ice sheets crashing into the sea. Decreasing amounts of sediment between the tectonic plates.

PETER   I think it's God.

FREYA   What?

PETER   Don't you think if there is a God, he's pissed off? Like when you leave a mug in your room too long and it grows into this rank horrible green pus. You throw it away when that happens don't you? You get a new one. Start again.

          STEVE *is in Victoria Station, a man in a polar bear costume approaches him. He is holding a bucket of money.*

STEVE   I'm in a hurry.

POLAR BEAR   I'm dying.

STEVE   Do you know where the Tube is?

POLAR BEAR   I know my whole habitat is disappearing down the tube, I know that.

STEVE   Right, excuse me.

POLAR BEAR   Melting icebergs, whole ecosystems eradicated, maybe you could spare a few pounds?

STEVE   I don't have any change.

POLAR BEAR   I'll do a dance.

STEVE   Can you get out of my way?

POLAR BEAR   It's a good dance.

STEVE   Who are you?

               The POLAR BEAR *reveals his face.*

POLAR BEAR   It's Rag Week. Greenpeace.

STEVE   Can you just / get out of the –

POLAR BEAR   Cheer up, might never happen.

               STEVE *struggles with the bear, pushes past and off.*

               A YOUNG MAN, *dirty and sweaty, runs up to* FREYA
               grabs her arm.

YOUNG MAN   Please! Please.

FREYA   Oh. You… How was –

YOUNG MAN   I'm sorry but my kid! My kid's in hospital, I've
               just found out, I need the bus fare to get down the road,
               I don't have any… change… I'm sorry, I'm really in a
               hurry, I'm really sorry. Shit. Shit.

FREYA   You asked me this yesterday.

YOUNG MAN   What?

FREYA   About your kid. I gave you five pounds. You said
               exactly the same thing then.

YOUNG MAN   Oh. Right, yeah yeah.

FREYA   You don't… have a kid, do you?

               The YOUNG MAN *looks at her – of course he doesn't.
               He runs off – the* POLAR BEAR *leaves as well. A
               rumble.*

PETER   Depressing, isn't it?

               Come on.

               FREYA *looks at* PETER.

FREYA   Peter. What's going on?

PETER   What?

FREYA   You don't make sense, following me.

PETER   I register very high on the autism spectrum. It's the sort
               of thing I'd do.

FREYA   You're not even that convincing. Shouldn't your voice have broken by now?

PETER   Yes, that's true, it should've broken by now.

FREYA   Right. So. Peter. What's going on?

PETER   I think I have some kind of purpose. Maybe it's to do with the earthquake. Sometimes people imagine a figure who represents death, the bringer of bad news, a man who will guide them from this life into the next. I could be Peter, at the gates of heaven.

FREYA   My version of death is a sullen fourteen-year-old boy with behavioural difficulties?

PETER   He takes many forms.

        FREYA *walks away, upset.*

        Or I maybe I'm a herald.

FREYA   What am I supposed to do?

PETER   Peter Rabbit. At the rabbit hole.

FREYA   I don't know why I'm here, or where I am, I don't want the baby –

PETER   Miss –

FREYA   – but I can't get rid of it, my family hate me, not a single friend has called me all week.

PETER   Miss –

FREYA   I'm a fuck-up, a fuck-up, on my own. A complete fucking MESS.

        She looks at her belly.

        I don't want you! Little fucking…

        She punches it.

PETER   Miss! I can feel it.

FREYA   What?

PETER   It's time.

FREYA   Peter, I've had enough!

PETER   I'm a carrier signal.

FREYA   A what?

PETER   Someone wants to talk to you and they're using me to get through.

          This is the moment when... The time has come. This is the moment.

FREYA   The moment?

          PETER *starts to remove his hoodie and his glasses.*

PETER   This is the moment when I...

          Who are you thinking of most?

          The moment when I...

          Who do you think of all the time?

FREYA   I don't –

PETER   Who are you thinking of right now?

FREYA   Emily.

PETER   Emily, yes.

          PETER *lets his hair down.*

          Now revealed is a sixteen-year-old girl.

EMILY   Hello Mum.

          A long pause.

          They look at each other.

          FREYA *starts to cry. Horrified. She backs away.*

          Mum –

FREYA   I don't... – Oh god... you're all *grown up*. Oh god.

          EMILY *looks upset.*

          FREYA *pulls herself together and tries to smile.*

          Sorry.

          Sorry.

          Your hair.

          It's a bit like mine.

EMILY   I've got dad's nose apparently.

FREYA   Yeah.

EMILY   His sense of direction too.

They look at each other.

FREYA   I look shit to you, probably.

EMILY   Well...

FREYA *reaches out and touches her on the arm.*

What are you doing?

FREYA   Maybe we could, have a coffee. Do you like coffee?

EMILY   We don't have time.

FREYA   But that's what mums and daughters do. They have a coffee together. They talk. Don't have time before what?

EMILY   No, we should go.

FREYA *follows* EMILY.

JASMINE *and* COLIN *are walking along the river.*

JASMINE   Five.

COLIN   Shut up.

JASMINE   Five girls so far, checking you out.

COLIN   Right.

JASMINE   How many before today?

COLIN   When I was twenty a girl came up to me pinched my bum she obviously thought I looked good from behind but when she turned me round and saw my face she went urrgh, and walked away.

JASMINE   You've had a tough life haven't you?

COLIN   Fuck it.

JASMINE   Exactly, you know where we're supposed to be going?

COLIN   The South Bank. This way.

A woman walks past and checks COLIN *out.*

JASMINE   Six.

COLIN   !

          She chases after him.

          FREYA *and* EMILY.

FREYA   What are you into?

EMILY   What?

FREYA   For fun. With your friends.

EMILY   I...

FREYA   ?

EMILY   Football.

          FREYA *tries to smile.*

FREYA   That's good.

EMILY   Mum I –

FREYA   Do you have a boyfriend?

EMILY   Am I gay you mean?

FREYA   No. I just.

EMILY   I play football so I must be gay.

FREYA   No. I didn't mean that.

EMILY   Yeah / okay.

FREYA   What do you want to do when you grow up?

EMILY   I'll finish school, get a job somewhere probably, I don't know.

FREYA   Ambitions...?

EMILY   No point is there? I mean there's nowhere to go. You don't understand. Look at you. Thought when you were younger you'd look better.

FREYA   What have I done? Why are you being like this?

EMILY   Are you joking?

FREYA   ...

EMILY   When you've been drinking, you sit on the sofa and apologise again and again. 'I'm sorry, I'm *sorry*

Emily.' Then you fall asleep, spill it everywhere. I have to put you to bed.

FREYA   What about your dad?

EMILY   Dad left ages ago. Only see him Saturdays.

              Come on.

FREYA   What?

EMILY   We don't want to be late.

              EMILY *escorts* FREYA *onwards.*

              STEVE *is on the South Bank.*

              A JOGGER jogs *past on the way to work.*

STEVE   Excuse me.

              She comes to a stop.

              I'm... meeting someone by the theatre, where's the... theatre?

JOGGER   The theatre? I don't know.

STEVE   Oh, okay –

JOGGER   I don't go to the theatre.

STEVE   Okay – I just...

JOGGER   Why would I go to the theatre?

STEVE   It doesn't matter.

JOGGER   It's just like TV. But more expensive. And further away.

              STEVE *stops and waits.*

              FREYA *and* EMILY *are walking along Waterloo Bridge.*

EMILY   You know where they've put the London Eye now?

FREYA   No.

EMILY   Bath.

FREYA   Why?

EMILY   Good question. After the flooding it was going to go on tour but no one had the money so they had a public vote and Bath it was instead.

You ever been on it? The wheel. I read about Bath in a book once. Looked nice...

FREYA   No.

They stop.

EMILY   So what have you done?

FREYA   What?

EMILY   What do you do? Day to day.

FREYA   I... don't really... I find it all quite...

EMILY   You find it all too much.

FREYA   Yeah.

EMILY   You can't cope.

FREYA   I've never found it as easy as I think you're supposed to.

EMILY *is looking out at the view.*

Have we stopped then?

Is this where you're taking me?

What am I supposed to do here?

EMILY   You've texted Dad haven't you?

FREYA   Yes but –

EMILY   And Jasmine, and Sarah.

FREYA   To meet me. I want to talk to them.

EMILY   Look where we're standing. Waterloo Bridge.

FREYA   ...

EMILY   You wanted them to watch you. Mum, if you could see what's going to happen. The buildings and the parks are shanty towns. Immigrants everywhere, gambling and drinking, the streets – covered in shit, the air thick with smoke, there's disease and rationing, blackouts and curfews. Every morning when we fetch the water we have to queue for an hour, and at night you keep a knife by the side of your bed, just in case. I hate it. So do you. Everyone has given up. You're passed out on the chair, but I'm in the bed, under the covers, desperately trying to get a message to you. It's what you tell me. It's what you say you should've done, for both of us.

FREYA   I'm sorry, I've really been trying.

EMILY   It's not too late. Just step over the barrier.

FREYA looks at her.

Then climbs over the barrier.

Get used to it. Breathe. I'm sat inside you. Warm and happy and I won't know anything about it. You have my entire support to throw yourself off. It's better you do. I promise.

FREYA looks out.

Breathe. And then, imagine there's a step. Just step out. They say most people die of shock before they hit the water.

A few people gather around, at a distance to watch.

EMILY stands amongst them, disappears in the crowd.

FREYA   Emily?

PASSERBY 1   Who is she?

PASSERBY 2   I don't know she just climbed over, but look at her.

PASSERBY 1   Yeah.

FREYA   Emily…?

PASSERBY 2   Just one of those women.

PASSERBY 1   / Yeah, god.

FREYA   Emily, please!

PASSERBY 1   Why does she keep on shouting?

PASSERBY 2   Who knows? Emily! Fuck! Sorry – shouldn't laugh. Has someone called the police?

STEVE is on the South Bank.

JASMINE and COLIN arrive.

STEVE   She texted you too?

JASMINE   Yeah she didn't say you were coming though, could've left you to it.

STEVE   Colin, you look –

COLIN   Yeah.

STEVE   She's supposed to be here supposed to be here by now but –

JASMINE   She gets distracted by bright colours. Don't worry, it's quite normal. She takes her time. Oh no.

           SARAH *appears*.

SARAH   Proper family gathering. Steve, she said you were away.

STEVE   I was.

SARAH   She's texted everyone. What's happened to you?

COLIN   Right.

JASMINE   Colin's got something / to tell you.

SARAH   So where is she?

STEVE   I don't know.

SARAH   Drags us all out here then doesn't show up herself, / pretty typical.

STEVE   I hoped she'd be waiting here, but –

SARAH   What do you mean Colin's got something / to tell me?

STEVE   Has anyone spoken to her? Sorry. / Has anyone actually spoken to Freya?

SARAH   Colin?

COLIN   Maybe we should –

SARAH   I didn't take the job. You were right. I turned it down.

JASMINE   He wants a divorce.

SARAH   Oh... you... For fuck's sake Jasmine he buys a new jacket, you think he's having a mid-life crisis. He doesn't want a divorce, we're just –

JASMINE   Ask him.

SARAH   I'm not going to ask him.

JASMINE   Ask him.

COLIN   I think perhaps we should...

SARAH   What? Should what?

COLIN   I think perhaps we should.

                    Yes.

STEVE   Is that...

JASMINE   What?

SARAH   We're, we're not going to talk about it here.

JASMINE   You mean on / the –

STEVE   / Yeah.

SARAH   In front of her and everyone else. We need to –

COLIN   Sarah.

JASMINE   / fuck, fuck, shut up. *Shut up*.

SARAH   I'm not doing this *now*.

JASMINE   On the bridge.

                    They all look.

                    A crowd has gathered on the bridge – traffic passes. It is noisy. A POLICE OFFICER *has arrived.*

FREYA   In 1844 Waterloo Bridge was called the bridge of sighs, there were so many suicides.

POLICE OFFICER   I want you to stay calm.

FREYA   Thomas Hood wrote a poem about a homeless woman who threw herself off.

POLICE OFFICER   You're going to be alright.

FREYA   One more Unfortunate,

POLICE OFFICER   Slowly come back/ over the barrier.

FREYA   Weary of breath,
                    Rashly importunate,

POLICE OFFICER   Help is / on its way.

FREYA   Gone to her death.

PASSERBY 2   / Come on. Fuck's sake, get on with it.

The crowd laughs.

FREYA   Make no deep scrutiny
          Into her mutiny
          Rash and undutiful:

          FREYA*'s phone rings.*

PASSERBY 2   JUMP JUMP JUMP JUMP...!

FREYA   Fuck fuck shit...

          The crowd chants. FREYA *answers her phone.*

STEVE   Baby, it's me. I'm here. I can see you.

FREYA   Steve... I'm scared. But I can't... They...

          FREYA *cries. Someone in the crowd starts playing
          'Jump' by Kris Kross. The crowd chant.*

STEVE   Please. Climb / back down on to the road.

FREYA   Who was her mother? /
          Had she a sister?

STEVE   Calm down, listen. / I'm on my way.

          *There is a rumbling drowning the rest of the noise. The
          ground shakes.*

          An earthquake. The bridge is moving.

FREYA   In she plunged boldly –
          No matter / how coldly
          The rough / river ran –

STEVE   Please don't. Freya. / I know what the problem is.

FREYA   Cold inhumanity, /
          Burning insanity,

STEVE   Freya. Freya. It's okay. I understand.

          The rumbling is loud now. The earth moving.

FREYA   Steve. I don't know what to do. I don't want the baby, I
          really can't have a baby.

STEVE   We'll work it out –

FREYA   There's a noise. It's moving. Shaking. The bridge.
           Everything's *moving*!

STEVE   Hold on and / just wait or

FREYA   I don't want to hold on – I can't wait any more – It's
           too late! This is important. Where have you *been*! This
           is *it*!

           The earthquake is very loud.

           Oh god oh god, it's the earthquake. Just like they said.

           I can't, I can't do anything.

           Please please no.

           Emily.

           It's breaking.

           I can't hold on! I... I can't!

           She slips.

           Blackout.

           The sound of destruction.

           An earthquake.

           End of Act Four.

ACT FIVE

Prologue

As the noise fades, an animation plays.

We see blackboard animation that illustrates the story. The narrator is old and wise.

NARRATOR It is said that in the old times, in the early years of the twenty-first century, mankind only thought of himself. The people would steal from the land and plunder the seas, they would kill the animals, tear out the minerals from the ground and poison the sky. And as the Earth grew darker, the Sun burnt brighter, and the sea began to rise, the people simply closed their eyes and drank, and danced, and attempted to ignore their certain destruction.

It was then, in mankind's greatest hour of need, that Solomon came. A young woman, accompanied only by one faithful companion, packed her bag, and came to the city of London. After three days, walking barefoot, she arrived on the bridge across the river, at the centre of the Earth, and she spoke. Her words proclaimed the new enlightenment.

She was young, and so full of hope and truth that her speech, her words, the power and the light, was relayed, repeated, across the world, by radio, by television, by powerful rumour and written instruction to every man and woman on the planet and slowly slowly, the tide turned. People listened and people changed. Solomon spent the rest of her life travelling the world, walking a new path, showing us the future, a new way to live.

And the people of the world were happy. They were saved and they rejoiced.

The blackboard bleaches to white.

Certain Destruction

2525, or possibly a hospital. A beeping sound.

A clean white space.

FREYA *is lying on a single white bed.*

A WOMAN *appears. She looks like* GRACE, *and wears a white version of the floral dress from the Act One Prologue. She also wears a veil.*

GRACE   Freya. Freya?

            FREYA *wakes. Tries to sit up.*

            No, you don't need to move.

FREYA   I was in the river.

GRACE   You're safe now.

FREYA   These aren't my clothes...

GRACE   How do you feel?

FREYA   Where am I? Where is everyone?

GRACE   It's just me. Try to focus. You've been asleep a very
            long time.

FREYA   What do you mean?

GRACE   You're in the future.

FREYA   The future?

GRACE   The year Twenty-Five, Twenty-Five.

FREYA   You're joking.

GRACE   You're alive. You're warm. You're safe. And now
            you're awake.

            Have a drink.
            Here.
            A glass of water.

            FREYA *takes it, and drinks.*

FREYA   Who are you?

GRACE   I'm Grace.

FREYA   My mum was called Grace.

GRACE   Yes.

FREYA   But she died. There was nothing they could do. It was cancer.

GRACE   We don't have cancer any more.

FREYA   Good.

GRACE   We don't have diseases or pain, we don't have suffering or death, we have only peace. Peace and life.

           GRACE *strokes* FREYA*'s hair.*

FREYA   She used to stroke my head like that.

           Can I...

           FREYA *removes* GRACE*'s veil.*

           Mum...

GRACE   Hello Freya.

FREYA   Mum!

           I was so scared! I didn't... I didn't know what to do.

           FREYA *hugs her and cries.* GRACE *hugs her tight.*

GRACE   You're safe.
           You're safe now.

           Hospital.

           FREYA *is in a hospital bed, on a ventilator,
           unconscious.*

           STEVE *is watching her. He paces.*

           TIM *enters.*

TIM   Mr Sullivan?

STEVE   Yes?

TIM   I was the doctor who treated your wife. They said you had some questions.

STEVE   When she came in, didn't you think there was something wrong?

TIM   She was worried about the baby but we tried to put her
           mind at rest, we let her stay in overnight, and then in
           the morning she checked herself out. We had no reason
           to think she would... well.

STEVE   You just let her go.

TIM   It was our assessment that she would be fine.

STEVE   Just let her walk out the door by herself.

TIM   She said she didn't have anyone to collect her.

           They look at each other.

STEVE   What do you think?

TIM   I'm sorry –

STEVE   Does she have a chance?

TIM   I'm sorry, it's not my department.

STEVE   I'm sure you've spoken to your colleagues before
           coming in here, you all *talk*, don't you? You wanted to
           know the situation before you confronted the husband.
           So you know the situation, what do you think?

TIM   They're conducting some tests.

STEVE   But what do you think?

TIM

STEVE   If there isn't a chance, you should tell me. If there's
           nothing any of us can do any more and we should all
           just give up, I'd rather know.

TIM   I'm sure there's a chance.

STEVE

TIM   You might want to talk to her.

STEVE   Why? She's in a coma. Why would I talk to her?

TIM   Some people find it helpful.

STEVE   ...

TIM   Is there anything else I can do?

STEVE   Her family are outside. Can you… make sure they
             have what they want, tell them what's going on, get
             them whatever they need.

             And keep them out.
             I don't want them coming in here.

             TIM *goes*.

             2525.

             The music plays again. GRACE *enters.*

             FREYA *is sat on the edge of the bed.*

FREYA   So – Dad bought into one of those cryogenic things
             and we've all been frozen at the point of death, you as
             well, revitalised only when medical science has the
             power to heal us.

             GRACE *smiles.*

             Is that right?

             GRACE *just looks at her.*

             Is that what's going on?

GRACE   You look better.

FREYA   I feel better. I want to have a look round. The future!
             Have you got flying cars?

GRACE   We don't need cars.

FREYA   And robots.

GRACE   You have no idea.

FREYA   When can I see?

GRACE   When you're well enough.

FREYA   I'm fine, look.

GRACE   We have some questions first.

FREYA   What about?

GRACE   Freya, the date of your preservation is of vital
             historical significance. It is said, that this was the
             turning point. The moment you fell, the place it
             happened, legend has it that it was from that place at

that time that the speech was made. From the bridge. From that moment. The tide turned. The world became better, and better until we solved the problems. All the problems. And we survived.

So. Did you hear it? Did you hear the speech? Is that why you were there?

FREYA   No. I don't know anything about it.

GRACE   This is important, you were on the bridge, in that time.

FREYA   Yes but –

GRACE   Why were you on the bridge, if not to hear Solomon's speech?

FREYA   Solomon?

GRACE   Yes.

FREYA   Solomon on the bridge?

GRACE   Solomon, the greatest woman in the world, she walked to London, stood at the centre of the Earth and changed everything.

FREYA   Solomon... Mum. It's not Solomon. It's Sullivan.

GRACE   What?

FREYA   It's me. I walked all the way to the bridge, I stood in the centre of the Earth.

GRACE   But Freya...

FREYA   I'm Solomon. I changed the world.

GRACE   Freya you can't be.

FREYA   Yes! Why not?

GRACE   Because you died.
             And Solomon...
             Solomon lived.

             SARAH *and* COLIN *are in the hospital café.* SARAH *brings back two coffees.*

SARAH   There.

COLIN   Thanks.

They drink.

How are you?

SARAH *shrugs.*

They drink.

SARAH   Do you remember the jacket you wore at Suzie's party?

COLIN   What?

SARAH   I just thought of it. You remember? It had shoulder pads.

COLIN   Yes.

SARAH   It was far too big.

COLIN   My lucky jacket.

SARAH   Well, that's what you used to call it –

COLIN   Yeah.

SARAH   Lucky in what way exactly?

COLIN   It got attention.

SARAH   You looked stupid.

COLIN   Like I said, attention.

SARAH   Well...

COLIN   From the birds.

SARAH   Birds. Jesus.

COLIN   Got your attention.

SARAH   You used to roll up the sleeves.

COLIN   Nothing wrong with that, not in the eighties.

He rolls up the sleeves of his jacket.

See?

She smiles.

Good look.

He unrolls them.

SARAH   Probably just ruined it.

COLIN   What?

SARAH   That jacket.

COLIN   What do you mean?

SARAH   Just... that it... looks expensive, you probably
          shouldn't –

COLIN   Not your problem now is it?

SARAH   Colin...

COLIN   What?

SARAH   I was trying to –

COLIN   What?

SARAH

COLIN   We shouldn't talk about this now.

SARAH   When you lost your job yes I probably thought I
          should compensate in some way. I know things aren't
          like they were, I know I'm *different* these days. But I
          don't think it's too late.

          I'll change.

          Or something.

COLIN   Do you like this suit?

SARAH   Yeah, I mean...

COLIN   Honestly.

SARAH   ...

          I don't think it's very... It's not who you are.

COLIN   I love it. I really do.
          It is absolutely, who I am.
          It absolutely is.

SARAH   ...

          SARAH *reaches to him.*

          He moves away.

SARAH   Do you even like me?
          I mean.

You say you've fallen out of love with me and
that's… fine… that's…
You don't want to see me any more.

COLIN

SARAH   But do you think I'm a nice person?
Because, with what everyone's said.
With Freya.
And what Jasmine says.

I don't have anyone else.

So this is kind of crucial.

Colin?

Do you like me?

COLIN   You live in a million-pound house with two cars.
You're a Liberal Democrat minister in a Tory
government. Then you tell me you want to join the
board of a multinational airline. It's not that I don't like
you Sarah. I hardly know you.

Jasmine was right.

SARAH   Jasmine's never been right about anything.

COLIN   …

SARAH   What did she say?

COLIN   Things change.

They look at each other.

2525. FREYA is on her feet now.

FREYA   Then… then I have to go back and do what I was
supposed to do.

GRACE   Back? Freya you can't go back. That world crumbled to
dust hundreds of years ago. This is all that exists now.

FREYA   But I was supposed to say something. That's why Peter
was there. And Emily. I wasn't supposed to fall, I was
supposed to speak. The crowd was there, ready to
listen, I was supposed to give them the message.

GRACE   Freya come and sit down.

FREYA   But I messed it up. There must be something you can do.

GRACE   It's too late.

FREYA   Mum!

GRACE   Sit down!

FREYA   No. I'm getting out. I've got to find someone who can help.

          I...
          Oh.
          Where's the door? There isn't a door.

GRACE   No.

FREYA   How do you get in and out?

GRACE   Freya.

FREYA   What?

GRACE   You don't need to go anywhere. Everything's good here. Everything's perfect.

FREYA   And where is everyone? You keep on saying we think this, and we're very interested, but I've only seen you. There should be hundreds of people wanting to talk to me, I'm historically important remember.

GRACE   I'm your closest relative and carer, of course I'm the one to look after you and if you give it time you'll –

FREYA   There's something going on.

GRACE   ...

FREYA   Please. Mum. Don't lie to me.

          GRACE *looks at her.*

          I always knew when something was wrong.

GRACE   Have you got a headache?

FREYA   How did you know?

GRACE   Sit down, with me, on the bed, and I'll explain.

          JASMINE *is in the waiting room.*

          ROBERT *enters.*

JASMINE	Er. This is a private room?
ROBERT	Really?
JASMINE	We've paid for it.
ROBERT	I'm sure you have.
JASMINE	Family only yeah?

She looks at him properly.

Oh. Shit. Shit.

Shit, didn't recognise you. Jesus. Seen pictures but they must be from a while back. You look... old. Shame we haven't met before something like this, isn't it?

ROBERT	You look... really –
JASMINE	What? Here you go, they said you like to answer back, okay yeah, I've been up all night, I'm not my best. What? I look like what?
ROBERT	Like your mother.
JASMINE	Do I?
ROBERT	When she was your age.

She's floored.

JASMINE	Yeah right well done. Good tactic. I look like my mum, put me off my – That must freak you out then. Sarah says Mum was never happy, often crying she said, looks like Freya got those genes.
ROBERT	Look, I know there's a lot to talk / about but –
JASMINE	And I got yours, apparently I've got a mouth on me reminds Sarah of you, yeah there's a fuck of a lot to talk about where do you want to start?
ROBERT	This isn't the time.
JASMINE	Never is, is it? Never is the fucking time by the sound of it.
ROBERT	Jasmine –
JASMINE	Such a lonely old fucking – look at you –

ROBERT   You're not a teenager so –

JASMINE   Actually I am.

ROBERT   Can you stop –

JASMINE   Technically I am? Nineteen, if you're counting, which
            you're probably not, so – stop what?

ROBERT   Stop being so fucking petulant.

JASMINE   Christ they said you got nasty quickly I thought they
            meant hours not minutes look at you, big red face.

ROBERT   Sit down.

JASMINE   I'm not the one getting angry Gandalf, you're
            shouting, I don't think you're allowed to do that I
            might call security.

ROBERT   I hate planes. I'm shattered. Fine. You're nineteen. I'm
            seventy. Sit down, and shut up. What are you wearing?

JASMINE   Whatever the fuck I want.

ROBERT   You look like prostitute.

JASMINE   You talk like this to everyone?

ROBERT   Yes. You?

JASMINE   Yes.

            A moment of respect.

ROBERT   Good.

            He sits.

            She reluctantly sits as well.

JASMINE   Read your books.

ROBERT   And?

JASMINE   Bit dry.

            He smiles.

            You told her to get rid of it.

ROBERT   I told her the truth yes.

JASMINE   Probably regret that now.

A moment.

ROBERT   I could do with a drink.

JASMINE *takes a bottle out of her bag. Gives it to* ROBERT.

What's this?

JASMINE   Ouzo.

ROBERT   Oh.

He drinks from the bottle. It's awful.

You want some?

She takes the bottle. Drinks. They continue to share it.

ROBERT   I should've put my work first, from the beginning.
            That's what I regret.

JASMINE   Even though Freya's nearly dead.
            Sarah's a fuck-up, getting divorced.
            And me… well… look.
            Even given all that?

ROBERT   Because of all that exactly.

            I should never have had any of you in the first place.

JASMINE   So why have you come now?

ROBERT   To say goodbye.

JASMINE   She's not –

ROBERT   Yes. From what I understand she doesn't have much of
            a chance.

JASMINE   No fuck off you don't know if anything had happened
            Steve would've told us, you don't know shit. Fuck's
            sake. Thought you'd have big eyes actually. We've all
            got big eyes. Suppose it must've been Mum.

ROBERT   Yes.

JASMINE   Right.

ROBERT   But she had your hair. Your hands.

JASMINE   What else?

ROBERT   …

JASMINE   What's in the bag?

ROBERT   One of your mother's dresses. Freya liked it, wanted it, years ago. I wouldn't let her. I thought maybe I could…

JASMINE   Bit fucking late now.

ROBERT   You're not like the other two.

JASMINE   No. You would've liked me.

ROBERT   Yes.

                I think I would.

                SARAH enters.

SARAH   You're here.

ROBERT   I am.

SARAH   You've met.

ROBERT   We have.

JASMINE   Where's Colin?

SARAH   Colin's gone.

                As the next scene continues, SARAH *sits with them and drinks the ouzo.*

                2525.

GRACE   When you fell in the river, Freya, you hit your head. You did some damage. And sometimes, when that happens, people become unable to see a distinction between their own particles and those around them. They can't see the edges of their body any more – where they stop and the world begins. They can instead understand instinctively that we are all just different recycled pieces of a larger, older creature. We are simply earthquakes ourselves, wonderful irregularities in an evolving system. We die and the Earth uses us for something new.

                YOUNG ROBERT *enters, dressed in white, and wheels in a cot.*

Yes Freya, this is the future, and I am your mother. But this is also the past and the present, and I am your father, your sisters, your friends, your husband, the table, the bed, the ground, we are everyone that is, was, and everything that will be. I'm nature all in one. So are you.

FREYA   This isn't real.

GRACE   Your brain is doing what it always does. Making sense of what it receives. Combining imagination, memory, information.

FREYA   I'm dreaming.

GRACE   You're on your way.

FREYA   Where?

GRACE   We're here to help you.

YOUNG ROBERT   Freya. Look.

The sound of a baby crying. FREYA goes and looks in the cot. She picks up the baby.

FREYA   Emily.

DR HARRIS is with STEVE, who sits on the bed.

DR HARRIS I'm sorry. Her condition is worsening.

STEVE   I...

STEVE doesn't know how to react.

DR HARRIS It's a matter of when to say goodbye. It should be soon.

STEVE   Alright. Yes.

DR HARRIS Alright then.

And what about the family? I know they're outside.

STEVE   ...

DR HARRIS Will they want to be here?

STEVE

DR HARRIS Or would you rather it was just you?

STEVE   Let them in.

The family goes through.

The NURSE *sits in a chair, exhausted. Turns on the radio. Music plays. A hymn.*

2525.

The worlds beginning to merge.

FREYA *frantic.*

FREYA   Wake me up... please.

GRACE   No.

FREYA   Please. I need to go back. I can't stay here. Emily's alive. I can hear her. She's calling for me.

GRACE   Freya. You can't.

FREYA   I made a mistake. I need to go back.

          Tell them all. Give the speech. Walk the Earth.

GRACE   No.

FREYA   You can't stop me. This isn't real. I need to wake up and tell them what's going to happen, or the world doesn't change. The world stays as it is!

          Darling!

She puts EMILY *back in the cot.*

          I'm going to be with you. I'm going to wake up.

FREYA *goes to the bed, lies down and shuts her eyes.*

GRACE   Freya. I'm sorry.

FREYA   Now!

          Yes!

          Now!

GRACE   It's over.

The music continues, the worlds blurring. The family gathered around the bed, GRACE *stood slightly apart.*

We can't hear what's happening – the music plays.

DR HARRIS *stands close by.* STEVE *sits on the bed with* FREYA, *holding* EMILY.

One by one the family say goodbye. ROBERT *stands back and watches.*

STEVE *gives* EMILY *to* SARAH, *and then lifts* FREYA *and hugs her. Crying.*

Some distance away... during this, EMILY *enters, sixteen, very different to how we saw her before. Bright, optimistic, intelligent.*

She wears the floral dress worn by GRACE *in the Part One Prologue. And she carries a backpack.*

Epilogue

The kitchen of a large house in the west Oxfordshire countryside. Night. On the table there is food out.

It is sixteen years later.

EMILY *is packing food into a backpack.*

Some of it doesn't fit. In the rearranging, we see a map, a torch. A knock on the door.

EMILY *goes and opens it.*

TOM *enters, now thirty-five, a man, rather than a boy. He is dressed much better, ready for a long walk. He is sure of himself.*

EMILY   Shhh – / Dad's asleep – you look nervous.

TOM   You've barely left the town on your own before, you don't know what it's like.

EMILY   I've done my research.

TOM   You should let me come with you.

          She smiles. Touches his arm.

EMILY   I'll be fine.

TOM   And what are you wearing?

EMILY   Do you like it? Before she died, Mum told Dad it was her favourite dress. Dad gave it to me this afternoon, for my birthday. I like the pattern. How about you? Did you get me a present?

TOM *gives her a small bag.*

TOM   Papers, ID, map, new phone.

EMILY   Good.

TOM   All in the bag, as ordered.

EMILY   Perfect. I'm thinking maybe I should go barefoot...

TOM   It's a long way.

EMILY   It is, and people should notice.

She takes her shoes off.

Definitely barefoot.

TOM   You'll call me if you get into trouble?

EMILY   There won't be trouble.

TOM   There might be, maybe we should tell your dad what you're doing. If he wakes up and you're gone –

EMILY   When did you care what he thought?

TOM   This is different.

EMILY   I've told them for years, over and over, when I'm sixteen, this is what happens. At dawn, I'll be on my way. Not my fault if they never believed me.

TOM   At least leave a note –

EMILY   Right. Toothbrush, bag, towel.

She puts the backpack on.

TOM   Speech?

EMILY   Don't need a speech. It's all up here... Tom! I'm half your age and you look petrified.

TOM   It's ridiculous.

EMILY   You know what I can do?

TOM   Yes.

EMILY   And you trust me?

TOM   Of course.

EMILY   Then smile. It'll be fine. Now, how do I look?

            He looks at her, takes her in.

TOM   Emily Sullivan.

            Magnificent.

            She smiles. He smiles too.

            She looks at him, goes to the kitchen blackboard, and writes, in large letters:

            'Gone to London'

            As she goes on her way, STEVE *finally lets go of* FREYA, *and she dies.*

            Blackout.

            End of Play.

LOVE, LOVE, LOVE

Love, Love, Love was first performed at the Drum Theatre, Plymouth, on 12 October 2010, as a co-production between Paines Plough and Theatre Royal Plymouth, before touring. The cast was as follows:

KENNETH	John Heffernan
HENRY	Simon Darwen
SANDRA	Daniela Denby-Ashe
ROSE	Rosie Wyatt
JAMIE	James Barrett
Director	James Grieve
Designer	Lucy Osborne
Lighting Designer	Hartley T A Kemp
Sound Designer	Tom Gibbons

The play was revived at the Royal Court Theatre Downstairs, London, on 27 April 2012. The cast was as follows:

KENNETH	Ben Miles
HENRY	Sam Troughton
SANDRA	Victoria Hamilton
ROSE	Claire Foy
JAMIE	George Rainsford
Director	James Grieve
Designer	Lucy Osborne
Lighting Designer	James Farncombe
Sound Designer	Tom Gibbons

This version of *Love, Love, Love* was first performed by Roundabout Theatre Company at the Laura Pels Theatre at the Harold and Miriam Steinberg Center for Theatre, New York City, on 22 September 2016, directed by Michael Mayer.

It received its British premiere at the Lyric Hammersmith, London, on 5 March 2020, directed by Rachel O'Riordan.

140

Characters

KENNETH
HENRY
SANDRA
JAMIE
ROSE

Note on the Text

The play should take place in a proscenium arch theatre. A red
curtain should close between scenes.

(/) means the next speech begins at that point.

(–) means the next line interrupts.

(…) at the end of a speech means it trails off. On its own it indicates
a pressure, expectation or desire to speak.

A line with no full stop at the end indicates that the next speech
follows on immediately.

A speech with no written dialogue indicates a character deliberately
remaining silent.

ACT ONE

Curtain up.

The sound of the Vienna Boys' Choir singing.

25 June 1967. A north London flat. It's a mess. Smoky. Unwashed glasses on table.

KENNETH *has the television on. He walks around wearing tweed trousers and a dressing gown. He comes out of the kitchen with a glass of brandy, puts it down on the side. Then moves back, runs and athletically jumps over the back of the sofa into the seat.*

He lights a cigarette. Watches the television. Relaxes.

Realises he's left his brandy on the side. Tries to reach it from the sofa.

Really tries.

Gives up, gets up, gets the brandy and sits back down. The door opens.

HENRY *enters. His hair is neat – he wears a black leather jacket.*

KENNETH   You're late.

HENRY   So?

KENNETH   You're missing the programme.

HENRY *takes off his jacket. Underneath he wears a black cardigan, shirt and tie.*

HENRY   What programme?

KENNETH   Look.

HENRY *does, for a moment.*

Twenty-six countries are broadcasting this, right now. Across the world.

Thought you were interested.

HENRY   Things to do, haven't I?

KENNETH   You said you'd be back for it.

HENRY   I've been working all day. I have to pay rent. Don't get
            a free ride.

KENNETH   A free ride.

HENRY   Not like some people.

KENNETH   You could go to university if you wanted.

HENRY   Bit old for that now.

KENNETH   No. You're not –

HENRY   Doesn't matter doesn't matter.

KENNETH   You're not too old you can get a grant, a scholarship
            you know.

HENRY   Doesn't matter.

KENNETH   You might get one. Even you.

HENRY   Shut it.

            He sits in an armchair. They watch for a moment.

KENNETH   This has never happened before in the history of
            mankind. Across the world four hundred million
            people, including us, are all watching this one thing at
            exactly the same time.

            They keep watching. After a moment –

HENRY   What's on the other side?

KENNETH   Henry, this isn't beyond you, this isn't a clever thing,
            this is for everyone, every single person across the
            world, you've got to understand the significance. It's
            America, Europe, Japan. It's twenty-six different
            countries, cultures and languages coming together. It's
            remarkable. It signifies a new age of international
            cooperation.

HENRY   What are they showing then?

KENNETH   The Beatles.

HENRY   That's not The Beatles.

KENNETH   Later on it will be.

HENRY   Who's that?

KENNETH   The Vienna Boys' Choir.

HENRY   The Vienna Boys' Choir?

KENNETH   Yeah.

HENRY   Bloody hell.

KENNETH   I know, but if you –

HENRY   Turn to the other side.

KENNETH   They illustrate the point, exactly what I'm saying,
                   Austria chose a choir, Britain chose *The Beatles*. Out
                   of everyone and anything in the whole country.

                   HENRY *takes one of* KENNETH*'s cigarettes.*

                   It could've been politicians or old men, an orchestra or
                   ballet or something old like that something old but it
                   wasn't. It was pop music. Young people, like us
                   dressed up as they want. Things are changing every
                   day at the moment.

                   HENRY *lights a cigarette.*

HENRY   You been out at all?

KENNETH   Once or twice…

HENRY   Right.

KENNETH   I got your beans.

HENRY   What?

KENNETH   Your beans.

HENRY

KENNETH   You said we needed beans.

HENRY   What about bog paper?

KENNETH   Do we need…

HENRY   Well there isn't any.

KENNETH   Really?

HENRY   Is there?

KENNETH   I don't know.

HENRY   Did you see any?

KENNETH   No but

HENRY   Well then.

KENNETH   Thought you might have it hidden away.

HENRY   Why would I –

KENNETH   Or something.

HENRY   Hidden it?

KENNETH   Or something. Yeah.

Beat.

HENRY   What about butter, milk? You get any of that?

KENNETH   Thought it was just the beans you needed.

HENRY   Just the beans…

KENNETH   Yeah just the beans. That's all you said to get, so that's what I got, following orders Henry, just following orders.

HENRY   Perhaps you should go home. Maybe your time in my flat is coming to an end, I think you should pack up actually.

KENNETH   You're tired I can tell.

HENRY   Yeah that's right Ken I am tired. Fucking knackered as it happens.

KENNETH goes and pours him a brandy.

Dad called me today.

KENNETH   At work?

HENRY   At work. On the telephone yes. Don't talk to him much like that. He speaks all properly, accentuates his vowels, like the Queen or something.

KENNETH   He thinks people listen.

HENRY   People?

KENNETH   Listen in. The government.

HENRY   Really?

KENNETH   What he said.

HENRY   He's a mad old man sometimes.

KENNETH   Something to do with the war I reckon.

HENRY   Mad old bastard.

            A moment.

KENNETH   What did he want?

HENRY   He said 'We were under the impression Kenneth was at
            Oxford over the summer.' Oh right, I said.

            'But when we tried to contact him it turns out he left at
            the end of term, got a lift somewhere, not a word from
            him… and then we receive this letter'

KENNETH   They got it then.

HENRY   Mum thinks you've been kidnapped.

KENNETH   I said I was alright, that's the only reason I bothered, to
            reassure her –

HENRY   She thinks they held you at gunpoint, forced you to
            write it.

KENNETH   They're insane, both of them.

HENRY   You should call.

KENNETH   No.

HENRY   You will. I have to put up with it otherwise. Telephone.

KENNETH   Hassle though.

HENRY   Or go home, that's your other option Kenneth, you
            could just go back home.

KENNETH   No. It's always the same, when I'm away they moan,
            they say they miss me, but soon as I arrive, they
            ignore me.

HENRY   They thought I might know something about your
            disappearance.

KENNETH   And you said?

HENRY	I said you don't tell me anything.
KENNETH	Right.
HENRY	Hadn't heard from you in ages.
KENNETH	Thanks. You're a brother, a real brother to me.
HENRY	I also said I thought you were a layabout little sod, an ungrateful little runt, that you should give them some of that grant you've got, give it back to them both.
KENNETH	Is that what you think?
HENRY	You're making as much as Dad and he works like a dog.
KENNETH	I'm the future of this country,
HENRY	My bloody taxes.
KENNETH	It's an investment.

Beat.

I appreciate you taking me in, Henry.

I needed to get away.

You know, break out for a bit, like.

The thought of spending all those weeks stuck in that house middle of nowhere, with Mum and Dad, can't drink, can't smoke, nowhere to go, nothing, absolutely nothing to do, it's like...

Like a prison sentence or something.

HENRY	You could get a job.
KENNETH	We're not supposed to get a job, supposed to concentrate on our studies. I don't need a job anyway got my grant so –
HENRY	That's right you don't need a job you've got your *grant*.

What about your friends, your lot from school, they're still around, must be.

KENNETH	They're just as bad, they're small, nothing. I needed somewhere exciting. I'm not being arrogant, but you understand, you moved away.

HENRY   Yeah well…

KENNETH   You came to where things are happening. You don't
             just hear about things in London, or read them in the
             papers, you see them, you're on the spot. It's the Post
             Office Tower, the river, The Stones, The Beatles –
             exhibitions, fashion, the cars, the *birds*.

HENRY   The birds are something yes.

KENNETH   Even bloody Harold Wilson. Saw him the other day.
             He's smaller than you'd think.

             HENRY *gets up and switches the TV off.*

             Oi. I was watching that.

HENRY   No you weren't.

KENNETH   It's important.

HENRY   It's a *choir*.

             Beat.

             So what you doing tonight? Out somewhere?

             Off out I presume?

KENNETH   No.

HENRY   You're not?

KENNETH   Thought I'd watch television actually.

HENRY   Said you wanted excitement. You could watch
             television at home.

KENNETH   No.

HENRY   Why not?

KENNETH   Mum and Dad don't have one.

HENRY   Yes they do, in the corner.

KENNETH   It blew up during the football.

HENRY   What?

KENNETH   The World Cup. Didn't you notice?

HENRY   Haven't been home for a while.

KENNETH   After that they said it was a waste of time and money
           getting another, said they'd rather listen to the radio.

           Pause.

HENRY   Plenty of skirt out there.

KENNETH   Yeah.

HENRY   Plenty of birds.

KENNETH   Right.

HENRY   Haven't you got a chum or something, someone you
           could meet?

KENNETH   You want me out.

HENRY   Well not to put too fine a point on it.

KENNETH   What's her name?

HENRY   None of your business actually though is it Kenneth?

           Pause.

KENNETH   I'm settled now.

HENRY   You're *settled*.

KENNETH   Got my brandy and fags, my house coat.

HENRY   Is that what it is?

KENNETH   Yeah.

HENRY   Thought you were ill or something.

KENNETH   Bloke at Oxford gave it to me.

HENRY   A present?

KENNETH   Yeah.

HENRY   Poof is he?

KENNETH   What?

HENRY   Was he a poof?

KENNETH   Don't think so.

HENRY   Are you?

KENNETH   What?

HENRY   A bender.

KENNETH   Hard to say isn't it?

HENRY   Is it?

KENNETH   What?

HENRY   Are you a poof?

KENNETH   No.

HENRY   You look like one.

KENNETH   Do I?

HENRY   In that. Look like a proper queer.

KENNETH   Nothing wrong with being queer.

HENRY   You are then.

KENNETH   No, but there's nothing wrong with it.

HENRY   Fucking Oxford, look at you.

KENNETH   Henry.

HENRY

KENNETH   Nothing like this has ever happened before. The laws
            are constantly being overthrown, the boundaries of
            what's possible, the music's exploding, the walls
            collapsing. That's what's going on. That's what's
            changing. We travel, do what we want, wear what we
            like. Enjoy it. Experiment.

            We're breaking free.

HENRY   Well you can break free right now and bugger off
            she'll be here in a minute.

KENNETH   No.

HENRY   Yes.

KENNETH   I don't have any money.

HENRY   …

            Beat.

KENNETH   I won't be in the way.

HENRY   You will be in the way.

KENNETH   She could bring a friend.

HENRY   I don't reckon she could actually Kenneth.

KENNETH   Make up a four.

HENRY   No.

KENNETH   Never done that have we, brothers with birds, the McLarens used to walk down the street, you remember, down the street, they used to wear jackets, looked the same, like just the two of them, there's strength in brothers, we've never done that. Do you remember the McLarens? Birds used to lap that up the two of them next to each other, birds used to love it.

I heard a story once about them, they were in this club, one of those places they used to go to, and this bunch of totty comes up to them and says we're going to make your day and they went back to their house and all the girls lined up, and the McLarens picked teams like football teams, till there were like five-a-side, then they took their side up to their room, and... well I don't know what they did. All that she said – Frank Jameson's sister Tracey, she was one of the girls – all she said was she had a great time.

A great time.

Do you ever feel you're missing out Henry?

Not saying we'd do that, but it makes you think we might be missing a trick.

HENRY *has taken some money out of his wallet – offers it to* KENNETH.

What?

HENRY   Here's a few bob, now fuck off.

KENNETH   No come on.

HENRY   Bit deaf tonight Kenneth are you?

KENNETH   What's her name?

HENRY *slaps* KENNETH *round the head, not hard, but enough. Then puts the money in* KENNETH's *hand.*

She has got a name?

KENNETH   What?

HENRY   You remember the fights we had?

KENNETH   What is it?

HENRY   You remember the fights?

KENNETH   Course I do.

He keeps his distance.

You always won I know that, I don't want to fight you I just want to know her name, won't make any difference, will it, you telling me, just saying what she's called, will it? Will it?

HENRY   Sandra.

KENNETH   Good name. Sandra.

HENRY   Yeah.

KENNETH   You and her been doing it long then?

HENRY   We're not doing it.

KENNETH   Oh right not doing it.

HENRY   Not yet, not so far. First time she's come round. Big moment you see? So I don't want some spotty bastard cluttering up the place, wearing his queer fucking coat of many colours.

You understand.

So.

Piss. Off.

Beat.

KENNETH   You're going to let her see it like this?

HENRY   What?

KENNETH   The flat.

HENRY   It's alright.

KENNETH   You let her see it like this, she'll run a mile turn right
          round off she'll go.

HENRY

KENNETH

HENRY   It was alright before you arrived.

KENNETH   Come on. I'll help.

          I'll help you tidy.

          HENRY *doesn't move*.

          Come on.

          I will, I'll help, then I'll go. Promise.

          They tidy.

          HENRY*'s efficient at it.* KENNETH *is slapdash.*

          Is she pretty?

HENRY   Yeah.

          Beat.

          Beautiful.

          They tidy.

KENNETH   Clever?

HENRY   Yeah.

KENNETH   Legs?

HENRY   Up to here.

KENNETH   Up to where?

HENRY   Where do you think?

KENNETH   Nice figure then.

HENRY   She's a piece of work all round, I'm telling you.

KENNETH   Classy?

HENRY   Bit posh yeah.

KENNETH   Yeah.

HENRY   Middle class, you know, dresses up nice, every time
I've seen her she's nice-looking. Makes an effort, hair,
and the face. You know. She's into all that anti-nuclear
wotnot, and women. Talks a lot about women. She
goes to groups.

Protests.

KENNETH   Where?

HENRY   University I think.

KENNETH   She's a student.

HENRY   Yeah. She's political. All that.

KENNETH   Thought you didn't like political women.

HENRY   I don't.

KENNETH   Right.

HENRY   But you should see her knockers.

KENNETH   Henry –

HENRY   Bloody marvellous. Size of footballs. More than makes
up for the political nonsense she comes out with.

KENNETH   You said that to her?

HENRY   Might've mentioned it yeah.

KENNETH   What did she say?

HENRY   That I was a chauvinist.

KENNETH   Bit unfair.

HENRY   I know. I told her, I'm not driving anyone around, they
can drive themselves.

KENNETH   That's not what chauvinist means.

HENRY   Bloody hell Kenneth you really think I'm a fucking
thick bastard don't you?

Beat.

I know what it means.

Maybe I didn't go to Oxford University, but I'm not a
bloody – no no don't leave those there.

> HENRY *takes some dishes* KENNETH *has put in a cupboard and takes them through to the kitchen.*

KENNETH   What time's she getting here?

HENRY   Nine o'clock. What time is it now?

KENNETH   Ten to.

HENRY   You going to bugger off then?

KENNETH   Yeah, I'll finish this, then go off to my room.

HENRY   Your room?

KENNETH   Leave you to it.

HENRY   You're not going in your room, you're going out.

KENNETH   Got books to read I'll be fine.

HENRY   You're going to stay in there all night?

KENNETH   They're long books lots of words you know me I'll be fine.

> *Beat.*

HENRY   Alright. But you better stay shut up in there. I'm telling you.

KENNETH   I will.

HENRY   Even if you want a piss. You do it out the window or something. In a bucket. Whatever. You stay put.

KENNETH   Alright.

HENRY   Understand?

KENNETH   Yeah.

> *They tidy.*

> Do you talk to him much then?

HENRY   Who?

KENNETH   Dad.

HENRY   He writes mostly.

KENNETH   What does he say?

HENRY   What?

KENNETH   When he writes.

HENRY   Him and Mum do a side each every other week. They
            check I'm alright. Get worried you know. He says
            how's things at work, I know what he means, he means
            am I making money. I write back and just say yeah
            Dad, yeah – everything rosy.

            Everything's peachy as a picture, don't you worry.

KENNETH   Says that to me too. 'All well and good you going on
            about Oxford, make sure you get yourself a job.' Wants
            me to go into the civil service when I graduate. I just
            laugh. That's as high as his imagination can reach.
            That's the pinnacle of ambition.

            Civil bloody service.

HENRY   Mum as well, every letter, how are things Henry? Any
            girls take your fancy yet? She thinks it's all tea parties
            and formal dancing. 'Take my fancy.' Bloody hell. If
            she knew.

KENNETH   Worried you're queer, probably.

HENRY   Watch it.

KENNETH

HENRY   Nah. She doesn't even know what that is.

            Pause.

KENNETH   What about this one tonight then?

HENRY   Hard to tell. Bit mouthy. Wait and see.

KENNETH   How did you meet?

HENRY   I was putting up a poster on the billboard, and I look
            down and there she is, staring up at me. I'm like 'Hello
            love.' She says I've been watching you. Big eyes. Says
            it you know – suggestively. 'I've been *watching* you.' I
            went a bit giddy if I'm honest. And she goes on, keeps
            on talking telling me about herself, turns out she works
            in this boutique, she's been watching all morning. She
            says she liked my shoes. I said they stop me falling off
            the ladder. We have a drink at the end of the day, met
            up a few times since then, you know, drink, pictures,
            the preamble, and eventually last time I say why don't
            you come round mine, we'll have dinner.

KENNETH   You haven't got anything in.

HENRY   I know, I'm aware of that. I wasn't thinking of the
            practicalities at that moment was I? But as a matter of
            fact she was, she says, 'You any good at cooking
            then?' I said 'As you mention it I don't know one end
            of a kitchen from the other but I'll have a go, I'll cook
            whatever you want, if you'll come over.' She liked
            that, and said it was alright, she'd bring the food and
            cook, if I got the drink.

KENNETH   Perfect lady.

HENRY   Exactly.

KENNETH   Looks better doesn't it?

HENRY   Suppose it does yeah.

            Beat.

KENNETH   A civil servant. Bloody hell. He doesn't have a clue.

HENRY   What then?

KENNETH   A writer.

HENRY   What sort?

KENNETH   A travel writer. I'm going to have a flat on the King's
            Road, full of ornaments, and carpets, collected from
            different countries and beautiful women, actresses,
            designers they'll all come over to visit.

HENRY   Believe it when I see it Kenneth.

KENNETH   At Oxford they talk like this all the time, saying what
            they're going to do and how they're going to go about
            it, they tell you, I'm going to be a doctor, prime
            minister, I'm an *artist*, all these clever bastards, when
            they say things like that, it doesn't sound stupid at all
            because you know, you look at them and you think yes,
            yes, they probably will be what they want to be.

HENRY   Rich most of them.

KENNETH   You've just got to want it enough.

            The doorbell goes.

HENRY   Right then.

KENNETH   What?

HENRY   Off you go.

KENNETH   What?

HENRY   In there.

KENNETH   Hang on.

HENRY   That's what you said.

KENNETH   I can't not *meet* her.

HENRY   I think you can.

KENNETH   It'll be rude if I don't even say hello.

HENRY   No.

KENNETH   I'll meet her and then bugger off. Promise. Say I've got all this work to do.

HENRY   …

KENNETH   …

HENRY   You better put something on then.

KENNETH   I'm sure she won't mind.

HENRY   She might not but I do. Scrawny little ferret running round the place.

The doorbell goes again.

At least do it up.

KENNETH *does.*

HENRY *goes.*

KENNETH *undoes the dressing gown and checks himself in the mirror.*

Comes back and lights a cigarette.

Pours himself a drink. Looks relaxed.

HENRY *enters with* SANDRA.

KENNETH   Hello.

SANDRA   Hello.

HENRY   This is my brother Kenneth.

KENNETH   Ken.

SANDRA   Hi Ken.

HENRY   This is Sandra.

SANDRA   How old are you?

KENNETH   What?

SANDRA   How old are you? What's your age?

KENNETH   Nineteen. How old are you?

SANDRA   Nineteen.

KENNETH   Coincidence.

Beat.

SANDRA   Can I have one of those?

KENNETH   Course you can.

He gives her a cigarette.

HENRY   Take your coat?

SANDRA   Thank you.

HENRY *takes her coat.* KENNETH *lights her cigarette.*

Why aren't you dressed?

KENNETH   Don't need to be.

SANDRA   You've been like that all day?

KENNETH   Yeah.

SANDRA   Interesting.

HENRY   He's a layabout.

SANDRA   I like this.

KENNETH   Do you?

SANDRA   Yes. It's very decadent. I like things that are decadent. Don't I Henry?

HENRY   Yeah right.

SANDRA   Henry's decadent.

KENNETH   Is he?

SANDRA   He wears a leather jacket like Joe Orton. It's splendid.
            You must be a very decadent family.

HENRY   Who's Joe Orton?

SANDRA   Or maybe not.

KENNETH   He's a writer.

SANDRA   Correct.

KENNETH   Our family's quite boring as it goes.

SANDRA   All families are boring. That's why London was
            invented. So you can move away.

KENNETH   Yeah.

SANDRA   Unless you're born in London. Then you're really in
            trouble.

KENNETH   Where are you from?

SANDRA   Saffron Walden.

KENNETH   Where's that?

SANDRA   It's a tiny little village in Essex, relatively pretty I
            suppose but the people are animals. Inbred most of
            them I think, couldn't wait to get out.

KENNETH   I know what you mean.

SANDRA   Do you?

KENNETH   I like your dress.

SANDRA   Do you live here?

KENNETH   I'm staying for a while.

SANDRA   I see how lovely but normally, normally Kenneth,
            where are you based normally?

KENNETH   Based?

SANDRA   Your *abode*.

KENNETH   I'm a student.

SANDRA	Henry you're very quiet. A student?
KENNETH	Yes.
SANDRA	Charming. Where?
KENNETH	Oxford.
SANDRA	How silly.
KENNETH	What?
SANDRA	Well I'm at Oxford too.
KENNETH	Henry didn't say.
SANDRA	Henry probably doesn't know, do you? Henry?
HENRY	
SANDRA	Did you know I was at Oxford University?

Beat.

HENRY	No.
SANDRA	You see? We don't know each other that well at all really. I only met him a few weeks ago.
HENRY	Two months now.
SANDRA	Is it?
HENRY	Yes.
SANDRA	Well we've been having such fun, I must've lost track. When we met, I was working in my summer job. He was up a ladder doing his thing with the posters. I was working in a shop on Baker Street, Apples and Oranges, do you know it?
KENNETH	No.
SANDRA	Delightful clothes. Wonderful colours. I simply adored it, but it's… well… it's turned into a complete disaster. Last week I got the sack.
KENNETH	Did you?
SANDRA	I've never had the sack before, well I've never even had a job before and I was outraged. All of a sudden they told me to leave.
KENNETH	Why?

SANDRA   I was smoking pot.

KENNETH   None of their business.

SANDRA   While serving a customer.

KENNETH   Cool.

SANDRA   That's what I thought, I thought that's in the spirit of
            the place, it's groovy, very now, they'll like it, but the
            customer complained didn't he, bloody bastard and
            they kicked me out on the street straight away. Don't
            know how I'm going to stay in London now with no
            job. Maybe I'll come here and live here with Henry.
            Would you like that Henry? Perhaps you'll still be
            hanging around Ken.

HENRY   Kenneth do you need to –

KENNETH   What?

HENRY   …

KENNETH   Oh. Right.

HENRY   How about a drink?

SANDRA   Whisky and ginger please.

HENRY   Alright then.

SANDRA   Kenneth are you having a drink?

KENNETH   No I… I'm going to go into my room actually. I've got
            some reading to get through. Great stack of books. I'll
            leave you and Henry to it.

SANDRA   Reading?

KENNETH   Yes.

SANDRA   You're joking?

KENNETH   Sorry.

SANDRA   Well that's a shame. A real shame, Kenneth.

KENNETH   Busy.

SANDRA   Why not stay for a little bit before you go all boring
            like that? Before you closet yourself away. Come on.
            Let's get to know each other.

KENNETH *considers*.

KENNETH   You don't mind, Henry, do you?

HENRY *looks at* KENNETH.

SANDRA   Kenneth, one drink?

KENNETH   Alright.

SANDRA   Lovely.

HENRY *gives her the drink and sits down, annoyed.*

SANDRA *and* KENNETH *then sit together on the sofa.*

I've got a confession to make actually. Can I tell you? I've been naughty.

KENNETH   Have you?

SANDRA   You're from Oxford I expect you'll understand.

KENNETH   Go on.

SANDRA   I'm completely gone.

KENNETH   Gone?

SANDRA   Stoned.

KENNETH   Oh.

SANDRA   Right this moment.

KENNETH   Yes.

SANDRA   Not drunk.

KENNETH   No.

SANDRA   Pot.

KENNETH   Good.

SANDRA   I smoke too much of it I think.

KENNETH   I don't think that's possible.

SANDRA   It's jolly isn't it?

KENNETH   I like it yes. Yes it is jolly.

HENRY

SANDRA	I smoked my last before I came out, now it's all gone.
	And now we're all here and what are we going to do? Do you have any?
HENRY	Did you bring dinner?
SANDRA	What?
HENRY	You were going to bring dinner, you were going to bring the ingredients and cook.
SANDRA	It's your house.
HENRY	We agreed.
SANDRA	Well I'm sorry but I just assumed you would cook.
HENRY	That's not what we said.
SANDRA	
HENRY	So we don't have anything in?
SANDRA	Do you have any weed?
HENRY	No.
SANDRA	Then no we really don't have *anything* in then, Henry, not a thing. Very well done on this evening, nothing to eat nothing to smoke, what a wonderful party.
HENRY	
SANDRA	Maybe you should get some fish and chips.
KENNETH	I've got some.
SANDRA	Fish and chips? Lovely.
KENNETH	Some weed.
SANDRA	Even better.
KENNETH	In my room.
SANDRA	Glorious.
HENRY	You didn't tell me.
KENNETH	You don't like it.
HENRY	You should've told me.
KENNETH	Why?

SANDRA   Don't you go in for grass Henry?

HENRY

SANDRA   ?

HENRY   Not legal is it?

SANDRA   Henry! You're so amusing. Isn't he? Not legal. The
           little policemen have got more important things to
           think about these days, than this, no one minds a bit of
           grass these days, it's like tea, it's like water, it's like
           fresh air these days, no one minds it at all. Go on
           Kenneth. Why don't you get yourself up and go and
           fetch it?

KENNETH   Right you are.

           He gets up and goes next door. A moment.

           SANDRA *looks at* HENRY.

SANDRA   I don't like your hair.

HENRY   It's always like this.

SANDRA   I know.

           Another moment.

           KENNETH *comes back, sits down next to* SANDRA
           and starts to roll. Pause.

HENRY   You didn't tell me you'd lost your job.

SANDRA   No.

HENRY   Why not?

SANDRA   We're not married Henry.

HENRY   Didn't say we were but –

SANDRA   Not even close. Don't want to get married. Probably
           never will. There's no loyalty to you Henry, I never
           promised anything.

HENRY   So you say.

SANDRA   So I do say that's right I say, I propose quite the
           opposite of marriage, I think you're very attractive and
           very nice, and all that but I don't feel the need to make

any kind of commitment, especially one that restricts the woman in the arrangement. I'm not ready to obey anyone. I mean really, I'm not twenty yet, neither's Kenneth, how old are you?

HENRY   Twenty-three.

SANDRA   Yes, well that's a bit older but we're not our parents. Things are different now. There's freedom.

KENNETH   Something's changing.

SANDRA   Something's changing yes, that's right, that's right Kenneth. You can feel it Henry, if you want to. Even you. You're part of it, even you, you moved to London, got your own place, did your own things. You didn't stay at home in the same town with your mum and dad, you're here and you're really living, aren't you? It's marvellous. What's the matter your face looks flat.

HENRY   What?

SANDRA   Don't you think?

HENRY   What do you mean flat?

SANDRA   All drooping, flat as a pancake, what's the matter?

            Beat.

HENRY   I'm over here on my own.

SANDRA   Oh.

            So you are.

            I'm sorry.

            She goes across and sits on the arm of his chair and hugs him. Kisses his head.

            Have you been getting jealous?

            You think I prefer your little brother, well he's nice I suppose but he's not a man is he? Not like you. He's a little boy.

HENRY   He's got to read his books. Got to go to his room.

KENNETH   What?

HENRY   Haven't you?

KENNETH   …

HENRY

KENNETH   …Yeah.

SANDRA   Henry?

           You want him to stay in there all night.

HENRY   Got his books.

SANDRA   He can't stay in there all night.

           Is he being simply gorgeous and getting out the way
           for us? Because I'm sorry but no, we can't do that.
           He's your guest, we can't evict him, turf him out, keep
           him all locked up in there, we can't do that.

HENRY   Thought we'd want the place to ourselves.

SANDRA   What if he needs the toilet?

KENNETH   He said I should use a bucket.

SANDRA   Henry.

HENRY   Thought you'd want some privacy Sandra.

           Thought that's what you'd be after.

           Up to you though.

           Do what you like.

SANDRA   We could have a little party instead.

           Couldn't we? The three of us. Two brothers. You two,
           and me.

           Yes. We should have a party.

           What do you think?

KENNETH   Alright.

           He lights the joint, and gets it going. Then gives it to
           SANDRA.

           She smokes it.

SANDRA   I was out in the park all last night, with a group, a
           whole group of us, I think, the others I don't know
           what they did, but I drank wine until the early morning

and then crawled under a tree and went to sleep. I slept
until ten o'clock this morning. I was found by a
policeman, by a little piggy, he said it's dangerous
sweetheart you could've been raped, all by yourself in
the park. I said the thing is *cunt*stable, the thing is you
early morning irritating *cunt*... stable, I'm a woman,
we could always be raped. At any moment, any minute
of the day or night. If we lived our lives like that,
trying to avoid it all the time, we wouldn't do
anything. I looked at him, right in the face – I think he
liked me – and I said, it's all about risk.

And then I turned and walked away. Went and had
lunch, a joint, a bath and came here, but you know the
thing – you two brothers – the thing was, I slept really
well, just there, on the grass under the tree, I slept
really well. I'm not sure about beds. I think we should
sleep outside. I really think we should. Do you want
some of this?

HENRY   No.

She gives the spliff back to KENNETH. *He smokes it.*

SANDRA   Do you like music?

KENNETH   Yes.

SANDRA   Henry doesn't.

HENRY   I do.

SANDRA   Classical music.

HENRY   Nothing wrong with that.

SANDRA   Not rock and roll.

HENRY   Well –

SANDRA   Do you like rock and roll Kenneth?

KENNETH   I do yeah.

SANDRA   What's your favourite rock and roll band?

HENRY   He likes The Beatles.

SANDRA   Is that right Kenneth? Do you like The Beatles?

KENNETH   Cream.

SANDRA   You like Cream?

KENNETH   Yes.

SANDRA   I like Cream.

KENNETH   Good.

SANDRA   Henry? Do you like Cream?

HENRY   …

SANDRA   I don't mean the thing from cows.

HENRY   Look, I'm rather tired of –

SANDRA   What's your favourite song of theirs?

HENRY   I don't know them very well that's true, I do prefer classical music, yes, but that's allowed.

SANDRA   It's allowed of course it is, but I think rock and roll is better, don't you? Kenneth, don't you think rock and roll is simply a better sort of music?

KENNETH   Yeah I do.

SANDRA   Do you know why Henry? Do you know why I prefer it?

HENRY   No.

SANDRA   You can dance to it. I want to dance. Do you have any music we can dance to? I love dancing. It's form and chaos all at the same time. Freedom and restriction combined. Anarchy and fascism. I love it. Do you have any rock and roll at all? You probably only have Mozart, Beethoven… Tchaikovsky. You don't have anything new. Do you?

HENRY   No.

SANDRA   That's a shame I felt like dancing. I really felt like it tonight.

HENRY

KENNETH   I've got some.

SANDRA   Oh look, Kenneth has some records as well. He's coming up with everything tonight isn't he?

KENNETH   Shall I get them?

SANDRA   Why not?

          KENNETH *goes*.

          Beat.

          Are you going to dance Henry?

HENRY   No.

SANDRA   Well why don't you go to the fish and chip shop then,
          because I'm getting hungry and you don't have any
          food I remember now because of the mix-up, so why
          don't you be a darling and go to the fish and chip shop
          and get us all fish and chips and while you're away, me
          and Kenneth, we'll have a bit of a dance.

HENRY   A dance.

SANDRA   Yes.

          You know what dancing is.

          HENRY *is angry. Stands up, gets his coat.*

          KENNETH *comes back in holding a small pile of
          records.*

KENNETH   Where are you going?

HENRY   Fish and chips.

KENNETH   Oh right. Good. You... Are you...?

HENRY   Back in ten minutes.

          He goes.

SANDRA   Never seen him so red in the face.

KENNETH   He gets angry sometimes.

SANDRA   He takes it all so seriously.

KENNETH   Nothing to worry about.

SANDRA   He's old-fashioned.

KENNETH   He likes you.

          Beat.

SANDRA   Are you old-fashioned Kenneth?

KENNETH   No.

I get bored easily. I like new things.

I like things that are fresh.

SANDRA   Fresh.

KENNETH looks through the records.

The world's going to be a different place in ten years, everything that's stopping us, what we're told to do, what we're told is the way to live, it'll all be different, you can feel it.

KENNETH   Yeah.

SANDRA   It's us, it's people like you and me Kenneth.

KENNETH   I know.

SANDRA   Young people, our age. We're the moment. Henry's just that bit too old he can't understand.

KENNETH   He's always been old.

SANDRA   I love being like this, I can feel the muscles in my body, I look in the mirror, there's not a wrinkle on my face, I wake up more vital.

KENNETH   Fresh.

SANDRA   Fresh yes. We don't need ties, we don't need jobs. We don't need these *structures*.

KENNETH   Yeah.

SANDRA   Or clothes. Looking like this, like we do, like you do under that look at you. You could walk around wearing nothing and you'd look better than most people when they're dressed up, you know that?

KENNETH   Well you too.

SANDRA

KENNETH   I don't want to be rude but I imagine you look quite lovely under that.

They look at each other.

SANDRA   My older sister, she's only five years older than me but she's falling apart. I know I'm not the most beautiful girl

in the world, and it's not about looks it's about feeling,
the feeling of now, I want to stay this age, in this
summer, doing what I'm doing, for the rest of my life.

KENNETH   You could be a model or something.

SANDRA   A model.

KENNETH   Yeah.

SANDRA   A model what?

KENNETH   In a magazine. Advertising holidays or perfume or
something.

SANDRA   A model woman you mean.

KENNETH   Yeah.

SANDRA   I wonder what you think that is?

KENNETH   What?

SANDRA   A model woman.

KENNETH   He said you were a feminist.

SANDRA   You and him ever shared?

KENNETH   Shared?

SANDRA   A woman.

KENNETH   No.

SANDRA   I don't mean shared.

KENNETH   I know what you mean.

SANDRA   I mean kissed.

KENNETH   Kissed.

SANDRA   Have you ever kissed the same woman.

KENNETH   No.

SANDRA   I like you Kenneth.

KENNETH   I know, I know that I can tell but he'll be back.

SANDRA   What do you mean?

            Beat.

KENNETH   He's my brother.

SANDRA   I know he is.

            But.

            Well.

            Here's what would happen. He'd be upset, in the
            moment, he'd be angry and leave, walk out the door,
            go to the pub, he'd call you a bastard want you to
            leave, to move out, but in a day or two, maybe even in
            a few hours, he'd get over it, think of it as a good thing
            that happened, because we're nothing me and him
            we're just passing through, he knows that really.

            You're running your hand through your hair, I think
            you do that when you get nervous, when someone's
            putting you under pressure, but there's no pressure
            Kenneth. You can do what you like.

            I like you.

            And let's be clear, Kenneth.

            You haven't stopped looking at me since I came
            through the door have you?

KENNETH   No.

SANDRA   Not since I came through the door.

KENNETH   No.

SANDRA   So we could just dance a little couldn't we? At least.
            Until he gets back.

KENNETH   …

SANDRA   We're going to die.

KENNETH   What?

SANDRA   We're going, to die.

KENNETH   Not now.

SANDRA   Eventually, and the world is terrible, with Russia,

            and the bomb

            and Vietnam,

            and all we're asking for, people like you and me, all
            we're asking for, is some humanity, is some freedom, is

to throw off everything that holds us down and explore
what we could do instead. Maybe it doesn't have to be
about power and guns and money, maybe it could just
be about the fact that underneath, underneath our
background and our countries and our clothes, like we
said, we're all the same. That's all that people like you
and me, that's all we're saying. We're going to die, and
we shouldn't waste our lives. Don't you agree Kenneth?

KENNETH   Yes I do.

SANDRA   The summer's only just started.

We could go off together, see what happens.

What do you think?

We could have adventures together you and me.

KENNETH   Adventures?

SANDRA   You chosen something to dance to then?

KENNETH *looks at the records and smokes, then
suddenly remembers, he smiles, looks at his watch,
gives the joint to* SANDRA, *runs, jumps over the sofa
again, and switches on the television.*

*We hear the opening of 'All You Need Is Love' by The
Beatles.*

SANDRA   What's this?

KENNETH   The Beatles.

SANDRA   It doesn't seem like music you can dance to.

KENNETH   I can dance to anything.

*He takes her hand and they dance close and smoke as
The Beatles play.*

They kiss.

He holds her hand and they look at each other.

HENRY *comes in the door.*

HENRY   They're shut.

He sees them. KENNETH *backs off.* HENRY *looks at
them.*

SANDRA   Henry. It's alright. It doesn't matter.

           It's alright.

           She goes towards him.

           Touches him.

           What's the problem?

           She touches his face.

           He looks at her.

           He turns to KENNETH.

KENNETH   I'm... we just... Sorry.

           HENRY *goes back out the door and shuts it behind him.*

           KENNETH*'s upset, goes and turns down the television.*

           Kneels by it.

SANDRA   Tomorrow he'll come back and you'll sort it all out. You'll explain how it happened. That we're better suited, that it's not a one-night thing, that we're going to live together in Oxford next term.

KENNETH   We –

SANDRA   We could do that, couldn't we? And you'll tell him that we're going to travel around together this summer, and he'll listen and understand and within a month he'll look back on this moment as being one of the best things that's happened to him, especially when he's found a new girl to go out with, one that's really suited to him, a slightly duller traditional kind of girl. When he finds her, at that point, he'll be really pleased this happened.

           Sometimes you have to do what feels right.

KENNETH   Yeah I know.

SANDRA   One day we'll laugh about this.

KENNETH   Yes.

           I mean...

I don't think he even liked you that much.

SANDRA   Oh.

KENNETH   I think you're lovely. All of you.

They move closer.

SANDRA   The whole of the summer, we can do whatever we want. So.

Are you ready?

KENNETH   For?

SANDRA   Adventures.

Lights fade.

Curtain.

End of Act One.

TWO

'She Bangs the Drums' by The Stone Roses plays.

Evening. March 1990. The dining/living room of a medium-sized terraced house on the outskirts of Reading. Reasonably tidy. A large table in the middle. Family photos. A television is muted, but showing scenes of the television news, riots in London.

The music is playing out of a stereo on the side.

JAMIE, fourteen, enters, performing and singing. Really enjoying himself. He jumps on the table, sings and dances to a surprising amount of the song. He knows all the words and intonation – he's talented.

Suddenly there's a noise from off, a key in the door, as it opens.

KENNETH   (*From off.*) Jamie?!

                 JAMIE *is surprised, nearly falls off the table, knocks over some flowers, crashes into a bookshelf.*

                 See it's still in one piece,

SANDRA   Alright

KENNETH   Hasn't exploded, blown over, burnt down, he hasn't taken it apart piece by piece it's exactly as you left it.

                 JAMIE *tries to tidy up as* KENNETH *enters. He's now forty-two, wearing a jacket, shirt and trousers. He still looks youngish. He takes his coat off.*

                 What are you up to?

JAMIE   Nothing.

KENNETH   What's this?

JAMIE   The Stone Roses.

                 KENNETH *listens for a second.*

KENNETH   He can't sing.

JAMIE   Neither can you Dad.

KENNETH   Watch it.

JAMIE   Doesn't stop you trying.

KENNETH   The ungrateful child.

JAMIE   No.

KENNETH   I give you all this. And you spit in my face.

JAMIE   I don't understand.

KENNETH   Switch it off.

He dumps his coat and goes out again.

JAMIE *stops the tape. Ejects it.*

(*From off.*) She could've been stuck there playing to no one, tears rolling down her face.

ROSE   It's alright.

KENNETH   She was trying to hide it but I could see, she was upset.

JAMIE *puts the tape carefully back in the box. Sits on the arm of the sofa and listens.*

KENNETH *comes back in. He's followed by* ROSE, *sixteen, in school uniform, with her violin.*

(*About the television.*) Turn that off too.

JAMIE   There's a riot going on.

KENNETH   Not tonight / there isn't,

ROSE   Dad –

KENNETH   She was upset!

JAMIE   It's in London, there's horses and skinheads.

ROSE   It doesn't matter.

JAMIE   Do you pay poll tax / Dad?

KENNETH   It's one day a year Sandra you know what I'm saying, she had a concert and it's nearly her birthday and it meant something to her.

ROSE *goes and sits in a chair.*

KENNETH *looks round.* SANDRA*'s not there.*

KENNETH   Where is she?

ROSE   Kitchen.

KENNETH   Thought she was following.

ROSE   She said she had something to prepare.

KENNETH   Oh.

He sits down.

Jamie you should've come, she was brilliant, like Jacqueline du Pré.

JAMIE   Jacqueline du Pré's / a cellist.

KENNETH   Solo and everything, little bit / she had to get right.

ROSE   You know what he meant. (*To* KENNETH.) It wasn't / a solo.

KENNETH   Everyone looking, everyone's asking, who's that girl with the cello?

ROSE   / Violin

KENNETH   She's amazing.

JAMIE   Don't like classical / music.

KENNETH   I was right there sweetheart, front row.

ROSE   Yeah.

KENNETH   Saved a seat for your mother, that was a waste of time.

JAMIE   Can I go upstairs?

KENNETH   No. We're doing a cake.

JAMIE   Why?

ROSE   A cake.

KENNETH   Yes.

ROSE   Mum said you were doing a surprise.

KENNETH   Oh.

Well.

It's a cake.

JAMIE   Why?

KENNETH   It's nearly your sister's birthday.

JAMIE   When?

KENNETH   Midnight.

JAMIE   How old is she?

KENNETH   Come on Jamie.

JAMIE   I don't know. How old?

KENNETH   …

JAMIE   Dad

KENNETH   Fifteen

ROSE   Sixteen.

KENNETH   I thought you were fifteen.

ROSE   Doesn't matter.

Beat.

KENNETH   What about your friends love? Were they there?

ROSE   It's a weeknight.

KENNETH   You getting on with them alright now?

ROSE   Dad…

KENNETH   What?

ROSE   Can we not talk about this please?

KENNETH   Why not?

ROSE   It's private?

KENNETH   It's only your brother.

JAMIE   I won't tell anyone. What happened?

ROSE   / Shut up.

KENNETH   Your music teacher, what's his name?

ROSE   Mr / Parsons.

KENNETH   You know he went to Oxford?

ROSE   Thought I saw you talking.

KENNETH   He must've been there the same time as your mother
                and me, an organ scholar apparently, don't remember
                him but organ scholars were strange.

ROSE   He is / strange.

KENNETH   We didn't really move in the same / circles.

ROSE   He smarms up to the parents, but in the classroom he's
                a total Hitler.

KENNETH   One of those?

ROSE   Yeah.

JAMIE   He's alright with me.

ROSE   Right.

JAMIE   Yeah. I like him.

ROSE   Do you.

JAMIE   It's probably cos you're stupid he only likes clever
                people.

ROSE   I really hate you.

                Beat.

KENNETH   Well if he gives you trouble, love, you let me know.

ROSE   What? Are you going to beat him up?

KENNETH   No I'll get him on the phone and have a word. The
                power of rhetoric, much forgotten.

ROSE   I can't imagine you hitting anyone Dad.

KENNETH   Definitely / not.

ROSE   But isn't that what dads are supposed to do?

KENNETH   What?

ROSE   Look after their daughters.

JAMIE   I can hit people. / I've got a really good punch.

KENNETH   Rosie don't be stupid you're looked after you get
                everything you want.

ROSE   / No.

KENNETH   Where is she? Thought we were having cake.

He gets up and goes out.

ROSE   (*To herself.*) He never *listens…*

JAMIE   I hit someone last week.

ROSE   Shut up.

JAMIE   After Maths Club we were giving each other dead arms.

ROSE   / 'Maths Club'.

JAMIE   Paul nearly cried when I got him.

ROSE   Can't believe you go to Maths Club.

JAMIE   What?

ROSE   Such a geek.

JAMIE   I'll hit you.

ROSE   You're too old to hit girls.

JAMIE   It's different with sisters.

ROSE   No it isn't. I'm a woman now. I can say what I want, and you can't do anything.

He looks at her.

JAMIE   Daniel's brother said that last Saturday at some party he burst into a bedroom and found Sarah Franks doing something to Mark Edwards that involved his penis.

ROSE

JAMIE   Isn't Mark Edwards supposed to be your boyfriend?

ROSE   …

JAMIE   Thought so.

You see? Don't need to hit you.

Happy birthday.

Cake makes you fat.

He goes out.

ROSE *sits there. Upset. Doesn't know what to do.*

A moment.

KENNETH *comes back in.*

KENNETH   Wish I'd learnt an instrument. But we didn't have the facilities you do these days, and anyway, we all wanted to play guitar or drums, you've seen the photo. Classical took a back seat. You've seen the photo?

ROSE   Yeah.

KENNETH   Where's your brother gone?

ROSE   Said he didn't want any cake.

KENNETH   Not the point.

ROSE   Doesn't matter.

KENNETH   Jamie come down here!

ROSE   Dad –

KENNETH   If you're not down in two minutes I'm sending your mother! That'll work.

He winks at ROSE.

Your uncle likes classical. We should invite him one day to see you. But anyway it's all the same thing now though isn't it? McCartney used to say it, these *divisions* between genres well they're pointless, I mean actually what's the difference between Mozart and Procol Harum, essentially they're the same thing.

ROSE   What's Procol Harum?

KENNETH   What?

ROSE   What's Procol Harum?

KENNETH   Who not what.

ROSE   They're a band then?

KENNETH   *What's Procol Harum?*

ROSE   Okay it doesn't / matter.

KENNETH   This weekend, we're getting the records out Rosie.

ROSE   Dad – really –

KENNETH   You and me.

ROSE	No.
KENNETH	Yes. If you haven't heard of Procol Harum you haven't lived.
ROSE	Just tell me
KENNETH	Impossible.
ROSE	Dad.
KENNETH	No. You have to hear them. In for a treat.
ROSE	...
KENNETH	Jamie! Now! We'll listen to it this weekend. Something to look forward to.
ROSE	I think there is a difference.
KENNETH	What?
ROSE	I think there is a difference between –

SANDRA *enters with a bottle of wine and a glass.*

SANDRA	I am completely dry. My throat is like Ethiopia or somewhere. Absolutely desperate for a glass or two. What's the matter love you look like you've been hit by a car.
KENNETH	Rose was talking love.
SANDRA	Were you? Go on then. Wasn't interrupting. Go on. Speak.
ROSE	I was just / saying about –
KENNETH	Did you get me one of those?
SANDRA	One of these?
KENNETH	Yes.
SANDRA	A *glass* you mean Kenneth?
KENNETH	A glass yes.
SANDRA	You want a glass.
KENNETH	Unless you expect me to drink it from the bottle?
SANDRA	I wouldn't mind.
KENNETH	I'm sure you wouldn't but some of us have standards.

SANDRA   You know where the kitchen is.

             He gets up.

KENNETH   You want one Rose?

SANDRA   Brilliant parenting Kenneth.

KENNETH   Celebration isn't it?

ROSE   I'm fine.

SANDRA   Perhaps she wants a fag too.

ROSE   No thanks.

SANDRA   Sarcasm love.

KENNETH   She's fifteen.

ROSE   Sixteen.

KENNETH   Sixteen there you are. We were drinking at that age, we
             drank for England both of us / you've told me the
             things you did.

SANDRA   Not with my parents, we drank secretly, and I bet she
             does that a lot, sure she's got places she goes –

ROSE   No / actually

SANDRA   She doesn't want to drink with us, we're *boring*.

KENNETH   We are boring, that's true.

SANDRA   We're like dinosaurs to her.

KENNETH   Jamie! Last chance!

SANDRA   You're like a mammoth Ken, and I'm… I'm one of
             those things.

KENNETH   What things?

SANDRA   One of those flying things.

             She mimes, and makes the noise.

KENNETH   Are you sure you don't want a glass love?

ROSE   Yeah.

SANDRA   What are they called?

             She mimes and does the noise again.

KENNETH   Shall I bring the cake in?

SANDRA   Ken! No. Let's wait till midnight. / What's –

ROSE   I'm tired.

SANDRA   It'll be fun. You can stay up. See it in. You're only sixteen once.

ROSE   Yeah but...

KENNETH   Alright.

        He goes.

        A moment.

SANDRA   What are they called those flying dinosaurs?

ROSE   Pterodactyls.

SANDRA   Terro-dactles. That's it! My daughter is a genius, she thinks and plays the violin, look at you. All dressed up.

ROSE   It's uniform.

SANDRA   Oh sweetheart, you're sulking, why are you sulking?

ROSE   I'm not.

SANDRA   Long face.

ROSE   Just because I'm not getting drunk doesn't / mean I'm unhappy.

SANDRA   I'm not drunk darling, I am / seriously not drunk.

ROSE   But you keep on / interrupting and that is getting quite annoying.

SANDRA   I am tired. I'll give you that, I am extremely exhausted from a long day... what?

ROSE   Nothing.

        Beat.

SANDRA   You have to learn, that sometimes, sometimes in life, people are late.

ROSE   I *know*. I've told you it doesn't matter. I'm / not bothered.

SANDRA   But obviously it does, it's this huge rift between us tonight I mean I'd give you a hug but I'm not allowed to touch you any more now that you're a teenager. I know I know that you are not happy I can see it. I am *concerned*. But your father and me we work hard and sometimes these things can't be avoided.

You're not a kid any more are you?

You can understand what I'm saying.

Yes?

ROSE   …

SANDRA   Are you seeing Mark / this weekend?

ROSE   It was just before, when all the other parents were all there. Before it began.

SANDRA   Oh – no. We're still / on this.

ROSE   It was embarrassing. All the other parents were there. Dad only got there at the last minute, and you –

SANDRA   I'm very busy Rose.

ROSE   You're a modern mother a working woman / I know I know

SANDRA   These other mums are probably at home all day, probably don't work the hours I do.

ROSE   I think they do actually. Most of them do work.

SANDRA   I drove foot to floor, top speed, all the way there, broke the law for you.

ROSE   Thanks that's really / nice of you.

SANDRA   And I got there for your bit. Didn't I?

ROSE

SANDRA   Didn't I?

            Rosie?

            Did you see me?

ROSE   No.

SANDRA   I was at the back, standing at the back.

ROSE   Didn't see you Mum.

SANDRA *looks at her.*

SANDRA   What's the matter with you tonight? Your father's right, have a glass.

           SANDRA *offers her the glass.*

ROSE   No.

SANDRA   Come on love you need it. Long face like that.

ROSE   What about you?

SANDRA   Don't worry about me, I am of a generation where we improvise wildly.

           ROSE *takes the glass.* SANDRA *swigs from the bottle as* KENNETH *enters with a glass.*

KENNETH   That's the woman I fell in love with right there. / Look at that.

SANDRA   You should keep it going.

ROSE   What?

SANDRA   The violin. What grade are you now?

ROSE   You don't know?

SANDRA   No I don't know that's why I'm / asking.

ROSE   We went out?

KENNETH   She's grade seven.

ROSE   *Six.*

KENNETH   Thought it was / seven.

ROSE   I passed last month. Remember?

KENNETH   I thought –

ROSE   We went out for dinner.

KENNETH   Oh right yes. You...

ROSE   I got a distinction we went out / to celebrate.

KENNETH   Thought that was seven.

ROSE   No.

SANDRA   Grade six that's really something. You could keep it
            going Rosie – a professional musician. Touring the
            world.

ROSE   Pays really bad –

SANDRA   It's not about the money, it's the passion, the
            audiences. You enjoy playing don't you? I can tell.

ROSE   Can we just have the cake now?

SANDRA   The look on your face when you get it right.
            Concentration. A little smile. I saw you. It's important
            to do something you love.

ROSE   Yeah. Can we do the cake / though?

KENNETH   We'll wait for midnight, it's what your mother / wants.

SANDRA   It's not all about money.

KENNETH   Do you remember that little orchestra at the Isle of
            Wight?

SANDRA   I do.

KENNETH   With a hangover it was / marvellous.

SANDRA   I remember the journey home.

ROSE   Can I / go upstairs then please?

SANDRA   Trying to hitch. Hungover, tired, smelling of crap, your
            father was irresponsible at that age love, please don't
            ever copy his behaviour. We nearly ended up murdered
            – this truck driver looking at my legs, your father
            encouraging him.

KENNETH   We didn't have any money.

ROSE   I've heard this story so many times.

KENNETH   He needed paying. That was the deal.

SANDRA   You were my pimp.

KENNETH   It was different, you could do things / like that then.

SANDRA   I suppose I did have very good legs.

KENNETH   All art aspires to the quality of music sweetheart, you
            know who said that?

ROSE   / Yes.

SANDRA   You could do it at university.

KENNETH   T. S. Eliot.

ROSE   / Walter Pater

SANDRA   A degree in music, you can do that at Oxford can't you?

KENNETH   You can, we were saying, like your Mr –

SANDRA   What?

KENNETH   Her music teacher I was speaking to Mr –

SANDRA   What are you talking about?

KENNETH   He was an organ scholar at Oxford, Mr –

ROSE   Parsons.

KENNETH   Parsons right.

SANDRA   Are you doing Music A level Rosie?

ROSE   Oh. – fucking...

SANDRA   Fucking. What fucking?

ROSE   Just –

SANDRA   Fucking, Ken, she's saying fucking.

KENNETH   Yes I know.

SANDRA   Love, why are you swearing you must be upset.

ROSE   We talked about my A levels *last week*!

SANDRA   Don't get offended Rosie. I've got a life of my own. I can't remember every detail. What did we say then? What did we decide? You're doing music then, yes?

              Yes?

ROSE   Yes.

SANDRA   Good. Well then you can keep that going, get your degree then join an orchestra, tour the world, perfect, all sorted out, get Jamie down here I'm on a roll.

KENNETH   Jamie!

ROSE	I'm going upstairs
SANDRA	Sweetheart no, we have a cake.

Beat.

ROSE	I'll come down for midnight, alright?
SANDRA	You don't enjoy our company.
ROSE	I'm going to make a phone call.
SANDRA	It's half-eleven, who are you calling at this time, it's too late, they'll be in bed.
ROSE	We're not in bed.
SANDRA	Who is it?
ROSE	I don't have to tell you / who I'm calling.
SANDRA	Have I offended you Rosie?
KENNETH	It's alright love, off you go, we'll call you when it's / time.
SANDRA	Did I bring you up like this? This look, this contempt?
KENNETH	Leave her alone.
SANDRA	Rejecting your parents it's an important part of growing up I understand that, teenage rebellion's important, but I have to say sweetheart tonight would not be the time, you don't seem grateful, your father and I we made a real effort.
ROSE	You nearly missed the concert Mum. When you came in late, everyone *looked*.
SANDRA	
ROSE	
SANDRA	I haven't told you this before but I'm not sure about Mark.
KENNETH	Sandra –
SANDRA	He's a nice boy I know but –
ROSE	What?
KENNETH	Sandra shut the mouth now / the mouth is doing things.

SANDRA   He flirts with me, and I know he's a / teenager, the
              hormones but –

ROSE   What are you talking about?

SANDRA   He flirts with me in the kitchen.

ROSE   No he doesn't.

SANDRA   He does, when he's here, I mean I'm not bothered by it
              but you should probably know. It's understandable,
              boys like real women at that age, fully formed, you
              know, and there's plenty more fish for you, in the sea,
              that's all I'm saying. Don't get too attached.

ROSE   Fuck's sake Mum you're a bitch.

KENNETH   Can't argue with that love.

SANDRA   I'm a *bitch*, I love this swearing, it's very sweet, isn't it
              Kenneth? She really is / growing up.

KENNETH   It's alright Rosie off you go, your mother's / showing
              off

SANDRA   Oh look at you, all little and upset and red – you're
              young is what I'm saying, and you're pretty, when you
              make the effort. You look so miserable. You should be
              having fun.

ROSE   Like you had fun you mean.

SANDRA   Well yes it's true we did have *fun* when we were your
              age we did.

ROSE   Fucked around a lot did you?

SANDRA   We certainly weren't hung up on sex no.

ROSE   Now you think I'm *hung up on sex*.

SANDRA   We didn't put all our eggs in one basket, it all seems so
              important for you, and you've got all these exams, I'm
              worried, you look depressed.

ROSE   Not my fault about the exams.

SANDRA   No but –

ROSE   So what are you saying?

SANDRA   …

ROSE

SANDRA   Fine. Don't listen to me. Do what you want. Make
             your mistakes and when you come running I'll be here
             to pick up the pieces, you've always got me darling,
             you'll always have me looking after you, that's what
             mothers do.

KENNETH   Off you go love.

ROSE   Don't shout yeah, while I'm on the phone.

SANDRA   Don't be silly.

ROSE   Cos you do sometimes and it's embarrassing.

             She goes.

             Pause.

             SANDRA *goes to a cupboard, takes out her cigarettes.*

             KENNETH *watches her.*

             She lights a cigarette.

KENNETH   You look tired.

SANDRA   Thanks.

KENNETH   That was a mess tonight.

SANDRA

KENNETH   It's not fair.

SANDRA   I've done the same for you Kenneth. Filled in for you.

KENNETH   Not like this, I've never just forgotten entirely.

SANDRA   It shouldn't have happened I know that.

KENNETH   Right, and when she called from the payphone asking
             where you were I –

SANDRA   You shouldn't have left Jamie by himself.

KENNETH   He's fourteen.

SANDRA   He's weird.

KENNETH   He's bright.

SANDRA   That's the problem.

KENNETH   It was a couple of hours. I told him not to touch anything. I gave him a number to call if he needed to. I couldn't leave her there playing to no one, it obviously means a lot to her. And he wouldn't come with me of course.

SANDRA   …

KENNETH   He could've gone next door in an emergency.

SANDRA   Next door.

KENNETH   Yes.

SANDRA   Don't want next door looking after him.

KENNETH   What?

SANDRA   Don't trust them.

KENNETH   Why not?

SANDRA

KENNETH   Why not?

SANDRA   They're loud.

KENNETH   Loud.

SANDRA   Always shouting.

KENNETH   Remind you of anyone?

SANDRA   Not like we do, nothing like us, they do it in public, out the door, they seem a bit violent if you ask me.

KENNETH   Up to them how they want to be, none of our business.

SANDRA   Up to them alright yes yes, although it's annoying first thing in the morning when you want some peace and quiet, sorting out your car first thing and there she is, the mum, shouting her face off out the front door.

           Not sure how they're even in that house. They can't have bought it.

           Not being…

           You know what I mean.

           It's not cheap round here.

           Pause.

KENNETH   The bill came today.

SANDRA   What?

KENNETH   School fees.

SANDRA   How much?

KENNETH   …

SANDRA   Christ.

KENNETH   I know. So.

            Beat.

            What was it tonight?

SANDRA   A meeting.

KENNETH   With?

SANDRA   Chris.

            Beat.

KENNETH   Chris again.

SANDRA   What? Chris again yes again Chris again yes. What?

KENNETH   These late meetings.

SANDRA   It's busy at the moment we don't get a chance in the days and then we bump into each other at five o'clock and we're like oh god there's about twelve things we need to sort out before tomorrow so we have to sit down and go through them there and then.

KENNETH   Sit down?

SANDRA   Yes, we sit down.

KENNETH   What do you mean?

SANDRA   A meeting.

KENNETH   You sit down.

SANDRA   Yes we sit down we tried standing up but our legs got tired.

KENNETH   Where?

SANDRA   What?

KENNETH   Where do you sit down together?

SANDRA   Alright Columbo.

KENNETH   Just a question. Don't make me / feel stupid asking.

SANDRA   'Sit down together.'

KENNETH   Sandra I'm not –

SANDRA   You're implying something.

KENNETH   When you arrived tonight you smelt of gin.

SANDRA   We had a drink together.

KENNETH   A drink together.

SANDRA   Together yes.

KENNETH   Always *together*.

SANDRA   It's kind of what a *meeting* implies, Kenneth.

KENNETH   So the meeting was...

SANDRA   Yes? The meeting was... what?

KENNETH   Where. Where was the meeting?

SANDRA   Well...

She looks at him.

Sometimes we go to the pub, shocking I know but it's the evening and we can't *bear* to stay in the office. Look at you. Your face quivering. Me and him in the pub. Ooo what might happen. Kenneth you think I'm having an affair.

KENNETH   How many?

SANDRA   Affairs? None.

KENNETH   Not affairs. How many –

SANDRA   Meetings? With Chris? We *work together*.

KENNETH   How many gins?

SANDRA   Gins.

KENNETH   Before you drove.

SANDRA   Oh how many gins. I see. I don't know.

KENNETH   That's the worst answer to that question.

SANDRA   A couple?

KENNETH   A couple like two, or a couple like five.

SANDRA   Like two.

KENNETH   *Like* two?

SANDRA   Oh stop.

KENNETH   Stop what? You're all over the place I think you're completely off the leash at the moment, I don't know what you're up to.

A moment.

SANDRA   Alright.

KENNETH   What?

SANDRA   What if I was?

KENNETH   What?

SANDRA   Having an affair, what if I was?

KENNETH   Are you?

SANDRA   Let's have a conversation.

KENNETH   So you are.

SANDRA   No. But what if I was?

KENNETH   I'm not playing a game. Not tonight. We can do this some other time.

SANDRA   Ken…

KENNETH   What? This is hypothetical or something.

SANDRA   Yes! Hypothetical. Exactly.

KENNETH   I'm serious. I want to talk to you, I want you to be honest, this isn't funny.

SANDRA   I'm just talking Kenneth. I'm just asking what you'd do if I was.

KENNETH   This is a test now?

SANDRA   This is a question.

KENNETH   You mean you want to.

SANDRA   There's something up with you tonight.

KENNETH   I've had enough. Yes, / I've had enough –

SANDRA   I want a conversation Kenneth. We've always been
           able to do that.

KENNETH   Alright.

SANDRA   You wouldn't want to trap me.

KENNETH   So you feel trapped?

SANDRA   Hypothetically.

KENNETH   Of course I don't want to trap you, / where does that –

SANDRA   We always said we've always said there's nothing
           worse than being stuck.

KENNETH   So what have you done?

SANDRA   Because we're going to die.

KENNETH   What have you done?

SANDRA   Nothing.

           Beat.

KENNETH   We're going to die, that's true Sandra, a rare admission
           on your part, death approaches, so what have you –

SANDRA   When I look in the mirror these days I see a ghost.

KENNETH   The cigarettes don't help.

SANDRA   Decay. All the time.

KENNETH   So what are you saying?

           A moment.

           You've found someone.

SANDRA   This is going round and round your head isn't it?

KENNETH   Someone younger.

SANDRA   Someone *younger*? No.

KENNETH   Or older. Chris.

SANDRA   I haven't found anyone I'm asking a question. I'm
            simply inviting a discussion about a subject but you're
            getting all jumpy and twitchy about it – *Chris*?

KENNETH   You can tell me.

SANDRA   *Chris?* No.

KENNETH   Really. Tell me honestly.

SANDRA   Kenneth.

KENNETH   Honestly.

SANDRA   Chris?

KENNETH   I'll go first.

SANDRA   Go first at what?

KENNETH   I'll lay it out.

SANDRA   Ken –

KENNETH   The truth. We haven't properly talked for –

SANDRA   We're very busy.

KENNETH   I have.

SANDRA   Have what?

KENNETH   I have slept with someone else.

SANDRA   You…

            Beat.

KENNETH   Your turn.

SANDRA   Wait wait.

KENNETH   Okay. I've said it. Your turn.

            A moment. She looks at him.

SANDRA   You…

KENNETH   I'm not the only one am I?

SANDRA   I was talking hypothetically.

KENNETH   Come on

SANDRA   What?

KENNETH   The meetings, the secrets.

SANDRA   What secrets?

KENNETH   We can talk about the details when / it's out.

SANDRA   No we can talk about the details now.

KENNETH   Who was it?

SANDRA   There isn't / anyone.

KENNETH   Chris?

SANDRA   No. Chris? No. Chris is ridiculous. For fuck's sake
           Kenneth.

KENNETH   Right.

           I thought...

SANDRA   No.

KENNETH   Right. Shit.

SANDRA   More wine?

           She pours more wine.

           So?

           Let's have it.

KENNETH   I was angry. I met a girl. Her name was Frankie.

SANDRA   That's a boy's name.

KENNETH   And a girl's name I believe.

SANDRA   Are you sure it wasn't a boy?

KENNETH   Yeah.

SANDRA   How do you know?

KENNETH   I know.

           She takes that in.

SANDRA   How old?

KENNETH   Does it matter?

SANDRA   I'm not angry here Kenneth.

KENNETH   Yes but –

SANDRA   Look at me, look at my body language my expression.

KENNETH   Alright.

SANDRA   You see I'm acting surprisingly calm considering I'm the victim.

KENNETH   You're never the victim.

SANDRA   You've messed me around.

KENNETH   Yes.

SANDRA   Yes so does it matter? It matters to me. So.

KENNETH   Alright.

SANDRA   How old?

KENNETH   Look –

SANDRA   HOW OLD?

KENNETH   Early twenties?

SANDRA   What does she do?

KENNETH   I don't know.

SANDRA   Did you catch a surname in the course of the evening?

KENNETH

SANDRA

KENNETH   Exactly. You're right. That's exactly what it was like.

SANDRA   In and out.

KENNETH   Bit more to it than that but –

SANDRA   In essence.

KENNETH   Yeah

SANDRA   BLOODY HELL KEN. BLOODY FUCKING HELL.

KENNETH   I'm sorry.

           Pause.

SANDRA   FRANKIE.

KENNETH   Frankie.

           She looks at him.

A moment.

SANDRA   Cigarette?

KENNETH   Don't be stupid.

She rolls a cigarette across the table.

He looks at it.

She throws him the lighter.

A moment.

He lights up.

SANDRA   Blonde?

KENNETH   No.

SANDRA   Redhead?

KENNETH   Brunette.

SANDRA   Tall?

KENNETH   Ish.

SANDRA   Looked like me did she?

KENNETH   No she –

SANDRA   From the little you remember?

KENNETH   From what I can remember she wasn't a patch on you.

SANDRA   Oh.

Beat.

KENNETH   But yes, she was…

SANDRA   She was… what? She was what?

KENNETH   Fresh.

SANDRA   Fresh.

KENNETH

SANDRA   Fresh *meat*.

KENNETH   If you like.

SANDRA   Right.

KENNETH   Yes.

SANDRA   Yes.

KENNETH   Yes she smelt different.

SANDRA   You're not sorry.

KENNETH   Not sorry.

SANDRA   Are you? You love me, your feelings towards me are exactly the same but you had a great time with her you just had a really good new kind of sex.

KENNETH   Yeah.

SANDRA   Then don't apologise then. If you're not sorry, take it back.

KENNETH   …

SANDRA   TAKE IT BACK!

KENNETH   Alright.

ROSE bursts in, crying.

ROSE   I told you both to shut up and you're shouting your bloody mouths off, I told you and Mark was on the phone and he was like what's that? And I tried to tell him it was the television but he thought you were shouting at me, he said it clearly wasn't a good time and hung up but we had to *talk* about something, it gave him an excuse to – now I have to go into school tomorrow and – Oh –

She sees KENNETH with a cigarette.

What, you're smoking now?

KENNETH

ROSE

SANDRA

ROSE   Fucking hell you two are the shittest fucking parents. I fucking hate you.

She storms out.

SANDRA   Five minutes sweetheart.

ROSE has gone.

KENNETH   You understand why I did it. I think you know.

SANDRA   No I don't know.

KENNETH   That's why you're not angry, there was a bit of you
that wanted this, you want me to do something exactly
like this.

SANDRA   I was happy with you.

KENNETH   No you wanted something more, that's why you started
this hypothetical thing you wanted me to say –

SANDRA   Kenneth I love you, I'm a lucky girl most men your
age are sagging, but look at you –

KENNETH   You could go for someone younger then.

SANDRA   What are you doing?

KENNETH   I'm talking hypothetically.

SANDRA   Yes. I could go for someone younger yes.

Beat.

KENNETH   We're in love.

SANDRA   I thought so.

Beat.

KENNETH   But something's gone wrong.

SANDRA   No.

KENNETH   We live in Reading.

Something's gone wrong.

SANDRA   …

KENNETH   It's all house. Children. Work. We never wanted it like
this. I'm not happy you're not happy so

…

They look at each other. It's true.

Right.

Yes. There.

SANDRA   …

KENNETH   Chris?

SANDRA   …

KENNETH   Yes?

SANDRA   We should get the kids down here it's nearly…

KENNETH   Sandra –

SANDRA   Jamie!

KENNETH   Sandra I can see –

SANDRA   Jamie! It's time.

KENNETH   I know what you've done why won't you admit / it?

SANDRA   Rosie, three minutes! Come down, we're doing the
             cake! If I have Ken, if I had done something as well,
             how would that help, if we'd both been lying to each
             other what are you suggesting we do?

KENNETH   Chris. Yes?

SANDRA   Jesus Ken leave it / alone

KENNETH   I don't know what we do but at least we could start
             with the truth. We were never like this, we were
             honest.

SANDRA   I'm getting the cake.

KENNETH   Chris.

SANDRA   No.

KENNETH   Yes.

SANDRA   NO!

KENNETH   Sandra

SANDRA   Alright!

             Yes. Fresh meat. Exactly. Four months. He's good. It
             helps.

             Alright?

KENNETH   Yes.

SANDRA   Good.

Now we're really in trouble. Well done.

JAMIE *enters*.

Come and sit down Jamie, would you like some wine?

JAMIE   What?

KENNETH   He's fourteen.

JAMIE   Okay. Is this because it's Rosie's birthday?

SANDRA   How about a cigarette?

JAMIE   Mum...

KENNETH   Ignore her.

SANDRA   He smokes anyway.

JAMIE   No I don't.

SANDRA   Oh come ON.

JAMIE   I've had a –

SANDRA   Just *take one*.

               He looks at her. She's serious.

JAMIE   Alright.

               He does.

               Got a lighter?

               She gives him one, he lights it effortlessly.

               Where's Rosie?

SANDRA   I'm just going to get the cake.

               She goes, shouting on her way.

               Rosie if you don't come down now there'll be trouble!
               We've made an effort for you don't want you sulking.
               I'll show her shouting.

               ROSIE!

               NOW!

               She goes out.

               Pause.

JAMIE *and* KENNETH *look at each other.*

JAMIE   Didn't know you smoked Dad.

KENNETH   Yeah.

JAMIE   It suits you.

KENNETH   Thanks.

               Beat.

               You too.

JAMIE   Thanks.

               They smoke.

               ROSE *comes in, very unhappy. She sits.*

               Do you want a cigarette?

ROSE   Shut up.

               Silence.

               They sit together.

               KENNETH *checks his watch.*

KENNETH   Thirty seconds.

               Silence.

               Then –

SANDRA   (*From off.*) Happy birthday to you!

               They all join in as SANDRA *enters with the cake.*
               Fifteen candles are lit. She puts it on the table.

ALL   (*Apart from* ROSE.) Happy birthday to you.
               Happy birthday dear Rosie.
               Happy birthday to you!

               A moment. They look at ROSE.

               Blow them out then.

               She does.

               They don't all go out.

               She sits for a moment.

She's about to do the rest when JAMIE *blows them out, with lots of smoke.*

Oh.

KENNETH   Jamie!

JAMIE   She didn't do it properly.

SANDRA   Ahhh! My little boy smoking in front of his mother.

A proper family at last.

Cake everyone?

She divides up the cake.

Now as you might've heard, your father and I have been having a conversation, an adult conversation but since you're both grown up now in your own way tonight I think we should lay it out for you what do you think Ken?

KENNETH   No I don't think we should actually / Sandra.

SANDRA   Your father went and found someone else and had sex with her. Her name was Frankie.

ROSE looks at her dad. JAMIE *smokes.*

She was young. It was revenge as he thought I was having an affair myself which if we're honest, if we're really laying this all out for you in the middle of the night, well… there's a man called Chris. Chris is not the sort of man you would expect me to be sleeping with, but it seems that both of us have felt in some way frustrated and we've found a way out – does everyone have a piece of cake?

No one replies.

KENNETH   Can we talk about / this later –

SANDRA   Now we still both love each other, don't worry about that. But we both feel trapped, we live, as you know, in Reading, and we never intended to be in this domestic situation we are both feeling that maybe human beings were not designed to be monogamous do you both know what that word means?

Neither answers.

We both feel that maybe sleeping around is our natural state, so that in itself might have been alright but the issue – and Ken do correct me – the issue is trust. We can't be lying to each other. That would be pointless.

As you grow up, both of you, you'll learn that in love as everything else there is no such thing as a happy ending. We're animals.

So the question we have is –

ROSE   Why are you telling us this?

SANDRA   Rosie I'm talking. Eat your cake. We're animals and what happens happens so the conclusion your father and I have come to is that we should get divorced that's right isn't it Ken? We didn't want to mention it to you until we were sure but having talked about it I think we've come to a joint decision now haven't we?

KENNETH   A divorce?

SANDRA   I know it must be difficult, but it's the right thing.

KENNETH   Sandra SHUT / UP.

ROSE   / I don't want to hear THIS!

SANDRA   It's really important we don't confuse our children and really a divorce is the only way forward.

KENNETH   It's what you want?

SANDRA   The only way we can be free. And we always said –

ROSE   Why are you telling us like this?

SANDRA   It's not fair on the children us going at each other / all the time.

ROSE   I asked a question.

SANDRA   Ken, we've made a decision really haven't we, and we'll stay in touch. We'll still be friends.

KENNETH   I don't know.

SANDRA   I think things are different now I think things have changed, we're entitled to do our own thing follow our own path, no one can tell us what's *right*, not church not the government, not even our children, it's no one's business but our own.

We've got our lives to live Ken, you, me, Rosie, Jamie, when it comes down to it we're all separate people these days. On our own paths.

There's a bit of you that's excited about this. Isn't there?

There's a little bit of you excited about the possibilities of striking out, on your own?

KENNETH   Yes.

Pause.

SANDRA   So there we are children. Mum and Dad are going to be happier.

And trust me. You'll be happier too.

ROSE *suddenly gets up and leaves.*

A moment.

KENNETH   Why?

SANDRA   Did you say something?

KENNETH   Why are you involving them?

SANDRA   Because technically we're a family.

Look. Jamie's still here.

JAMIE *is smoking and not looking at them.*

He's pleased I've laid it all out.

He's pleased we're up front so he knows what's coming. They know about their parents. They're not children. He smokes. Rosie's doing all sorts of thing with her *boyfriend* I bet she's having a whale of a time.

JAMIE   She's split up with him.

KENNETH   What?

JAMIE   He slept with Sarah Franks last weekend. She's only just found out. That's what she was doing on the phone. Heard her crying. He doesn't want her any more.

SANDRA   Well… Proves my point. No happy endings.

           Pause.

           ROSE *screams from upstairs.*

           What was –

JAMIE   It's Rosie.

KENNETH   She sounded –

           Another scream. KENNETH *goes.*

           SANDRA *waits for a second, unsure, then goes after*
           KENNETH. *Another scream. Sobbing.*

           From off:

           Rosie!

SANDRA   Rosie!

KENNETH   Are you alright? It's not important. What your mother
           was saying…

           Sobbing. Banging. JAMIE *lights another cigarette.*

           Open the door Rosie.

           A banging.

           Rosie!

           More banging and shouting.

           JAMIE *goes and puts the tape back in.*

           *'She Bangs the Drums' plays again – picking up from
           where it left off.*

           JAMIE *sings along quietly.*

           Underneath the banging and the shouting continues.

           JAMIE *gets the rest of the wine and drinks from the
           bottle.*

           *As the curtain falls and the lights fade the music mixes
           with the banging on the door.*

           In the dark just a thumping.

           Interval.

THREE

Thumping.

We hear 'Sexy Chick' by David Guetta feat. Akon.

As the drums come in... curtain up to reveal...

2011. A living room in a large country house. French windows open out onto a large garden. Light pours in. An iPad is plugged into a dock – playing the music and the video to the song.

ROSE *enters, with a bag, having come in the front door. She is now thirty-seven, lives in London, and is dressed in slightly old, dark clothes.*

She looks around – where is everyone?

JAMIE *enters through the French windows with his iPhone. He is thirty-five, unshaven, and wearing a grey hooded top. He tips the iPhone around, playing 'Labyrinth' intently. Doesn't look up. Nods in time with the music.*

He stops. Still doesn't look up.

Then she goes over and switches off the iPad. JAMIE *turns round.*

JAMIE   Oh.

          ROSE *smiles.*

ROSE   Hello.

          She goes over and hugs him.

JAMIE   Aren't you coming this afternoon?

ROSE   It is this afternoon.

JAMIE   Dad said you were coming back when it finished

ROSE   It has finished.

JAMIE   Oh. Have you seen this? It's a game, you... you have to get the ball in the hole.

ROSE   Right.

JAMIE   You've got a phone though?

ROSE	Yeah.
JAMIE	Yeah you should download it then.
	He goes back to playing it.
ROSE	How's things?
JAMIE	Yeah good.
ROSE	The job?
JAMIE	Yeah it's alright. You know, it's you know it's flexible.
ROSE	Been there a while now.
JAMIE	What?
ROSE	Been driving for them a while.
JAMIE	Yeah six months or whatever.
ROSE	You like it?
JAMIE	Yeah yeah.
ROSE	You still doing your course?
JAMIE	What? No.
ROSE	You…
JAMIE	Didn't… teacher was shit.
ROSE	Right.
JAMIE	Giving it all – Didn't know what he was talking about. I was I was cleverer than him I could tell I was like, er have you have you thought of the social factor he didn't know what I what I was talking about I was like this guy's a fraud this guy doesn't know anything. I get bored quickly.
ROSE	I know.
JAMIE	Didn't like it so I stopped.
	Beat.
ROSE	So what is it now?
JAMIE	Gonna go travelling.
ROSE	You said that before.

JAMIE   Saving up.

ROSE   Where?

JAMIE   Australia. My my my friend – you remember – Kate.

ROSE   You're still in touch with her.

JAMIE   Yeah Facebook. Gonna go and stay with her, for a bit.

ROSE   Right.

JAMIE   Supposed to be mental out there.

ROSE   Right.

          Mental.

JAMIE   Yeah.

          Beat.

ROSE   You didn't want to come today?

JAMIE   How did he die?

ROSE   Didn't dad tell you? Cancer.

JAMIE   Yeah didn't want to come. Not my thing.

ROSE   Right.

JAMIE   That okay?

ROSE   Yeah.

          Beat.

          How's dad?

JAMIE   Alright.

ROSE   Must be around the house a bit more now.

JAMIE   Yeah.

ROSE   Annoying is it?

JAMIE   No it's good. He picks me up.

ROSE   What?

JAMIE   From the pub.

ROSE   Right.

JAMIE   We get on so. Yeah. Can be annoying but you but you. You get used to it.

ROSE   Right. Jamie?

JAMIE   What?

ROSE   Can you stop playing that for a minute?

JAMIE   What? Oh… what? Is it is it? I'm not being rude.

ROSE   I haven't seen you in months.

JAMIE   I'm not being rude. Don't get annoyed.

          She sighs.

          Don't get annoyed with me.

ROSE   I'm asking you Jamie.

JAMIE   Right, right. Hang on.

          Pause.

          He stops.

          Puts it away, walks around a bit.

          What then? What do you want then?

ROSE   Nothing, just… do you want a cup of tea?

JAMIE   Nah I'm alright.

          Beat.

ROSE   What happened with the flat?

JAMIE   What? Oh.

ROSE   Last time I was here you were trying to find somewhere.

JAMIE   Too expensive it's like I could spend all my money on the rent you know or I can live here and have money no contest and as I as I said Dad's cool, he's like a mate, but I don't have to

ROSE   Don't have to pay rent.

JAMIE   Yeah exactly. It's expensive. Costs loads.

ROSE   I know.

JAMIE   Yeah. Do you rent?

ROSE   Of course.

JAMIE   Yeah right so you so you know.

ROSE   It's more expensive in London.

JAMIE   I couldn't live in London. I went there the other day,
              we went there went there to see a play.

ROSE   What?

JAMIE   *Wicked.*

ROSE   That's a musical.

JAMIE   Yeah it was good, but we went to the pub and it was
              like five quid for a pint and we were we were like I
              said I said I think there's a mistake you're charging us
              five quid and the guy – everyone in London's rude you
              know? You know?

ROSE   Who did you go with?

JAMIE   What?

ROSE   To see *Wicked.*

JAMIE   Dad.

ROSE   You didn't say.

JAMIE   What?

ROSE   I'm in London. You didn't call I could've met you.

JAMIE   Didn't... what? Didn't think of it. So. What? Shit.
              Don't get annoyed with me yeah?

ROSE   I'm not.

JAMIE   What is this?

ROSE   No.

JAMIE   Sounds like you you were so so

ROSE   It doesn't matter, I'm glad you liked the show.

JAMIE   Yeah it was good. Interval, it was good it had an
              interval you can go out have a smoke.

ROSE   Right.

              JAMIE *hears something. Looks out the window.*

JAMIE   Dad.

ROSE   Right.

JAMIE   Out there.

          Suddenly JAMIE *goes out the French windows.*

          ROSE *is left on her own.*

          She looks around.

          The house is beautiful.

          Expensive equipment, art, ornaments. Perfect.

          She goes to the wall.

          Touches it.

          Leans on it. Something's wrong.

          KENNETH *enters through the French windows. He is
          now sixty-four, and wears a dark suit and a black tie.
          He is still looking healthy.* JAMIE *follows behind him.
          He has a black bag.*

KENNETH   My favourite daughter.

ROSE   Your only daughter.

KENNETH   This is true. Sharp as a button.

ROSE   Buttons aren't sharp.

KENNETH   I meant bright.

ROSE   I think you did.

KENNETH   Bright as a button.

ROSE   There you are.

KENNETH   My favourite daughter.

          He kisses and hugs her. Then takes his jacket and tie off.

          That went okay, didn't it?

ROSE   Yeah.

KENNETH   Sorry we didn't get to talk but... stuff. All okay getting
          there?

ROSE   Got a taxi from the station.

KENNETH   You didn't want to drive?

ROSE   Got rid of my car.

KENNETH   Oh right.

ROSE   Ages ago.

KENNETH   Suppose it's not worth it in London?

ROSE   Well...

KENNETH   And the train was alright?

ROSE   Yeah.

KENNETH   I can't stand them, not these days. Wait – how did you get here. Afterwards.

ROSE   Taxi.

KENNETH   Again? I could have given you a lift. Had to say goodbye to everyone but –

ROSE   I thought I'd get out the way.

Out of the bag, KENNETH *gets out a small black functional urn, and puts it on a shelf. Then, over the next dialogue, he goes to a small fridge and produces a bottle of wine, from which he pours a glass.*

KENNETH   That pub wasn't bad though in the end. Not a bad place for it. Good view. You want a drink?

ROSE   I'm alright thanks. Got water.

KENNETH   We're on white wine at the moment. Aren't we Jamie?

JAMIE   Yeah. Yeah.

KENNETH   Colin got back from France on Monday. You know Colin?

ROSE   No.

KENNETH   Plays golf, he went on a bit of booze cruise, we put in an order didn't we?

JAMIE   Yeah.

KENNETH   And here are the fruits, of his labour, bottled up, he went for quality, all the way to the south and you really can taste the difference. Sit down sit down.

They do. ROSE *looks at the urn.*

ROSE   Didn't he want to be buried?

KENNETH   I don't know, he didn't leave instructions.

ROSE   You never discussed it?

                    Where are you going to scatter them then?

KENNETH   We'll work something out.

                    So. Anyway.

                    Exciting.

ROSE   What?

KENNETH   Your news.

ROSE   It's not news.

KENNETH   I loved it, calling us up, 'Since we'll be together
                    anyway, I want a moment to talk.'

ROSE   Right.

KENNETH   'Since we're all in the same place for once.'

ROSE

KENNETH   'I have something to say'

ROSE   Yeah.

KENNETH   It's good. It's a good excuse – haven't properly spoken
                    to your mother in months. Did you see her?

ROSE   What?

KENNETH   Just now. At the pub. Did you see what she was up to?

ROSE   No.

KENNETH   Flirting with the barman. Clive couldn't make it in the
                    end so she took the opportunity. Flirting away with this
                    bloke behind the bar.

ROSE   She was getting drunk.

KENNETH   That's what she's like.

ROSE   Yes.

KENNETH   Uncontrollable.

ROSE   Uncontrollable.

KENNETH   Got to admire her really.

ROSE   She's not driving here is she?

KENNETH   No. I'm sure... she. Actually yes she probably is.
              Fingers crossed! Get out the way!

ROSE   So irresponsible.

              Pause.

KENNETH   You alright love?

ROSE   ...

              Beat.

KENNETH   Jamie's still got his job.

ROSE   Yeah I know. He said.

              It's good.

KENNETH   Yeah.

              They're both looking at JAMIE, *who's not been
              listening.*

JAMIE   What?

KENNETH   How's the flat?

ROSE   Fine.

KENNETH   And Sarah?

ROSE   What?

KENNETH   It is Sarah? Your flatmate.

ROSE   She moved out last year.

KENNETH   Oh right, who is it now then?

ROSE   This bloke Paul.

KENNETH   A bloke – what does Andrew make of that? – who's
              Paul?

ROSE   Some guy from Gumtree.

KENNETH   Gumtree?

ROSE   You advertise on it if you've got a room going.

KENNETH   So Paul's really just some bloke?

ROSE   Yeah.

KENNETH   Is that. That's…

ROSE   What?

KENNETH   You're happy with that are you?

ROSE   Not really.

KENNETH   Wouldn't have been allowed when I was your age, sharing – man and a women. Together like that, would've been an outrage. A sin.

ROSE   Well the rent needs paying.

Beat.

KENNETH   You know if you need any help with anything.

ROSE   Yeah.

KENNETH   Good good.

Suddenly JAMIE *unzips his hoody, takes off his T-shirt and strides out into the sun of the garden.*

He's off then.

Beat.

ROSE   Is he alright?

KENNETH   What do you mean?

ROSE   He seems worse.

KENNETH   Don't know what you mean.

ROSE   The repeating. The – he's going round in circles.

KENNETH   Rosie, you always say this, I think it's cruel.

ROSE   He used to be bright.

KENNETH   He's his own person. He's very intelligent.

ROSE   But he's not Dad. He really isn't. Not any more.

KENNETH   He's just – he doesn't fit in to what people want. But he's wonderful. When he had that thing in the centre with the disabled kids.

ROSE   He never turned up.

KENNETH   It was early mornings, but when he was there he was brilliant. Why do you want to get at him?

ROSE   I just wonder if he should... get help or something.

KENNETH   Leave him alone. He's happy.

ROSE   But that's not –

KENNETH   What?

    Beat.

ROSE   Nothing.

KENNETH   Are you alright?

    ROSE *turns away.*

    A strange moment.

    Then she turns back.

ROSE   How's retirement?

KENNETH   I don't know why I didn't do it before. Time's my own. Me and Jamie we do the garden, he likes it, then we go to the pub. It's bliss. Golf. Perfect.

ROSE   Good.

KENNETH   You know I worked out with the pension and the payments, and the income from the Birmingham house, I'm making over eighty thousand a year.

ROSE   Right.

KENNETH   Not bad for doing nothing.

ROSE   Yeah.

KENNETH   And I mean now you're all out of university or whatever, and everything's paid off so the money's my own. Good isn't it?

ROSE   Yeah.

KENNETH   Life of luxury.

ROSE   Eighty thousand.

KENNETH   Yep.

ROSE   Almost three times what I make now.

KENNETH   What? No. Is it?

ROSE   Yeah, and I'm working all the time.

KENNETH   Really?

ROSE   …

KENNETH   Well at least you're doing what you want to do aren't
            you?

ROSE   …

            A doorbell.

KENNETH   There she is. Safe and sound but a trail of destruction
            in her wake, no doubt. Pretty much sums her up…

            He goes out.

            ROSE *nearly cries, but stops herself.*

            Voices offstage.

SANDRA   You've done something to the front?

KENNETH   Landscaped the drive.

SANDRA   Looks cheap.

KENNETH   My choice.

SANDRA   Just saying Kenneth, no need / to snap at me.

KENNETH   I know, I know you're always / just saying.

SANDRA   Is she here?

KENNETH   She's in a mood.

SANDRA   Oh good, just what I want to contend with after a
            funeral, one of Rosie's *moods*.

KENNETH   Be careful.

SANDRA   I'm always careful. Through here?

            They enter. SANDRA *is now sixty-four, dressed
            expensively and tastefully in black for the occasion and
            the weather. Her skin is amazing. She has looked after
            herself.*

            Hello!

ROSE   Hi Mum.

SANDRA *goes and kisses and hugs* ROSE.

SANDRA   Look at you. My baby. Were you at the wake just now?

ROSE   Yes.

SANDRA   I didn't see you. But here we both are, your father and
          your mother together again isn't it something? You
          look healthy.

ROSE   What does that mean?

SANDRA   Healthy. Healthy. Not ill. Healthy. What do you think it
          means?

ROSE   Fat?

SANDRA   Don't be silly you're not fat, why haven't you got a
          drink?

ROSE   I don't want one.

SANDRA   Diet?

ROSE   No.

SANDRA   Pregnant?

ROSE   No.

SANDRA   Because you've called us all together to tell us
          something and now you're not drinking.

ROSE   I'm not pregnant.

SANDRA   You're sure?

ROSE   Mum –

SANDRA   I was convinced that's what this was about, well never
          mind, I know I could do with a drink.

KENNETH   We're on the wine.

SANDRA   Are you? You never had any taste for wine. Your dad,
          Rosie, he never had any taste for anything, except
          women – he didn't do too badly there.

KENNETH   I'll get you a glass.

SANDRA   That's an idea, and music, I suppose he knew a thing or
          two about his music. Come on sit down then. How are
          you? Not pregnant we know that. How's it going?

ROSE	Good.
SANDRA	How are the gigs?
ROSE	On and off.
SANDRA	I loved it at Christmas.
ROSE	Yeah it was good you came.
SANDRA	I loved it. We both enjoyed it.
ROSE	How's Clive?
SANDRA	Not well.
ROSE	Right.

SANDRA   But we ply him with booze and it does the trick. Doctor says it won't help but I think Clive's long past that, and we say will it actually kill him? All the booze and doctor says not immediately so off we go, gin, sherry, this whisky we got from Islay. You've not been to Islay have you Ken?

KENNETH   I haven't had the pleasure no.

He gives her some wine.

There you are.

SANDRA   Well you've should. Why don't you go with Kerry?

KENNETH   Not with Kerry any more.

ROSE   They split up.

SANDRA   What?

KENNETH   I split up with Kerry months ago.

SANDRA   Why?

KENNETH *shrugs.*

You're such a *man* Ken, look at him. You should update me. Put it on Facebook. I'm on Facebook now. I love it. Ken you should join now you're single.

KENNETH   Jamie tried to set me up but it's all nonsense really isn't it? Poking and walls and everything else.

SANDRA   Baby I looked you up, why aren't you on it?

ROSE   I was.

SANDRA   All your friends are. You were? What happened?

ROSE   I deleted my account.

SANDRA   Why?

ROSE   …

SANDRA   Well I love it. Photos, all of that. It's good for flirting
              too and Clive doesn't understand computers won't go
              near one, so it's entirely safe. You know you can
              actually chat to people on it? I love it. This wine isn't
              bad Ken.

KENNETH   Told you.

SANDRA   Where's it from?

KENNETH   France. Got twenty bottles in the garage. You can take
              one with you.

SANDRA   You can give me a couple when I go.

KENNETH   I just said that.

SANDRA   What?

KENNETH   I'll give you a case.

SANDRA   Lovely. This isn't bad. Where's Jamie?

ROSE   Sunbathing.

SANDRA   He knows what's good for him. Bless him.

KENNETH   Shall I…

SANDRA   No don't disturb him wouldn't get any sense out of
              him anyway, away with the fairies, see him later.

ROSE   It was a shame he didn't make it today.

KENNETH   Not his thing.

SANDRA   Shall we get started? Get it over and done with? Very
              exciting.

              Isn't it?

              You want to talk to us.

ROSE   Dad can you sit down?

KENNETH   Oh right.

SANDRA   He's always the same isn't he? No attention span.
            Look at him.

KENNETH   I just can't concentrate any more. No need to. I love it.
            Freedom! At last!

SANDRA   Your father, still all over the place. Come on Ken. Sit
            down. She's getting annoyed. She wants us all to *talk*.

ROSE   I'm not annoyed.

SANDRA   See?

            He sits down.

KENNETH   I have now sat down.

SANDRA   Alright then love.

            All yours. Off you go.

ROSE   Don't…

SANDRA   What?

ROSE   Don't patronise me.

SANDRA   What?

ROSE   I'm not a kid.

SANDRA   I know. We all know that. What a strange thing to say.

            Of course you're not.

ROSE

SANDRA   I'm just saying, I'm here for you. We're listening.
            Gosh.

KENNETH   Let her speak.

SANDRA   I am. That's what I'm doing. I'm prompting.

            Speak.

            Go on love.

            Pause.

ROSE   I want you to buy me a house.

            SANDRA *smiles.*

KENNETH *laughs.*

SANDRA   A house?

              KENNETH *laughs some more.*

KENNETH   You've got a house.

ROSE   I'm renting.

KENNETH   Your flat.

ROSE   I rent it.

KENNETH   Thought you liked it.

ROSE   I... No.

              ...I...

              Oh.

KENNETH   What's the matter love?

SANDRA   Something's wrong isn't it? I can tell.

              ROSE *laughs.*

ROSE   Yeah one or two things yeah one or two things have
              gone a bit wrong.

SANDRA   Come on then.

KENNETH   We've got nothing else to do this afternoon love.

ROSE   Don't get drunk.

SANDRA   I've only just arrived. Look as I said we're here for
              you, but we don't need to be insulted.

              Yes?

              We're well past that. Aren't we Ken? We can do
              without.

              Yes?

              Let's make that clear.

KENNETH   We won't get drunk love.

              Pause. ROSE *gathers herself again.*

ROSE   I'm thirty-seven.

SANDRA   Yes we know. My baby.

ROSE   It was my birthday, in March.

SANDRA   We sent you a card. Didn't we? Clive and I did
            anyway, Kenneth did you?

ROSE   Mum!

KENNETH   Course I / sent her a card

ROSE   Shut up yeah?

SANDRA   Okay, alright, we've been having fun, having a good
            time up till now but maybe it's not clear Rosie I don't
            have to be shouted at, you understand? We could all be
            doing lots of / other things –

ROSE   Do what you like.

SANDRA   Just carry on.

ROSE   So... my birthday. I had a little thing in a bar in
            Clapham, hired out this little bar, and all my friends
            came, and two days before I didn't tell you this, but
            two days before my birthday I broke up with Andy.

KENNETH   You didn't... oh... you're not with.

ROSE   No.

KENNETH   You didn't say.

ROSE   You never asked.

SANDRA   You don't like us asking.

ROSE   Yeah so I'd already booked this bar, and I went ahead
            with it anyway even though I was quite... *lonely*... you
            know.

SANDRA   Oh baby.

ROSE   And everyone turned up and some of them with kids
            and stuff and we had a bit of a dance you know, kept
            the smiles going but then suddenly I found I was sat on
            a chair at the side of the room, all on my own, at my
            own party, and I was crying.

SANDRA   Were you drinking gin?

ROSE   No.

SANDRA   Gin can do that.

ROSE   I wasn't drinking at all Mum but I found I was crying,
            and it was because I realised as I was sat there, I
            realised I'd completely fucked it up.

SANDRA   What?

ROSE   I... thought I'm thirty-seven and I've had a good time
            in London, sort of – but what have I got? No flat, no
            kids, no partner, no car, ten thousand in unsecured debt.

SANDRA   You're doing what you wanted darling, not many
            people can –

ROSE   What I wanted at seventeen but I'm nearly forty and
            I've got nothing.

            And I was sat there at the side of the room and I
            thought where did it go wrong? And walking down the
            street it hit me and the more I thought about it the more
            obvious it was.

            It's your fault. All of it.

            I wanted to tell you. I thought you should know.

KENNETH   Our fault.

SANDRA   Baby.

            You're upset I understand, you're obviously in some
            kind of state we can see that but don't turn this at us,
            you're being ridiculous. / We've given you
            everything –

ROSE   Don't get *offended*. Listen to me.

SANDRA   Well you're accusing us of –

ROSE   I've done everything / I was told to do.

SANDRA   Just stood there and accusing us of ruining your life,
            this melodramatic streak / it comes from your father.

ROSE   I worked hard at school, / got my results.

KENNETH   What's that supposed to mean?

ROSE   You said go to university to get a job so that's what I
            did, but when I came out there weren't any jobs.

SANDRA   A degree was something to fall back on.

ROSE   A degree means nothing.

SANDRA	Well you didn't need it in the end anyway you –
ROSE	Yeah right exactly, as you said I should, as you *encouraged* me to do, I followed my dream, did what you said was *important*, following my *passion*.
SANDRA	You're really talking look at her Ken.
KENNETH	I am
ROSE	I didn't settle down too early, didn't compromise and I *thought* I really believed, because you *told me* Mum, you *assured* me, that a woman can have it all, you were my example.
SANDRA	I'll take / that as a compliment –
ROSE	– you said, as did everyone else, there's no hurry to have kids these days, so I waited until I had built up my career, but the problem was my career never happened.
KENNETH	You weren't to know how / things would turn out.
ROSE	Well I was to know
SANDRA	You've done alright.
ROSE	I was to know for a simple reason which is that *I'm not very good*. But you always encouraged me. Everyone did, my teachers, you, the college, all of them said I should keep going when obviously, looking back, *clearly* –
KENNETH	It's just difficult, it's a difficult / profession –
ROSE	Everyone knew. All the time, you knew I wasn't great, but out of *kindness*, you didn't say and instead just watched me entirely fuck up waste my life away.
SANDRA	
ROSE	All my friends who got proper boring jobs have a brilliant time – for fifteen years they've been able to afford parties, drinks, holidays while I'm still temping between gigs, and then they had babies but I waited, I was working too much, too hard, with music, this *hobby*, but now I'm old, really old. You know where Andy's gone?

SANDRA	Look –
KENNETH	Andy? What do you mean?
ROSE	She's twenty-four and desperate for kids. That's where he's gone.
	To her. She doesn't want a career.
	So where does that leave me?
KENNETH	Love –
ROSE	Stuck on the bottom fucking shelf.
	Beat.
KENNETH	You said it was what you wanted.
ROSE	I needed guidance, real honest guidance when I was young – perspective, but instead you let me, you encouraged me to –
SANDRA	Is this getting to a point darling?
ROSE	Yes it's getting to a *point*.
SANDRA	Because it sounds like a moan.
ROSE	Well sorry for taking up your time Mum.
SANDRA	I can think of better ways to spend my afternoon.
ROSE	Granny and Grandad lived through the war, lived through rations, their lot built the welfare state. They *worked* hard.
KENNETH	We've worked hard. Forty years, both of us, every day –
ROSE	And what have you lot done? Climbed the ladder and broke it as you went.
SANDRA	Kenneth top me up. This is good stuff.
	He does.
ROSE	You got your cheap flights and your nice cars but never looked at what they were doing to the environment, you hate immigrants, love the *Daily Mail* – voted in Thatcher, destroyed the unions, reduced taxes, Tony fucking Blair –
SANDRA	/ Politics!

ROSE   – now surprise surprise you've voted in the Tories
                again. All because you want to cling on to your money
                but here I am, your own daughter, and I can't afford a
                house, a car – a child.

SANDRA   It's not too late, you're not even forty.

ROSE   At my age you had a house, half paid off, two kids,
                holidays, money.

KENNETH   It was different then.

SANDRA   That's right, completely different.

ROSE   Look at you… 'If you can remember the sixties you
                weren't really there.' What a smug fucking little thing
                to say. You didn't change the world, you bought it.
                Privatised it. What did you stand for? Peace? Love?
                Nothing except being able to do whatever the fuck you
                wanted.

SANDRA   What about our divorce you haven't mentioned that
                yet, I'd bring that in if I were you.

ROSE   Yeah okay – right, Granny and Grandad made an
                effort. To stay together. For you. But you just… one
                night. Over. Done. Not even what happened to me
                made you think about it. You still said you didn't want
                to be trapped. It's not a trap, it's called responsibility. I
                don't think Jamie ever got over it all falling apart.

KENNETH   Jamie's fine actually. Jamie's perfectly happy. It's you
                I'm worried about now.

SANDRA   So *dramatic*.

ROSE   It was dramatic. To me. To both of us. At the time. It
                was a big fucking deal. I promise you.

SANDRA   You must be exhausted.

                Are we having lunch? Or do you want to get to the
                point?

ROSE   My point is you should buy me a house.

KENNETH   Why?

ROSE   What?

KENNETH   Why should we buy you a house?

SANDRA   We can't afford it love. Either of us.

KENNETH   But even if we could. I'm sorry Rosie, you know we
            love you, you know we'd do almost anything for you,
            but there has to come a day when you live your life.

            Most of what you're saying has nothing to do with us.

            As you said you're nearly forty. You've had
            opportunities. You've made choices.

            Better or worse. No one made you play the violin.

            No one made you keep going.

ROSE   But you always said what a shame it would be –

KENNETH   Why did you listen to us?

            We're your parents.

            Sandra and me, we never listened to a word our parents
            said.

            Why the hell did you take any notice of what we told
            you?

            You're supposed to rebel.

            That's what you're supposed to do.

SANDRA   I remember telling my mum to fuck off.

            I was seventeen. It was the best moment of my life.

            Love, you've never told me to fuck off have you?

ROSE   Yes.

SANDRA   No.

ROSE   You don't hear me.

SANDRA   Well then that's the problem.

            Isn't it?

ROSE   Mum?

SANDRA   Darling.

ROSE   Fuck off.

            Beat.

KENNETH   It's your life Rosie.

It has to be.

He drinks from the wine.

We love you.

But you can't blame us.

You want us to give up our retirement, our independence, our holidays, our security as we get older, you want to take all of that away from us and just *give* you a house.

ROSE   It's not fair.

KENNETH   Life isn't.

ROSE   …

KENNETH   I'm surprised you don't know that by now.

ROSE   …

SANDRA

KENNETH   Isn't your mother quiet?

Beat.

Look, why don't you have a glass of wine and we'll –

SANDRA   At least your father and me we never went crawling back to our parents.

KENNETH   Alright Sandra –

ROSE   I'm not crawling

SANDRA   Looks like it to me –

KENNETH   Sandra –

SANDRA   I'm a woman, you don't know what I faced for thirty years every place I went to work, we didn't just climb the ladder women like me, we made it, we built it all, you don't understand the world as it was Rosie, I'm sorry but you have no idea –

ROSE   It's not just me. Everyone I know has less than their parents did at their age. They're bringing their children up in these little houses, these tiny flats, the best they can afford, while their parents sit on all the money, in huge houses, with big empty rooms. It's disgusting.

SANDRA   It's not all about money.

ROSE   YES IT IS! IT IS *ALL* ABOUT FUCKING MONEY.

SANDRA   I pity you. If that's what you think Rosie. I really pity you.

ROSE   Mum. It's simple. Buy me a house.

    You can.

    Either of you could.

    Please.

SANDRA   What's this really about?

    Darling?

ROSE   You're supposed to look after your children.

    JAMIE comes in.

JAMIE   What's going on? I don't I don't... I can't... I'm getting a headache! The SHOUTING! I'm trying to relax. I can't I can't – I can't I can't –

SANDRA   Jamie –

    She goes to him, but he deliberately moves away from her, nearer to ROSE *and* KENNETH.

ROSE   Come on Jamie. Jamie, it's alright. We'll go into the garden.

JAMIE   What?

ROSE   Go for a walk. You can have a smoke. Or, whatever. We'll catch up yeah.

JAMIE   Yeah, right. Yeah.

    He looks at her, trusts her.

ROSE   Dad?

    Dad.

    You understand.

    You get what I'm asking.

And you can afford it.

…?

A moment. Is he considering?

Then he looks at her. Hard.

KENNETH   No.

She grabs JAMIE *by the hand.*

They go.

KENNETH *picks up the urn. Looks at it. Then out the window where his children have gone.*

SANDRA   I thought our children would be heroes.

I imagined they would soar. Standing on our shoulders I assumed that our kids would reach heights we never imagined, change the world entirely. I thought they would solve the great problems, become prime ministers, scientists, academics.

But look at them. They sit on computers, not living, typing messages about nothing. Watching meaningless videos, and waiting for Friday night, they want to be rich and famous, in fact that's all they want to be, but they never lift a fucking finger.

Do they?

They don't read, they don't work and they don't *think*. They want it all on a plate.

And then strangely when nothing arrives, it's our fault.

What happened?

I thought you're supposed to be proud of your children.

KENNETH *puts the urn down.*

Can we buy her a house?

But no, NO! you're right – Sometimes I go into the garden, you've seen our garden, I go out there and lie on the grass, And I think I haven't done this since I was young. For forty years it's been hard graft. We've worked ourselves to the bone.

Pause.

Top me up Ken.

KENNETH *does*.

Maybe it was me

KENNETH No.

SANDRA I've got a mouth like a train, you know that, I'm a very confident person, maybe I was overbearing.

KENNETH We never went to bed with an argument still hanging. They weren't unhappy growing up.

SANDRA Our daughter slit her wrists.

KENNETH

SANDRA I still think of it.

I dream of the blood. On the floor.

She might do it again, I still see her as a little girl.

KENNETH She'll be alright.

SANDRA I don't know Ken we've been saying that for twenty years, don't worry, she'll be alright but now she's here saying what she's saying and she's nearly forty and I'm starting to think maybe she's got a point.

Maybe she won't be...

Alright.

Maybe she has wasted her life.

As you said. It isn't fair.

Perhaps we just got lucky.

Pause.

They drink the wine.

KENNETH Have you got a fag?

SANDRA Ken! You don't.

KENNETH Well.

SANDRA Not for years.

KENNETH Well.

They get out cigarettes.

KENNETH *lights one. Then gives it to* SANDRA.

He smiles and lights one himself.

Pause.

They take in the room.

SANDRA   What do we do?

KENNETH   She knows we love her.

Beat.

She'll calm down, come back.

Beat.

She always does.

Pause.

You alright?

SANDRA

They smoke.

What happened with you and Kerry?

KENNETH   She wasn't on my intellectual level.

SANDRA   She was fat.

KENNETH   Thank you.

SANDRA   Well she was you know as well as I do she was rather overweight.

KENNETH *smiles.*

KENNETH   You look great.

SANDRA   Got a gym at home now. Every day, hour in the gym, Pilates, pool.

KENNETH   Got a pool here.

SANDRA   I know.

KENNETH   I could build a gym too.

SANDRA   What?

KENNETH   Just saying.

SANDRA   I know you.

KENNETH   You do.

SANDRA   Never just saying. You could *build a gym*.

KENNETH   Well I could.

SANDRA   What do you mean?

    KENNETH *looks at her.*

KENNETH   You don't like Clive.

SANDRA   I...

KENNETH   Come on.

    He's fun but –

    You don't like him really.

    Do you?

    She smiles.

    He smiles.

    A connection.

    I want to die with you.

SANDRA   That's a big thing to say.

KENNETH   I've always said big things.

SANDRA   You stop me in my tracks sometimes Kenneth.

    They look at each other.

    Sometimes I don't think you'll ever end.

    The way you look.

    You're still –

    Your eyes are bright.

    They stare at each other.

KENNETH   Do you miss me?

SANDRA   Clive doesn't dance.

KENNETH   Why not?

SANDRA   His feet.

KENNETH   Never stopped me

SANDRA   No. Medically. He has sores.

Beat.

KENNETH   We never travelled.

SANDRA   Our fair share.

KENNETH   I mean the world.

SANDRA   Right.

KENNETH   We never saw the world together.

SANDRA   No.

KENNETH   I'm retired now.

SANDRA   So I hear.

KENNETH   You could leave Clive with a bottle of booze and a nurse. He won't know the difference.

SANDRA

KENNETH   I'll sell this place, and off we go, you and me, world tour, whatever we want.

SANDRA   What about Rosie?

If we did that, if we spent all our money like that what would she…

What would Jamie do?

What sort of people would that make us?

KENNETH   We've worked hard. It's our money.

Sandra…

We're all going to die.

This would make us *alive*.

SANDRA   Yes but…

KENNETH stands and goes to a cupboard.

He looks through his records.

What are you doing?

Ken?

What are you up to, burrowing around down there?

Ken!

Ken!

He finds a record and puts it on.

'All You Need Is Love' plays.

Oh no.

KENNETH   You can dance to this.

SANDRA   I'm married.

KENNETH   I thought you were the sort of girl that did what she wanted.

SANDRA   Ken –

KENNETH   Henry said you were a goer.

The song plays. They both glance at the urn.

SANDRA stands up and goes towards KENNETH.

SANDRA   Henry knew a good thing when he saw it.

They dance, as before.

It's kind of beautiful, with the sun, and the smoke.

SANDRA and KENNETH kiss.

ROSE enters, looks at them.

ROSE   Fuck's sake.

I thought you were divorced.

They smile, turn and look at her, warm – loving.

She cries, then picks up her bag and storms out towards the front door. KENNETH and SANDRA keep on dancing.

JAMIE walks in, sees the smoke and then goes to SANDRA's packet of cigarettes. Lights one, then goes and sits down.

ROSE *comes back in.*

Okay. I need a lift, to the station.

Can one of you give me a lift?

Mum.

Dad?

Mum.

Dad.

Mum.

Dad.

As the music descends in chaos, fade to black.

Curtain down.

Music continues to madness.

End.

THE ENEMY

The Enemy was first performed as part of Headlong's *Decade* at Commodity Quay, St Katharine Docks, London, on 1 September 2011. The cast was as follows:

Kevin Harvey
Samuel James

Director	Rupert Goold
Set Designer	Miriam Buether
Costume Designer	Emma Williams
Choreographer	Scott Ambler
Lighting Designer	Malcolm Rippeth
Composer & Sound Designer	Adam Cork
Associate Director	Robert Icke
Assistant Director	Nadia Latif
Technical Sound Design	Sebastian Frost
Casting	Pippa Ailion

Characters

JOHN
MAN

Note on the Text

(/) means the next speech begins at that point.

(–) means the next line interrupts.

(…) at the end of a speech means it trails off. On its own it indicates a pressure, expectation or desire to speak.

A line with no full stop at the end indicates that the next speech follows on immediately.

A speech with no written dialogue indicates a character deliberately remaining silent.

Blank space between speeches in the dialogue indicates a silence equal to the length of the space.

JOHN *is waiting. The* MAN *approaches him.*

JOHN	Hi
MAN	Hi
JOHN	Okay.
MAN	What?
JOHN	No no. So you're the…
MAN	What?
JOHN	You're the one who…
MAN	What?
JOHN	It's just –
MAN	Okay.
JOHN	I'm John.
MAN	Right.
JOHN	They said –
MAN	Can I?
JOHN	Yeah.
MAN	Thanks.
JOHN	They said –
MAN	What?
JOHN	Wait here.
MAN	Okay.
JOHN	Stay here and he'll find you.
MAN	Right.
JOHN	He'll find you.
MAN	Yeah.

JOHN	So you're –
MAN	Yeah.
JOHN	Him?
MAN	Yeah.
JOHN	Okay
MAN	Okay
JOHN	So what's your –
MAN	What?
JOHN	Your –
MAN	I can't –
JOHN	Your name
MAN	I can't tell you.
JOHN	Of course.
MAN	Of course not.
JOHN	But you're –
MAN	Yeah
JOHN	The one who –
MAN	Yeah.
JOHN	Okay.
	Okay.

MAN	So what?
JOHN	No.
MAN	What now?
JOHN	I've got
MAN	Cos I –
JOHN	I've got
MAN	Other places.

JOHN	No I'm just
MAN	Okay
JOHN	Nervous.
MAN	Why?
JOHN	Why am I –
MAN	Nervous. Why would you be –
JOHN	Be nervous?
MAN	Yeah.
JOHN	Well –
MAN	What?
JOHN	It's a big –
MAN	What?
JOHN	You.
MAN	What?
JOHN	You're –
MAN	What?
JOHN	Him.
MAN	Just a job.
JOHN	I know but –
MAN	Trained.
JOHN	Come on.
MAN	What?
JOHN	You must
MAN	What?
JOHN	Feel it.
MAN	What?
JOHN	Pride.
MAN	No

JOHN	No pride?
MAN	No.
JOHN	Joy.
MAN	Joy?
JOHN	Anger.
MAN	Control.
JOHN	Did you –
MAN	What?
JOHN	Have any –
MAN	Have any?
JOHN	Know any –
MAN	What?
JOHN	Anyone who –
MAN	What?
JOHN	Died.
MAN	Of course.
JOHN	No. But –
MAN	Jesus.
JOHN	On that.
MAN	What?
JOHN	That day.
MAN	Oh.
JOHN	In the –
MAN	The Towers.
JOHN	The Pentagon?
MAN	Yeah.
JOHN	Either.
MAN	Yeah.

JOHN	You did?
MAN	Yeah.
JOHN	Who?
MAN	…
JOHN	Who?
MAN	What?
JOHN	Who was –
MAN	You want…
JOHN	What was –
MAN	A name?
JOHN	No who was he?
MAN	He?
JOHN	Your
MAN	What?
JOHN	Who died.
MAN	She
JOHN	She?
MAN	Yeah.
JOHN	Okay.
MAN	Yeah.
JOHN	What was *she*?
MAN	I don't.
JOHN	To you.
MAN	No.
JOHN	To you I mean.
MAN	She was –
JOHN	A friend?
MAN	I don't.

JOHN   You knew her

MAN   She was good.

JOHN   A good –

MAN   Yeah.

JOHN   A good friend?

MAN   Good girl.

JOHN   Good girl.

MAN   Yeah.

JOHN   And you.

         You knew her from.

         From…

         What?

         School?

MAN   No

JOHN   College

MAN   No.

JOHN   What?

MAN   Why?

JOHN   Just a

MAN   Yeah.

JOHN   A friend.

MAN   Yeah.

JOHN   Not a

MAN   No.

JOHN   You and

MAN   No.

JOHN   Her.

MAN	No.
JOHN	You didn't.
MAN	No.
JOHN	Ever.
MAN	Not your
JOHN	Close?
MAN	Business.
JOHN	You were –
MAN	Sarah
JOHN	Okay.
MAN	That's –
JOHN	That's her name.
MAN	Yeah
JOHN	Yeah.
MAN	Pentagon.
JOHN	Okay.
MAN	Yeah.
JOHN	She worked –
MAN	She worked in the –
JOHN	Yeah. There.
MAN	There.
JOHN	Yeah.
MAN	Okay.
JOHN	Yeah.

	You didn't...
MAN	What?
JOHN	Did you ever...

MAN	No.
JOHN	You and.
MAN	No.
JOHN	Her?
MAN	Stop.
JOHN	Cos they'll
MAN	What?
JOHN	Want to know.
MAN	Who?
JOHN	Readers.
MAN	Why?
JOHN	Human.
MAN	What?
JOHN	This is
MAN	Human?
JOHN	All about the
MAN	No.
JOHN	Human side
MAN	Human side
JOHN	All about –
MAN	*What?*
JOHN	You.
MAN	No.
JOHN	So this.
MAN	Not what I
JOHN	Her.
MAN	No.
JOHN	*Sarah.*

MAN   No.

JOHN   You loved

MAN   Not the

JOHN   Loved her?

MAN   Not the story.

JOHN   It is.

MAN   The mission.

JOHN   No.

MAN   That's the

JOHN   No.

MAN   Story.

JOHN   I say.

MAN   What?

JOHN   I say what's

MAN   Tell you

JOHN   What's the –

MAN   Feeling

JOHN   The story and

MAN   the gun.

JOHN   this.

MAN   weather.

JOHN   This is

MAN   anything

JOHN   This *is*.

MAN   tactics…

JOHN   What they

MAN   angle.

JOHN   Want to

MAN	Shot
JOHN	What they want to know.
	So.
	Sarah?
MAN	Sister.
JOHN	Oh.
MAN	Yeah.
JOHN	Not…
MAN	No.
JOHN	Oh.
MAN	Yeah.
JOHN	I'm
MAN	Okay.
JOHN	Sorry.
MAN	Yeah.
JOHN	But you
MAN	What?
JOHN	You see?
MAN	What?
JOHN	That's
MAN	Yeah.
JOHN	A story.
MAN	I get it.
JOHN	Guy who
MAN	I get it.
JOHN	Shot him.
MAN	Gets revenge.

JOHN	Revenge?
MAN	I get it.
JOHN	Is that –
MAN	What?
JOHN	What you…
MAN	No.
JOHN	Felt.
MAN	No.
JOHN	Revenge?
MAN	No.
JOHN	You said.
MAN	Your story not –
JOHN	Revenge.
MAN	Not mine.
JOHN	So when you –
	In the
	The
MAN	What?
JOHN	The moment.
MAN	No.
JOHN	When you.
MAN	No.
JOHN	Did it.
MAN	No.
JOHN	Did she?
MAN	No.
JOHN	You thought.

MAN	No.
JOHN	Of her?
MAN	Not at all.
JOHN	No?
MAN	A target. A mission. A target. A shot. No.
JOHN	Her face.
MAN	What?
JOHN	In those.
MAN	You don't –
JOHN	Those last
MAN	Don't care.
JOHN	Moments.
MAN	Do you?
JOHN	Pain.
MAN	Jesus.
JOHN	Death.
MAN	I follow.
JOHN	Do you.
MAN	Orders.
JOHN	Do you?
MAN	What?
JOHN	Feel?
MAN	What? Feel what?
JOHN	Do you feel?
MAN	I'm a guy.
JOHN	Guys feel.

MAN	I know.
JOHN	You do.
MAN	I do.
JOHN	You seem.
MAN	What?
JOHN	Cut off.
MAN	From.
JOHN	Feelings?
MAN	No.
JOHN	Emotions.
MAN	Next.
JOHN	Sarah.
MAN	Next question.
JOHN	Sarah.
MAN	Sarah.
JOHN	Your
MAN	Yeah.
JOHN	Sister, what would she.
MAN	Think?
JOHN	Yeah.
MAN	Of me.
JOHN	Yeah.
MAN	That I'm
JOHN	You're
MAN	The one.
JOHN	Yeah.
MAN	She'd be
JOHN	Yeah.

MAN	Glad.
JOHN	Yeah.
MAN	I'm alive.
JOHN	Okay.
MAN	she always
JOHN	What?
MAN	Said I'd
JOHN	Okay.
MAN	Die.
JOHN	Yeah.
MAN	In war, she said.
JOHN	Yeah.
MAN	War.
JOHN	Right.
MAN	But in the
JOHN	Yeah.
MAN	In the end it was her.
JOHN	Yeah.
MAN	In war.
JOHN	You think?
MAN	What?
JOHN	That that
MAN	What?
JOHN	– what happened
MAN	You mean
JOHN	Was that?
MAN	Yeah.
JOHN	War?

MAN   Looked like it yeah.

             Looked like war to me.

JOHN   You're married?

MAN   No.

JOHN   No.

MAN   You?

JOHN   What?

MAN   Tell me.

JOHN   What?

MAN   Why this?

JOHN   I don't.

MAN   Why me?

JOHN   You're

MAN   Why this?

JOHN   Important.

MAN   Two years.

JOHN   Yeah.

MAN   Two years.

JOHN   Two years yeah.

MAN   To find me.

JOHN   That's right.

MAN   Two years.

JOHN   Yeah.

MAN   Just this.

JOHN   That's right.

MAN   Why?

JOHN   The story.

MAN	Do you care?
JOHN	Do I care?
MAN	Or is it just –
JOHN	The story.
MAN	The man.
JOHN	Yeah.
MAN	Who shot.
JOHN	Yeah.
MAN	Bin Laden.
JOHN	Yeah.
MAN	Some story.
JOHN	Some story.
MAN	You'll be rich.
JOHN	No.
MAN	Famous.
JOHN	Yes.
MAN	Rich.
JOHN	Maybe.
MAN	No maybe.
JOHN	Maybe.
MAN	You will.
JOHN	Okay.
MAN	I want to know.
JOHN	What?
MAN	My question.
JOHN	What?
MAN	To you.
JOHN	What?

MAN	Do you?
JOHN	What?
MAN	Care.
JOHN	Care?
MAN	Yes.
JOHN	About?
MAN	Me. The shot.
JOHN	Yes.
MAN	The man.
JOHN	Of course.
MAN	Bin Laden.
JOHN	Look –
MAN	Revenge.
JOHN	Well
MAN	Do you.
JOHN	Okay.
MAN	Care.
JOHN	Okay.
MAN	Or is this just.
JOHN	Of course.
MAN	Is this just the way you –
JOHN	I'm American.
MAN	Is this just the way you make your mark?
JOHN	I'm as American as you.
MAN	Not nervous.
JOHN	What?
MAN	You were –

JOHN   What?

MAN   Nervous.

JOHN   Well –

MAN   Not nervous any more.

JOHN   You're a

MAN   What?

JOHN   Seal.

MAN   Yeah.

JOHN   The best.

MAN   Yeah

JOHN   Degree

MAN   Degree

JOHN   MA

MAN   Yeah.

JOHN   Languages

MAN   Four.

JOHN   Bright.

MAN   The best.

JOHN   So you must

MAN   What?

JOHN   Think.

MAN   Think?

JOHN   Yeah.

MAN   Think…

JOHN   About why?

MAN   What?

JOHN   Why it happened.

MAN   What the

JOHN	Yeah
MAN	The Towers
JOHN	Yeah, the –
MAN	The Pentagon.
JOHN	Yeah.
MAN	Do I know –
JOHN	What do you –
MAN	Why it happened?
JOHN	What do you –
MAN	Is that your –
JOHN	No.
MAN	Your question?
JOHN	Your thoughts.
MAN	My…
JOHN	Yeah.
MAN	My thoughts.
JOHN	Yeah…
MAN	Why?
JOHN	The readers.
MAN	The story.
JOHN	Unique. Viewpoint.
MAN	The things.
JOHN	Okay.
MAN	The things I believe.
JOHN	Yeah.
MAN	Are important.
JOHN	Okay.

MAN	For me.
JOHN	Yeah
MAN	My family.
JOHN	Yeah
MAN	My sister.
JOHN	Okay

MAN   Freedom to think, freedom to act, the rule of law, intellectual development, equality of opportunity, eradication of corruption, a free market, freedom to worship freedom to express your opinion if it does not inhibit other opinions, equality of men, of women, regardless of gender, race, or sexuality, the separation of church and state, the ability of every citizen to vote in free and fair elections to decide their own government, these things don't come free, these things have to be earned with war and blood, it's the only price. They said my sister was killed by the blast as the plane hit the building, they think she died quickly and I don't know I won't ever know for sure about that, but what I do know is that the man who ordered my sister's death did not want anything I could give him. I know that he was, according to the criteria I've just laid out for you, the enemy. He was the enemy of everything I believe. He was the enemy of everything that allows you to do your job and everything that keeps you safe and gives you life. He ordered the attack as retaliation, yes, but not against bombs or bullets but against music, and movies and sports and life. And my sister loves those things. I didn't kill him because he killed my sister, I didn't kill him because of the country he came from or what he believed, I killed him because I know what the enemy looks like and it had his face.

JOHN	Okay.
MAN	Okay.
JOHN	Thanks.
MAN	Yeah.

JOHN   Yeah.

MAN   You want –

JOHN   No.

MAN   Anything else?

JOHN   No.

MAN   Worth it?

JOHN   Yeah.

MAN   Two years?

JOHN   Yeah.

MAN   You're gonna be rich.

JOHN   Yeah.

MAN   With this.

JOHN   Yeah.

MAN   God bless.

JOHN   Yeah.

MAN   God bless America yeah?

JOHN   Yeah.

MAN   God bless America.

JOHN   God bless America.

MAN   Okay.

        He goes.

13

13 was first performed in the Olivier auditorium of the National
Theatre, London, on 18 October 2011. The cast was as follows:

JOHN   Trystan Gravelle

THE TWELVE
RACHEL   Kirsty Bushell
AMIR   Davood Ghadami
HOLLY   Lara Rossi
EDITH   Helen Ryan
RUTH   Geraldine James
STEPHEN   Danny Webb
SHANNON   Katie Brayben
ZIA   Shane Zaza
MARK   Adam James
SARAH   Genevieve O'Reilly
MARTIN   Nick Blakeley
ROB   Matthew Barker

ALICE   Natasha Broomfield
RUBY   Grace Cooper Milton/
                              Jadie-Rose Hobson
DENNIS   Nick Sidi
TERRY   John Webber
PAUL   Nick Blakeley
ESTHER   Barbara Kirby
LIAM   John Webber
CAROL   Sioned Jones
SIR CHRISTOPHER   Martin Chamberlain
FIONA   Zara Tempest-Walters
SALLY   Esther McAuley

All other parts played by members of the company

Director   Thea Sharrock
Designer   Tom Scutt
Lighting Designer   Mark Henderson
Music   Adrian Johnston
Movement Director   Steve Kirkham
Sound Designer   Ian Dickinson

Characters

JOHN

THE TWELVE
AMIR
EDITH
HOLLY
MARK
MARTIN
RACHEL
ROB
RUTH
SARAH
SHANNON
STEPHEN
ZIA

ALICE
CAROL
DENNIS
ESTHER
FIONA
LIAM
PAUL
RUBY
SALLY
SIR CHRISTOPHER
TERRY

BUSKER
HECKLER
PEOPLE IN THE PARK
PROTESTERS
RIOT POLICE
OTHER POLICE
PASSERSBY
VARIOUS CROWDS

OTHER MEMBERS OF THE ALPHA GROUP

Note on the Text

The play should be performed with a circle.

Although the scenes are numbered separately, they should flow continuously.

(/) means the next speech begins at that point.

(−) means the next line interrupts.

(...) at the end of a speech means it trails off. On its own it indicates a pressure, expectation or desire to speak.

A line with no full stop at the end indicates that the next speech follows on immediately.

ACT ONE

One

Darkness.

Laurie Anderson's 'Someone Else's Dream' plays… the whole song.

Some light.

We see twelve people asleep in bed.

A little more light…

The twelve suddenly wake up.

AMIR, RACHEL, HOLLY, ZIA, SHANNON, STEPHEN, RUTH, SARAH, EDITH, MARK, MARTIN *and* ROB. *All petrified. Disturbed.*

An alarm clock flashing. 7.13 a.m.

JOHN *enters.*

Two

JOHN *is standing with a travelling bag.*

Everyone clears except SARAH *who's joined by* RUBY. RUBY *drags her own small case, takes her mother's hand.* SARAH *checks her emails, they wait for a taxi.* RUBY *stares at* JOHN.

JOHN *smiles at her. Then looks back out front.* RUBY *continues to stare.* SARAH *notices.*

SARAH	Ruby…
	Ruby…
	Ruby!
RUBY	What?
SARAH	Don't stare. (*To* JOHN.) I'm sorry.
RUBY	He smells.

SARAH	Ruby! (*To* JOHN.) I do apologise.
RUBY	He smells bad.
SARAH	She's isn't normally like this.
RUBY	I am.
SARAH	She's not been sleeping.
RUBY	I have, I'm just precocious. It's you Mom. You never sleep any more.
SARAH	Ruby! (*To* JOHN.) I get bad dreams. I tried to sleep on the plane –
RUBY	Mom?
SARAH	But when I did –
RUBY	Where's Dad?
SARAH	When I did, I…

A moment. SARAH *stares at* JOHN. *He looks at her for the first time.*

Oh.

DENNIS *enters with the bags.*

DENNIS	Hey! Munchkin! What's up?
RUBY	Mum's weird.
DENNIS	What?
SARAH	She's being rude again.
DENNIS	Come on sweetie! It was a long flight, I know, but we're back home now.
RUBY	This isn't home. This is Britain.
DENNIS	You like Britain.
RUBY	No I don't. *Britain?*

She looks at JOHN.

Britain's ugly.

Three

RUBY, DENNIS *and* SARAH *clear and the stage is charged by a group of protesters and policemen. They clash – shouting. Banners saying 'No fees!', 'We won't pay!'*

SHANNON *enters hoovering, listening to her iPod.* AMIR, *one of the protesters, is arguing with a* POLICEMAN, *both on megaphones. People film it.*

CROWD   We won't pay! We won't pay!

POLICEMAN   Get back!

AMIR   We're allowed / to be here!

POLICEMAN   Back! / Now!

AMIR   This is a / peaceful protest.

POLICEMAN   Get back!

AMIR   I'm not pushing! You're acting / aggressively! This is a –

POLICEMAN   Fuck you –

        The POLICEMAN *pushes* AMIR. AMIR *pushes back. The tussle continues as…*

Four

RUTH *arrives in her office with three advisers –* MARTIN, LIAM *and* CAROL. SHANNON *hoovers.* MARTIN *yawns, loudly.*

RUTH   If you're flagging Martin, I'd get some coffee.

MARTIN   I'm fine.

RUTH   National Insurance and income tax, that's a conversation we haven't had, where's Andrew?

LIAM   What?

RUTH   Liam is this skirt working?

LIAM   Er…

MARTIN   Andrew's at the conference.

RUTH   I'm sorry?

CAROL   The skirt's good, Prime Minister.

MARTIN   In Brussels!

CAROL   It goes with the jacket!

RUTH   What?!

MARTIN   Brussels!

CAROL   Jacket!

RUTH   Excuse me! Do you have to do that now?

          SHANNON *looks up, leaving the hoover on.*

SHANNON   Oh hi! You alright?

RUTH   What?!

SHANNON   Well – Not being funny but you look a bit...

          She does a face.

RUTH   I couldn't sleep.

SHANNON   Bad dreams?

RUTH   What?

SHANNON   Me too. It's the weather. Makes you sweat like a horse.

CAROL   Prime Minister –

RUTH   Look can you do this tomorrow please... er...

SHANNON   Shannon.

RUTH   Sharon

SHANNON   Shannon.

RUTH   Just switch it off. Alright?

          SHANNON, *slightly offended, switches off the hoover.*
          We hear the protest outside.

          What is it this morning?

LIAM   Student fees.

RUTH   ...still on that? – Thanks Sharon.

SHANNON   Shannon

RUTH   They've started early.

LIAM   Haven't we all?

SHANNON   I didn't vote for you.

              She goes.

RUTH   Can she work here?

MARTIN   What?

RUTH   If she didn't vote for me.

MARTIN   As a cleaner, she's technically a civil servant. She can vote for whoever she likes.

RUTH   Carol's a civil servant.

MARTIN   Yes.

RUTH   Well did Carol vote for me?

              They all look at CAROL, *who's suddenly on the spot. Fortunately for her,* EDITH *walks past, grabs a trolley and pushes it through a bank window, then runs off. The police run towards the noise…* RUTH *despairs.*

              Martin – Tell them to get that under control. I've got a headache.

Five

The police grab hold of RACHEL, *who is near the window.*

RACHEL   Hey!

AMIR   Get off her!

              He grabs the trolley and hurls it at a police officer, who falls to the ground. AMIR's *then jumped on and arrested. As this happens…*

Six

…STEPHEN *walks through, to give a lecture to some students at a London university.*

STEPHEN   At least some of you have bothered to turn up. I'm Stephen Crossley, and today I want to talk about God.

The police charge, scattering the protest, as JOHN *walks centre-stage. People walking past…*

I have here a box. Inside is the Lord Almighty himself. You have a choice. Do you open it?

If you do, you will look God in the face, and know for certain his existence, dimensions, his absolute power and glory. But unfortunately, once that moment has happened, you will then burn in his omnipotence and omniscience. Your free independent life destroyed, you will be gone forever.

Therefore, perhaps you think it's better that you don't open the box. Instead you live a life of horror and worship, always under the power of what might lie inside, waiting for you, in the dark.

So. Do you open it? Do you stare God in the face? Or shy away.

People in suits, tourists, walk past. HOLLY *on her phone.* SHANNON *coming home from work.*

For me. Every time, turn on the lights, open the box – face the truth. Because when you do…

He opens it. Nothing.

There's nothing there. Never is.

Seven

ALICE *enters with* MARK. *A* BUSKER *sets up nearby… his head is down, we can't see his face.*

MARK	A toothbrush, a new shirt and a double espresso. What's his name?
ALICE	Mr Hamidi.
MARK	And what's his thing?
ALICE	His thing?
MARK	Yeah. What's his –
ALICE	I have literally no idea what you're talking about.

MARK   What's he *done*?

ALICE   *I don't know.*

MARK   Alright, look –

ALICE   If you mean what's he *accused* of then maybe I have some –

MARK   Oh for Christ's sake.

ALICE   You're a lawyer Mark. What he's *done* is a question for the jury.

MARK   Alice, as you rightly say, I'm a lawyer. What are you?

ALICE   I'm good with words. Warwick University, excellent degree.

MARK   2.2

ALICE   So I had a good time.

MARK   A toothbrush, a new shirt and a double espresso.

ALICE   (*Giving him the file.*) Assault of a police officer.

MARK   Okay. Give me an hour then burst in, say you need me. Say I've got another meeting, it's an emergency, my brother's ill –

ALICE   You don't have a brother.

MARK   Alice, just get me out of there – I'm not at my best

ALICE   I'll say. What happened? You're *late*. You're never late.

MARK   …the train.

ALICE   And your clothes.

MARK   *My* clothes, Alice don't go there, Yellow jumpers, trainers, leggings, you're supposed to be at work.

ALICE   That's my thing, my style but you're normally so *fastidious*.

MARK   I had bad dreams okay –

ALICE   *Punctilious* – Oh! A nightmare? Wow! Were there monsters?

MARK   Monsters yep. Can we –

ALICE   An explosion?

MARK   Yes… an explosion… monsters – why? Did you have the same thing?

            The BUSKER *plays notes on his guitar…*

ALICE   The same?

MARK   The same *dream*.

ALICE   Yes I did!

MARK   That's weird.

ALICE   I know.

MARK   Really?

ALICE   Yeah.

MARK   *Really?*

            Beat. The BUSKER *pauses for a moment, lifts his head up – a strange expression – deep, depressed… then continues…*

ALICE   No! Course I didn't have the same dream, I don't remember dreams. I spent the night with my boyfriend.

MARK   Lionel.

ALICE   Leon. We had lots of sex.

MARK   He's a big chap right?

ALICE   Absolutely he's a big chap yes.

MARK   I meant fat.

ALICE   I meant his cock.

MARK   You're odd.

ALICE   I'm alternative.

MARK   Get my things.

ALICE   Go to your meeting.

MARK   What's his name again?

ALICE   Amir Hamidi.

             ALICE goes. MARK has a searing headache. He
             leaves, just as…

Eight

…RACHEL enters on the phone.

RACHEL   Amir Hamidi. Amir. Hamidi, he's been arrested, no I
             don't want to hold I've been holding already don't you
             dare fucking put me on hold okay if you transfer me or
             move me or do anything with me I'll scream I'll call
             you back and just scream down the phone or
             something – all I want to know is where he is and
             you're going to find out and tell me now yes? Now.
             That's what you're going to do. So.

             Hello? Hello?!

             They've hung up. She screams, throws her phone away
             in anger – JOHN catches it.

JOHN   Rachel?

             The busker stops playing. RACHEL looks at JOHN.

RACHEL   Oh God.

             God…

             John? How can…

             She looks at him. Hits him.

             We thought you were dead.

             She hugs him. Tight.

Nine

A meeting in Number 10. RUTH and DENNIS shake hands.

RUTH   Mr Harrison. Your reputation precedes you.

DENNIS   Thank you Prime Minister. Please call me Dennis.

RUTH   Did you have any trouble getting here, through the
             crowd?

DENNIS	No, they threw some eggs but –
RUTH	Well you can't make an omelette.

A tiny beat.

DENNIS	I'm sorry?
RUTH	It's an expression – you can't make an omelette without –
DENNIS	I can –
RUTH	Okay –
DENNIS	I can make an omelette, I'm pretty good –
RUTH	What?
DENNIS	Two eggs, cheese, mushrooms.
RUTH	Ah. You're joking.
DENNIS	Yeah.
RUTH	Ha ha.
DENNIS	Thought I'd break the ice.
RUTH	This isn't official is it? This visit?
DENNIS	No Prime Minister. If it were official you'd be talking to the Ambassador. The President felt perhaps if the two of us were to speak instead it would be more... informal.
RUTH	Well he's right so far. I'm told you have the President's ear. Apparently you go way back.
DENNIS	Way back yeah.
RUTH	The President's an interesting man, Dennis. I thought we were getting on and there was mutual respect, but recently – nothing. Suddenly there's silence. And that's not on.
DENNIS	He's a busy man. That's the Ambassador's message.
RUTH	I know that's the Ambassador's message but no one likes the Ambassador, no one tells him anything. I assume the President sent you informally like this because he knows I've had enough of the *message* and at last you're going to give me a *reason*.

She smiles. DENNIS *likes her.*

DENNIS   It's Iran. The talks. The President hopes the Iranians
           will believe there is distance between our two
           countries. He doesn't want it to seem like we're
           secretly building a coalition to invade.

RUTH   We're not.

DENNIS   Not yet. Right now he's still in the 'extending the hand
           of peace' stage. He's talking about new global
           alliances. But if that fails the old alliances will be as
           important as ever. So what I'm saying is, you're right,
           there is silence, but you can read something into it.

RUTH

DENNIS   The silence contains an implicit friendship. He can't
           articulate that friendship or it would defeat the point.

RUTH   That's why you're here.

DENNIS   That's right.

RUTH   You're asking for patience.

DENNIS   Yes.

RUTH   Faith.

DENNIS   Exactly. Yes. Yes Prime Minister. Have faith.

RUTH

DENNIS   When the talks are over, it'll be the special-est
           relationship we've ever had. Press opportunities,
           private conversations. Whatever you need, you get, but
           at the moment things between Britain and America
           have to seem... cold.

           The talks are working. We stand a chance of averting
           the inevitable. And that's rare. No one wants a war.

           Beat. RUTH *smiles.*

RUTH   Alright. Tell the President he has my support.

DENNIS   Thank you.

RUTH   For now.

DENNIS   Understood.

RUTH   And you'll keep me updated.

DENNIS   Yes we'll make sure we –

RUTH   No. You. Dennis. You're the President's man, I think
              you know what's going on better than anyone, so
              you'll keep me updated, you'll be on the phone all the
              time, here when I need you, as long as this goes on.
              That's the price for my patience. Okay?

              DENNIS *smiles*.

DENNIS   Okay.

RUTH   Good. Martin will show you out.

              DENNIS *goes*.

Ten

…RACHEL *walks in front of* JOHN, *angry.*

RACHEL   He's been arrested, we were out protesting and got into a
              fight and they took him off. I don't know where he is.
              And you know, then you're just… standing there
              looking like a fucking – How did you know I'd be here?

JOHN   I didn't.

RACHEL   Where did you go? Why did you leave us? Don't *smile*
              don't – We have things to deal with John big fucking
              things hanging in the air the air is thick right now with
              this – don't think we're friends –

JOHN   It's good to see you.

RACHEL   I'd forgotten but it's coming back quickly how
              annoying you can be.

JOHN   You and Amir. Still together.

RACHEL   Yeah we are. Still together. Yeah.

              Beat. She looks at him – so?

JOHN   What are you up to?

RACHEL   Huh! Okay – Yeah John – let's catch up, let's sit down
              and have a proper good old chat about how things were
              and where we are now and what's gone on. So I'll start

– Amir was working as a lecturer which was nice but then they lost funding, shut the department so now he's miserable as fuck and as for me, well, I was doing my PhD but gave it up cos one of us had to earn something. So now I have a job. I work for a charity. Women's rights in developing countries.

JOHN   Your sort of thing.

RACHEL   I sit on the phone and call people up and ask them for money.

JOHN   Like sales.

RACHEL   It's begging. So! What about you John? What have you been *up to recently*?

         Beat.

JOHN   Things are difficult.

RACHEL   That's perceptive of you yes difficult is a word that's a good word to describe it literally every day I get a call, an email, this person's ill, that one's depressed, I'm a walking Samaritan people think I can deal with their problems but for some reason they never imagine I might have some of my own cos I'm not sleeping at the moment.

JOHN   Bad dreams?

RACHEL   No not bad, horrific, if you want the truth, which I remember you always did – so why did you go then? Leave us. How could you? No one understood it.

         Beat.

JOHN   There's a Starbucks over there. I need to wash. I'll sort myself out, come back in a minute? Alright?

         She looks at him.

RACHEL   You'll come back?

         He smiles and turns to go.

         John?

         He looks at her.

         I'm glad you're not dead.

Eleven

AMIR *is sat at a table.* MARK *walks in.*

MARK   I'm Mark, your solicitor.

AMIR   You?

MARK   Yeah.

AMIR   I've changed my mind. I'm pleading guilty.

MARK   Look, I don't want to be here either mate, but you
        phoned your girlfriend, she called your dad, he checked
        the Yellow Pages, and here I am, underpaid,
        overqualified, you might as well use me. I'm really good.

AMIR   You're a wanker mate.

MARK   What's the charge?

AMIR   Those papers, doesn't it say?

MARK   Can I make a confession?

AMIR   Okay.

MARK   I haven't read the papers.

AMIR   Fuck's sake.

MARK   I *know.* I haven't read them. What a *dick.* So. The
        charge.

AMIR   I was protesting, and this police officer was kicking my
        girlfriend so I got this trolley and sort of pushed it at
        them. One of them goes down and I'm like shit. We
        weren't being violent, it was them, one of them calls
        me Al-Qaeda, he's swearing all of that, and I'm trying
        to stay out of it but –

MARK   What were you protesting against?

AMIR   Student fees.

MARK   Aren't you a bit old for that?

AMIR   I was a lecturer. I got fired.

MARK   Well you should be all in favour then. Bit more money
        in the system you can keep your job.

Over the next speech, MARK*'s nose slowly starts bleeding.*

I had a great time at university. Parents paid for it of course. And I got in just before they started charging so *ker-ching*. What do you want instead then? What's your alternative?

AMIR   A graduate tax would be more / successful in –

MARK   Yeah but that's the same thing. You pay as tax, you pay off a loan, doesn't make any difference. Either you want properly funded universities or you don't. It's a competitive world these days. India. China. We're on the way down.

AMIR   Oh – you've got –

MARK   I just think it's funny that essentially you're protesting because they *called it the wrong thing*. You got into a *fight* – I thought you must really mean this stuff but no, you're just unemployed and pissed off. Anyway. We can get you out of it, if you say the right things.

AMIR   Your nose is bleeding.

MARK   What?

AMIR   There's a whole load of blood coming out of your nose.

MARK smiles, then puts his hand to his nose.

MARK   Shit...

AMIR   Is it stress?

MARK   What?

AMIR   Or coke?

MARK   No.

AMIR

MARK   ...

AMIR   You want to go and sort yourself out.

Twelve

Thirteen members of an Alpha course enter and sit in a semicircle.

HOLLY*'s with them but a bit mistrustful.* SALLY *is the leader.*

SALLY So in this half, I thought I might ask a few questions of those who have contributed a little less so far. Holly! Maybe you could tell us what brought you here and what you hope to get out of these sessions?

HOLLY Er yeah. So I want something good to happen? Cos my dad's a shit, and my mum gets anxious, about things? And I'm not liking university cos I haven't got any money or... well, friends. I don't know why, I'm a good person I think but anyway my gran, she goes to this church and I was telling her and she said I should try the Alpha course cos you only work out what you want to do in life when you know what your core beliefs are so...

SALLY Alright. Terry – perhaps the same question to you.

TERRY Well, I suppose it was my ex-girlfriend who first –

HOLLY Okay wait you ask me this big question then we move on? I thought we were here to talk?

SALLY We are, and it was important to hear that Holly but –

HOLLY I was opening up. I was answering.

SALLY And I appreciate that but –

PAUL You know sometimes the questions are more important than the answers.

HOLLY What?

PAUL Sometimes the *questions* are more important than the *answers*.

HOLLY What does that mean?

SALLY It's a very good point and worth considering, for all of us. Maybe real belief isn't about facts, certainties, *answers*. It's questions, possibilities. Who are we? What are we doing here?

HOLLY	I'm definitely starting to ask what I'm doing here.
SALLY	Terry do carry on.
TERRY	My ex-girlfriend had this dress and –
HOLLY	But it is about certainties. It all is.
SALLY	Holly –
HOLLY	There's one God, original sin, Jesus, the Trinity, Heaven, Hell. Those aren't questions, they're given as facts.
SALLY	You sound very familiar with Christianity –
HOLLY	My dad was a priest.
SALLY	I thought you said your dad was a shit.
HOLLY	Bible in one hand, bottle in the other.

They're all quiet for a moment, intimidated, HOLLY *presses on…*

I have trouble believing in any of it. Why would God let me be born into a fucked-up family with no money and a shit life when I've done nothing, absolutely *nothing*, to deserve it?

A moment.

ESTHER	Can I say something?
SALLY	Esther – of course.
ESTHER	It seems to me Holly. Holly, is that your name?
HOLLY	Been here all afternoon *Esther* –
ESTHER	It seems to me that God allows us freedom to make *our own* decisions. Yes? If you're having difficulty and torment in your life maybe that's more about your *attitude*? Your *approach*.
PAUL	But, to be fair to Holly, it's a big question that every Christian struggles with. If there's an all-powerful, all-loving God, why is there evil in the world?
ESTHER	And that's what we're here for, to ask those big questions.

SALLY   Yes, Esther, that's right exactly.

HOLLY   So what's the answer?

Beat.

ESTHER   Well...

HOLLY   Yeah and here's another big question – Why did Jesus
           turn up then? Right then? He could've freed the
           African slaves, or stopped Hitler killing the Jews, but
           no, he came to Earth at that point and did a few small
           miracles. He could actually come down right now, do
           some miracles today, help us all out with the climate,
           money, terrorism, we could do with that but I don't see
           him anywhere.

PAUL   Well, Jesus never claimed to *solve* / our problems.

SALLY   So you're basically saying you don't believe in God.

HOLLY   What?

SALLY   That's what your questions imply.

PAUL   Er... Sally, I don't think that is what she –

SALLY   That's what *all* your questions imply.

PAUL   Maybe we should / take another break?

SALLY   This is a Christian group, a Christian discussion
           group –

HOLLY   I know. It's a discussion group and we're / discussing
           it.

SALLY   I'm in charge of how it runs and I want to make it
           constructive, and open but you're just – You're just sat
           there and –

           She starts crying. PAUL *comforts her.*

PAUL   It's alright. Hey... Hey...

SALLY   Sorry but she's... I know she probably doesn't
           understand, but she's horrible – Terry. It's your turn. I
           want to hear from Terry.

           Terry! Say something! Please!

Pause. TERRY *isn't sure. The pressure is huge.*

TERRY   Sometimes I hear voices.

          They all look at him. A moment.

HOLLY   Wow.

          ESTHER *turns to* HOLLY, *sweetly.*

ESTHER   Holly?

          Look...

          Maybe you should just fuck off?

          HOLLY *grabs her bag and goes.* EDITH *starts practising the piano.*

Thirteen

RUTH *is making a speech.*

RUTH   It's tough for everyone at the moment so I think some
          plain speaking is called for. I'm not an old Etonian,
          I'm not one of the boys. My father was a postman, my
          mother a primary school teacher. I've come a long
          way, and I'm proud. Under my leadership, the
          Conservative Party has modernised, root and branch.
          Just as Labour grew up from outdated socialism, so we
          have moved on from the days of Thatcher. We get,
          now, the importance of the NHS, of comprehensive
          schools, of a state which looks after people. We don't
          hold up the *market* as a solution to everything, but
          unlike many currently in opposition, we're also not
          frightened of it. We stand for opportunity. We want
          people to get on and I promise you we'll get this
          economy back on track – this time through hard work,
          not gambling and speculation. This time through
          enterprise and getting out there and getting it done.
          That's what I'm all about. Nothing was ever handed to
          me on a plate. I like hard work. Every minute. Every
          hour. To make this country great again. That's what
          you voted for. That's what you're going to get. Okay?
          Hard work!

          She smiles. Cheering as...

Fourteen

*…*RUBY *runs on and sits at a table.* SARAH *brings dinner over and she eats.*

RUBY I prefer it when Amelia cooks.

SARAH You're so lucky Ruby

RUBY I know.

SARAH Most children don't have a cook.

RUBY I know but I do have a cook and I prefer her food to yours.

SARAH Some children don't even have a mommy.

RUBY What does that mean? Is that a threat?

SARAH No. A threat? Of course it's not a threat.

RUBY You have food you like and don't like. The cook's a professional, you're not. It makes sense that I prefer her food. I'm allowed to express my opinion.

SARAH I'm saying you should be grateful.

RUBY To who?

SARAH That you have food and shelter at all.

RUBY *Thanks Mom.*

SARAH Not to me Ruby, not to us, grateful you were born into such a well-off background in the first place.

RUBY You mean grateful to God.

SARAH Yes, absolutely. Grateful to God.

RUBY I don't believe in God.

SARAH I beg your pardon?

RUBY When you say grace, I don't shut my eyes, I just wait for you to stop.

    Beat.

SARAH Ruby, you should be careful.

RUBY What do you mean?

SARAH   It's.

             It's

             It's all a matter of responsibility is what I'm saying
             sweetheart, beliefs come with responsibilities. You
             can't just sit there and say something like that,
             something like 'I don't believe in God' you have to
             have a philosophical basis for it, you have to be able to
             justify it.

RUBY   I can believe what I like.

SARAH   Where do you get this from? It's not me certainly, it's
             not your father.

RUBY   I read a book.

SARAH   When you open your mouth and these things come out
             – it's not the Ruby I like.

RUBY   I appreciate a multiplicity of voices in my life rather
             than simply relying on my parents.

SARAH   What book?

RUBY   I read lots of books.

SARAH   *What book?*

RUBY   *Fairytale God* by Dr Stephen Crossley.

             Pause.

SARAH   I would really appreciate it, Ruby, if as a favour to me,
             you ate your chicken.

             RUBY *reluctantly does.*

RUBY   You were shouting last night.

SARAH   What?

RUBY   You were shouting in your sleep. God. God! Help me.
             Save us! Save us!

SARAH   It was a bad dream.

RUBY   That's what religion is.

SARAH   What *are* you?

RUBY   Just a *bad dream.*

Fifteen

AMIR *walks with* RACHEL *from the interview room.*

RACHEL   He said it was a coincidence.

AMIR   I don't believe in coincidence.

RACHEL   Neither do I but there he was.

AMIR   Didn't you say like what the fuck?

RACHEL   Of course but he wouldn't tell me. He asked about these dreams – anyway then when we found out where you were and when we got here, he marched straight up to the desk and I don't know what he said but after a couple of minutes they let you out – I mean actually of all people he was the one we needed but –

AMIR   Is he alright?

RACHEL   What do you mean?

AMIR   He's not ill, or –

RACHEL   No he's not ill, he's just the same, he's... John.

         They've arrived at JOHN. AMIR *looks at him.*

         JOHN *looks at* AMIR. *Smiles.*

JOHN   You're okay?

AMIR   Yeah.

JOHN   You look good.

AMIR   Thanks.

         MARK *enters with a tissue.*

MARK   I go to the bathroom to sort myself out, when I come back they tell me you've been let off. What happened?

AMIR   John got me out.

MARK   John? Okay. This is John. And he's what? A friend? A wizard?

JOHN   I asked them if they were going to press charges.

MARK   They hadn't pressed charges?

JOHN   Did you check?

MARK   Well, I assumed since his daddy was willing to pay –

JOHN   They didn't have any evidence. It's good. He's out.
         What's the problem?

         MARK *looks at them.*

MARK   Nothing.

JOHN   You wanted to help him.

MARK   Help him? No. Sorry. Heart of stone. I'm very happy
         he's out of my life. Fucking over the… you know…

AMIR   Moon?

MARK   *Rainbow.* Seriously. Can do without it.

JOHN   Is that a latte?

MARK   Cappuccino.

JOHN   I haven't had a cappuccino in ages. Do you mind?

         He takes it and drinks.

         You look tired.

MARK   Don't look so great yourself –

JOHN   Bad dreams?

MARK   I'm *sorry*?

JOHN   Monsters. Darkness. What did you say Rachel?
         Something moving? An explosion? What's your name?

MARK   Mark

JOHN   Mark.

         JOHN *gives the coffee back.*

         How did you sleep last night?

         MARK *takes the coffee – looks at* JOHN. *Unsure for a
         second.*

MARK   Have you been talking to Alice?

JOHN   Who's Alice?

ALICE *enters, out of breath.* MARK *looks straight at* JOHN.

ALICE   Oh! Mark! There you are! You've got to come right now because something really terrible has happened to your... er... brother... he's really... dead... what?

MARK   Come on.

             MARK *leaves.* ALICE *follows.* RACHEL *and* AMIR *look at* JOHN. *He smiles.*

AMIR   You're alright?

JOHN   Yes.

AMIR   Cos we thought since you never called us or told us anything, we assumed there must be something wrong with you.

JOHN

AMIR

RACHEL   You know what we did?

AMIR   Rach, give it a minute – let's find somewhere to –

RACHEL   No I'm going to tell him right now actually – the morning you'd first gone no one knew anything but we assumed you'd turn up but then there was another day and the next day and course the assumption was that eventually you'd come back but once it was months and then years it was like, how long do we keep on waiting?

JOHN   I'm sorry if it was / difficult.

RACHEL   Too late. So in the end we had a funeral. Me, him, and whatever other people remembered who you were and cared which by then it wasn't many if we're honest but we got together and said goodbye cos we thought he has to be dead because if he *isn't* dead then we don't know him at all. Doing that to us. So we said goodbye and we buried you, didn't we?

AMIR   Yeah.

             Beat.

JOHN   Do you want to come out? Tonight. I haven't been out in a long time.

RACHEL   No, of course we don't want to come *out*. John –

AMIR   It's been a long day.

JOHN   Of course. I'll see you later then. Is it alright to stay with you?

RACHEL   For how long? I don't see why –

AMIR   Yeah, it's okay.

JOHN   Thank you.

            He turns to go.

RACHEL   What are you going to do? Do you even have any money?

JOHN   I'm fine.

RACHEL   You want to borrow some?

JOHN   No. I'll be fine. Thanks though.

            And he's gone.

Sixteen

HOLLY *is with* EDITH. EDITH *is giving her some money.*

EDITH   How much do you need? Thirty?

            There. Have a nice time. Just this once.

HOLLY   Thanks Gran.

EDITH   Yes. Go for your life. No regrets. You're young.

HOLLY   Yeah.

EDITH   You've always got to remember in life, the most important thing… The most important thing you'll ever learn…

HOLLY   What?

EDITH   …

            Oh! Look at you. Holly! Dressed up. Lovely. You're going out tonight?

HOLLY   Yeah.

EDITH   Are you alright for money?

HOLLY   No... Gran... it's...

EDITH   How much do you need love?

          HOLLY *looks at* EDITH.

HOLLY   Thirty?

EDITH   Alright.

          There. Just this once. Have a nice time.

          She goes into her handbag, gives her thirty quid,
          HOLLY *takes it, and goes.* EDITH *plays on the piano*
          and it becomes music under the next scene.

Seventeen

RUTH *is having a drink with* STEPHEN.

STEPHEN   I don't mind admitting, I was surprised. You told me
          you've started praying again, so I just assumed this
          would be it. But I listened to every word and once
          again, no God.

RUTH   People don't want to hear what I believe, it's about
          what I think.

STEPHEN   People want you to be honest.

RUTH   About my judgement, my views on the world.

STEPHEN   And your belief in God informs that of course it does,
          and if your belief informs your decisions it's dishonest
          not to mention it in a speech on standards, it's actually
          anti-democratic.

RUTH   This was supposed to be a relaxing evening for me.
          One night off in two months, I think what shall I do? I
          know, I'll get Stephen round, he's a laugh.

STEPHEN   Ignore me Ruth – keep doing whatever you're doing
          because you're loved. The masses trust you, and vox
          populi vox dei.

RUTH   You think Latin's sexy don't you?

STEPHEN   Latin's wise. Greek is sexy. I can explain your success Ruth. You are your work. You're a woman of the people, for the people. I mean it's a strain for you from minute to minute I'm sure, but your greatest strength?

RUTH   Enlighten me.

STEPHEN   No husband. No children.

RUTH   Thank God my son is dead and my husband left me, how lucky am I?

STEPHEN   You've got nothing to fight for except your country. It's like you're a priest. No commitments, distractions, you're married to us. People like that. Thatcher was the same.

RUTH   Thatcher had kids.

STEPHEN   But she didn't give a shit about them. The public think men are better at detachment. Separating their work decisions from their home life.

RUTH   That's rubbish.

STEPHEN   Well you don't have a home life.

RUTH   I do, I get in, I put the television on.

STEPHEN   Friends?

RUTH   Never seen it.

STEPHEN   *Do you have any friends?*

RUTH   Of course.

STEPHEN   Who?

RUTH   You're a friend.

STEPHEN   Who else?

RUTH   ...Oh Stephen I don't have time.

STEPHEN   Don't worry. You'll manage with the two of us. Me and Uncle Pinot. We'll be there for support when you need it.

He tops up her wine.

And you will. In the next few months you're going to need all the support you can get.

RUTH   I've got support. You said, I'm popular –

STEPHEN   Personally. You're going to need solid personal back-up when you're sending other people's children to their death.

                Beat.

RUTH   Let's talk about something else. How's your sex life?

STEPHEN   My sex life?

RUTH   Or something, *anything*, I don't know!

STEPHEN   Currently my sex life is tepid. How's yours?

RUTH   Like a mammoth.

STEPHEN   Woolly?

RUTH   Extinct.

STEPHEN   Must be tricky for a woman like you.

RUTH   Sometimes I get so horny I have to go for a walk.

                The music changes to a club beat – throbbing noise…

STEPHEN   What's this?

RUTH   I don't know. Radio must've retuned itself. It's one of these digital ones, sometimes it just does its own thing.

STEPHEN   You still dance?

RUTH   What? No.

STEPHEN   I remember as a student you dancing so hard you knocked the rector's teeth out.

RUTH   He got in my way.

                No. After Simon died, I never saw the point.

                The music and momentum builds… builds…

                I'm not sleeping at the moment Stephen. That's the problem.

                Every night, this dream…

Eighteen

People are dancing – the people of London, out on the town – drunk and letting go. It's tribal and free and open. Full-hearted shouting and release. The student party after the protest maybe, or a dream, a memory… It builds and builds and then… with a ripping… voice and voices… the world explodes… white light – a nuclear blast and then…

Blackout.

ACT TWO

One

The same music as before: Laurie Anderson's 'Someone Else's Dream'.

Then it's cut short –

The twelve awake in bed, as before. Terrified. Breathing. A terrible vision.

Bright light – the alarm going – 7.13 a.m.

Two

Everyone clears except JOHN *reading on an iPad,* MARK *making coffee and* RUTH *with a cup of coffee.* CAROL *reads from a paper, bored, annoyed...*

CAROL   The thirteen steps is... a paragraph of the Final Document of the 2000 review Conference of the Nuclear Non-Proliferation Treaty. It provides a set of... 'practical steps for the systematic and progressive efforts to implement Article VI', which is the part of the –

                A big sigh.

                – treaty that provides for nuclear disarmament. So... that's what you need to know when it comes to Iran. The thirteen steps are the proof that we've... er... made an effort.

RUTH   What's the matter Carol?

CAROL   It's rather early.

RUTH   Well no rest for the wicked.

CAROL   I wouldn't know.

                Beat.

RUTH   What are they? Specifically. The thirteen steps.

CAROL   You want all of them?

RUTH	Of course. Is it long?
CAROL	Well there's thirteen of them.
RUTH	We'll do it in the car.
CAROL	The Foreign Secretary's in the car. You asked to see him this morning?
RUTH	Alright. Good. Bring my coffee. We'll test him.

She goes with her BlackBerry. CAROL *picks up her coffee and follows.*

Three

JOHN *is in* AMIR *and* RACHEL*'s flat.* AMIR *hasn't slept – he's slightly wild, fidgeting, restless…*

AMIR   I don't want to sleep. I stay up, putting it off, but eventually you do and there's figures in the dark, this *feeling*, something horrific – thousands of voices, insects. And I'm there with Rachel, in the dream and something terrible's about to happen, there's an explosion and then we wake up, facing each other, screaming. Every night.

JOHN   I'm sorry.

AMIR   How can it be both of us? Exactly the same thing? Do you get them?

JOHN   No.

He looks at AMIR.

What are you doing today?

AMIR   I've got some job applications I'm supposed to fill in, and eventually I have to sign on… I don't know…

He sits on the sofa.

Yesterday was this big moment, we all went out, an early start, we were like 'get it back on the agenda, in the headlines' – but then you get there and the turnout's not as many as you think, the police are aggressive and then everything that happened and you come home and you just *know* you haven't made any difference at all.

They just sit up there in that fucking building and they really – I really don't think they give a shit.

He switches on his laptop.

JOHN I thought you were going out?

AMIR shrugs.

I need a box.

AMIR What kind of a box? A cardboard box?

JOHN Probably needs to be wood. It might rain. I suppose no one has wooden boxes any more do they?

AMIR What for? We've got a bucket?

JOHN That'll do.

AMIR Under the sink. Why? What are you doing?

JOHN I'm going to the park.

AMIR Why?

JOHN You should come along.

AMIR What are you doing?

JOHN looks at him.

HOLLY walks towards MARK's breakfast table, wearing a dressing gown with hood up.

JOHN Come with me.

AMIR looks at him for a second – Then –

AMIR Nah. I'm tired. I'll just stay here.

JOHN looks at him and goes.

Four

MARK *comes up to the breakfast table.*

MARK Thank God you're alive, I thought I might've actually fucked you to death. Good way to go. As long as you orgasm first. Can you imagine having a heart attack before you come? Coffee?

HOLLY takes off her hood.

Jesus. Some girls look great first thing, no make-up, fuzzy hair, some girls look really sexy in the morning. But you? Not so much.

He gives her the coffee.

HOLLY   I didn't mean to sleep over – but it was late…

MARK   It's fine. Like having a girlfriend. I was up at four. Bad dream, explosion, monsters, all kinds of shit, I went to the living room and binged on *CSI: Miami*, five episodes, don't even like it, fell asleep, the dreams again, woke up –

HOLLY   I had a dream too, the same thing… Monsters, an explosion. It's the weather. Apparently it happens in February? Because people are stuck inside, in their jobs doing the same kind of things with the same kind of problems, so we all have similar dreams.

MARK   It's June.

He drinks his coffee.

You getting up then? Work to do. You mind fifties?

How's the course going?

She shrugs as he puts some money down and goes out.

Hope it's worth it.

Five

DENNIS, RUBY *and* SARAH *are having breakfast.*

SARAH   Ruby tell your father what you're doing at school.

RUBY   Dinosaurs.

DENNIS   Dinosaurs? That's great. I love dinosaurs.

RUBY   Yeah.

DENNIS   Like *The Flintstones*!

RUBY   I beg your pardon?

DENNIS   You know. Fred Flintstone, Barney Rubble. We used to watch it munchkin, you remember?

RUBY	It's not like *The Flintstones* at all. The fossil record shows that humans and dinosaurs never existed at the same time.
	SARAH *drops her knife on her plate.*
DENNIS	Well sure honey but it's a cartoon.
RUBY	I know.
DENNIS	These Flintstones, they go to the movies, they have cars powered with their feet, I don't think the fossil record has much to say about that either.
RUBY	Yeah.
DENNIS	But it's okay, because it's a story. It's not real.
RUBY	Then it's not like what I studied at school, is it?
DENNIS	Well.
RUBY	What I studied at school is fact.
SARAH	You see what I mean?
DENNIS	Honey –
SARAH	She's like this with me all the time.
RUBY	Like what?
	DENNIS *finishes his breakfast. Puts his napkin down on the table.*
DENNIS	Have you read books?
RUBY	I'm always reading books.
DENNIS	I mean fiction.
RUBY	Yeah.
DENNIS	What?
RUBY	…
DENNIS	What about… Harry Potter! Have you read that?
RUBY	Yes.
DENNIS	Did you like it?
RUBY	No.
DENNIS	Why?

RUBY   It was stupid.

DENNIS   Well that's the idea. It's like using your imagination.
            It's not real. That's the point.

RUBY   I know what fiction is. I don't mean imaginary I mean
            it's stupid. It's not intelligent. It's for children.

DENNIS   Well sure but your mother and me –

RUBY   Really stupid children who only understand short
            words like 'cat' and 'apple' and 'house'

DENNIS   Your mother and me, we like it – the story's interesting.
            It takes us out of the real world and shows us something
            else, something more that makes the real world better.
            Maybe you should give it another go? It's fun.

RUBY   Dad? Have you seen what's going on? A man kills
            seventy people with a gun, hundreds of protestors
            executed by the Syrian government, thousands of
            children starving in the Horn of Africa.

            There's evil Dad. There's so much evil in the world.

            I don't have time for fun.

Six

*The park. Green open space. People milling about. It's a weekday, so
not that busy.*

ZIA *is with* FIONA.

ZIA   What about Friday?

FIONA   I'm sorry?

ZIA   We could go out on Friday? There's this new film, it's
            a documentary about the larger asteroids. Some of
            them are bigger than the planets and they reckon that –

FIONA   Listen –

ZIA   – instead of manned missions to Mars next, we might
            go to one of them, some of them might have ice, water,
            maybe life, what do you think? I know it sounds geeky
            but it's good and we can get popcorn.

FIONA   It's not working.

ZIA   Pepsi.

FIONA   I don't want to see you again.

ZIA   Shitload of nachos. What?

FIONA   Zia. We don't get on.

ZIA   Yeah we do.

FIONA   No.

ZIA   I do.

FIONA   Exactly.

ZIA   Oh.

           Beat.

FIONA   I want to call it a day.

ZIA   Why?

FIONA   Zia –

ZIA   Cos you can't just say that say it's not working and
           leave it like that you can't – okay give me one proper
           reason yeah?

FIONA   The shouting. In your sleep. It wakes me up.

ZIA   Oh. Right. The shouting.

FIONA   Yeah.

ZIA   Yeah. Well.

           FIONA *turns to leave –*

           Wait! Please. Wait a –

           JOHN *arrives, places the bucket on the ground and
           stands on it.*

JOHN   Okay okay okay.

           ZIA *turns, at first irritated, then starts to listen.*

           I know this is weird and you're having a good time but
           I've had a thought about a battery hen.

           FIONA *leaves.*

           Okay. So this hen has lived in this box her whole life.
           She's never seen anything else. She just sits there and

the food arrives and the eggs get taken away. Now of course her brain is much smaller than ours but I'd like to imagine she has some thoughts on her situation.

What would she think about the world?

She hears noises, so she thinks there are others outside. On the evidence she's got, she'd probably assume these are other chickens. She's unlikely to work out that her keepers are people – she'd have no concept of us, the world, the ground, the Sun or the Moon. Limited by what she could sense, and what her brain could deduce, she would get it all very, very wrong.

ALICE *crosses the park, watches for a moment, and leaves.*

My thought was that, like that hen, we go around thinking eventually we'll work everything out – but limited by what we can sense and what we can deduce, surely it's possible there are things that leave no evidence and no trace? That we have no concept of.

So when people say they are sure that there can't be a God, even when they say that it's unlikely, they're like a battery hen denying the existence of the Moon. They can't know. None of us can, for sure. What was there before the universe? What happens when we die?

ROB *hears this...*

LIAM *crosses the park, stops to listen to* JOHN.

It's all open.

Same time tomorrow.

A slightly embarrassed silence. LIAM *walks off.* JOHN *gets down off the bucket and picks it up.* ROB *approaches him, nervous – distracted.* HOLLY *hangs around.*

ROB   Hi. Are you – from a group – an organisation?

JOHN   No. Just me.

ROB   I'm... going away – we're all heading off and...

Have you got a book?

JOHN   No.

ROB   A leaflet?

JOHN   I'm here tomorrow.

ROB   I'm going away.

HOLLY   I'll film it.

ROB   What?

HOLLY   I'll film it tomorrow, put it online, then you can watch
           it, yeah?

ROB   Oh. Right. Thanks.

HOLLY   What's your name?

JOHN   John.

HOLLY   John in the park. That's what I'll call it.

ROB   Right. Thanks.

           He goes.

HOLLY   I'm Holly by the way.

JOHN   Good to meet you.

           They shake hands and she goes, leaving ZIA.

ZIA   Have you heard about the graph?

JOHN   What?

ZIA   There's this graph and if you plot scientific progress
           against time you see it's an exponential curve. The rate
           of progress doubles every ten years and if you plot this
           curve it gets to a point where it's a straight line, which
           would technically mean infinite progress in a single
           moment. According to the graph it is going to happen
           in ten years. This moment. The singularity.

           Thought it was interesting. Sorry, I'm a bit – my
           girlfriend just left me.

           Apparently I'm shouting, at night and… It puts them
           off.

           Tomorrow yeah?

JOHN   Yeah.

Seven

A large table, around which are gathered, for a briefing – SIR
CHRISTOPHER (*Head of the Armed Forces*), DENNIS *and* RUTH,
who's with CAROL, MARTIN *and* LIAM.

CAROL   The Head of the Armed Forces Prime Minister –

RUTH   Sir Christopher thank you for coming. Always nice to
               have a uniform in the building, engenders some much-
               needed formality in the ranks don't you think Carol?

SIR CHRISTOPHER   Glad to be of service.

RUTH   This is Dennis Harrison.

DENNIS   Sir Christopher, good to meet you.

SIR CHRISTOPHER   You're from the Embassy.

RUTH   Dennis is working with us on this. He's close to the
               President. Shall we make a start?

MARTIN   Everyone's been given the background to look over –

SIR CHRISTOPHER   Good because in the past political advisors
               have been strangely uninformed –

RUTH   Liam, are you strangely uninformed about Iran?

LIAM   I worked in Arab countries for five years?

SIR CHRISTOPHER   Iran isn't an Arab country.

LIAM   Well…

SIR CHRISTOPHER   This is what I mean.

RUTH   Very good. Liam, read the file. Sir Christopher?

SIR CHRISTOPHER   Three months ago, Iran pulled out of the
               Nuclear Non-Proliferation Treaty. The withdrawal is a
               clear sign the regime has the intention and potentially the
               technology to develop a nuclear weapon – which of
               course, would change everything – the ability of the
               regime to act against its own people with impunity, the
               balance of power with Israel. It would also allow the
               fundamentalist religious faction in Iran to propagate their
               anti-Semitic and anti-Western agenda with even more
               vigour. But our biggest concern is terrorism. If nuclear

        material and technology fell into the hands of a terrorist
        group, it would destabilise the entire civilised world.

DENNIS   What terrorist group?

SIR CHRISTOPHER   I beg your pardon?

DENNIS   Can we be specific?

SIR CHRISTOPHER   Iran funds and supports enemy factions in
        Iraq and Afghanistan. Their money kills our soldiers.

DENNIS   But no links with Al-Qaeda.

SIR CHRISTOPHER   No.

DENNIS   I'm just clarifying because when you say terrorism –

SIR CHRISTOPHER   I'm sure the Prime Minister understands the
        difference – Prime Minister, perhaps we should have
        this meeting on our own –

DENNIS   The Prime Minister likes perspective.

SIR CHRISTOPHER   Yes. That's what I provide.

DENNIS   You have an opinion.

SIR CHRISTOPHER   And you don't?

RUTH   Of course he does. That's what I want. Opinions. Both
        of you.

SIR CHRISTOPHER   Alright – the US military is looking at an
        initial campaign potentially beginning in approximately
        four weeks' time. We concur with the Americans that
        anything less than a full-scale occupation would have
        little effect to the nuclear programme, in fact it may
        simply encourage them to speed it up.

RUTH   There's not a way of standing back? Providing military
        support for some kind of… home-grown / revolution?

SIR CHRISTOPHER   Much too slow and unreliable I'm afraid. No,
        the only way to do it is to get in the country quickly
        and physically dismantle every last piece.

RUTH   All or nothing.

SIR CHRISTOPHER   That's correct.

        Fractional beat.

LIAM   Can I…?

RUTH   Liam?

LIAM   The British people will ask why we're spending
              millions on a war a long way away when their
              hospital's in crisis, the library is closed and their son
              can't go to university. They will protest in their
              thousands. I don't know if you could survive it.

SIR CHRISTOPHER   The public don't have the long view, Prime
              Minister, that's why they elected you. If we get this
              wrong, there will be serious consequences for decades
              to come. We've tried everything else but the Iranian
              intentions are clear. They want the bomb.

DENNIS   They want respect. It's not so long ago Britain and
              America were funding a war against them. So we're
              trying to build up trust.

SIR CHRISTOPHER   Your talks. How are they going?

DENNIS   They're going well.

SIR CHRISTOPHER   My counterparts at The Pentagon don't have
              much hope. A waste of time. That's what they said.

DENNIS   That remains to be seen.

              Beat.

RUTH   If we did it. Casualties?

SIR CHRISTOPHER   Minimum.

RUTH   Not just our troops. I mean in total, the invasion, the
              aftermath, Iranian, American, British, if we proceed,
              how many people would die?

SIR CHRISTOPHER   Prime Minister I'm reluctant to confidently
              predict –

RUTH   Sir Christopher, in the end I may well have to pick up
              that phone and condemn a large number of people to
              death, so is it not reasonable to ask if you know
              roughly what that number will be?

SIR CHRISTOPHER   Of course, but –

RUTH   A hundred? Five hundred? Five thousand?

SIR CHRISTOPHER   We'd hope that the Iranians themselves
would welcome action like this and –

DENNIS   A hundred thousand. That's what they're telling me.
On previous experience, assuming this will take years
to achieve, over a hundred thousand dead.

Beat.

Prime Minister, the talks are progressing. We sincerely
hope this will all be academic.

Beat.

RUTH   Keep me updated. Thank you everyone. Carol – give
me the room for a minute, yes?

They go, leaving RUTH *on her own.*

We hear the sound of a hoover… SHANNON *enters.*

SHANNON   Oh hello!

RUTH   No.

No!

Not. Now. Go.

Go away.

SHANNON *looks at her, leaves the hoover running, a
strange moment. Then she takes off her apron, throws
it on the ground, and leaves.*

RUTH *goes across, slowly, and switches the hoover off.*

Eight

AMIR *is watching a video of* JOHN *on a laptop.*

JOHN   (*Voice-over.*) 'We've given up and now we wave it all
through – class, inequality, unkindness, we glamorise
violence, lust after infinite riches, and we all feel it but
the question is why?'

RACHEL *comes in.* AMIR *stays watching the video.*
RACHEL *goes to switch on the lamp.*

AMIR   Alright?

The lamp doesn't work. AMIR *doesn't see.*

Good day?

He keeps watching the video.

RACHEL   I really don't want to be the boring one?

AMIR   What?

RACHEL   Pause it.

AMIR   What? Oh –

He stops the video.

RACHEL   Thank you I really don't want to be the boring one and
          I know we're in very different places at the moment in
          our lives – you've been on the internet all day reading
          the *Guardian* website, watching your videos – how's
          John getting on?

AMIR   Good – people are starting to write about what he's
          doing –

RACHEL   Yeah and you've been posting and tweeting and all of
          that and you've had a nice day which is good but I've
          got work, and this is the bit where I really don't want
          to be the boring one in this relationship but did you call
          about the washing machine?

AMIR   Okay –

RACHEL   Did you pick up the shopping?

AMIR   …

RACHEL   Do the light bulbs? Well no we can see the answer to
          that.

AMIR   I just got… I've got into this. Have you watched him?
          Have you actually sat down and heard what he's got to
          say?

RACHEL   When would I have time to do that?

          Beat.

AMIR   Rach, we've always talked – look I know this sounds a
          bit mad – but we've talked ever since university about
          the moment when something changes, and John's
          saying these things, and… you know… he's open, he's

passionate and he means it. And it's only just started,
but people are listening because he's taking everyone
out of all of this – exactly what you're talking about
our little houses and things we buy and washing
machines and light bulbs and he's making them feel
like there could be something more.

RACHEL   Have you left the sofa today?

AMIR   …

RACHEL   What?

Beat.

Anyway. I *like* our house. What's wrong with our
house?

AMIR *looks at her, a bit crushed.* JOHN *enters.*

John, we were just talking about you. Had a good day?
Amir's saying you're becoming famous.

JOHN   You've been working hard.

RACHEL   Yeah I have.

JOHN   That's good.

But I think you should stop now.

RACHEL   What?

JOHN   For the evening. Stop.

RACHEL   Stop what – what are you talking about, weird abstract
instructions. What, is my energy a bit high at the
moment, you're going to sort out my *chakra*. Okay. I'll
stop. What? What now?

Beat.

Shall we do a *trust exercise*?

JOHN   You find it difficult, don't you?

RACHEL   I… No.

Beat.

What?

JOHN   See?

RACHEL   Oh fuck off John.

            JOHN *smiles – he knows her.*

JOHN   I've done the shopping. Got everything we need.

            I'll cook tonight. You put your feet up.

AMIR   I was going to get it.

JOHN   No. It's fine. You two stay there. My turn.

            He goes.

            AMIR *and* RACHEL *sit for a moment.*

            Then as EDITH *starts playing,* RACHEL *pulls the
            laptop over and starts to watch the video.*

Nine

EDITH *goes to the piano. There's a cross on the top.*

She begins to play a tune. 'The Only Girl in the World' by Rihanna.

As she does, SARAH *appears outside her house, smoking.*

Ten

Morning. SARAH *is smoking outside her house. She sees* JOHN
walking past.

SARAH   Hey!

            JOHN *looks up and walks over.*

JOHN   Hello

SARAH   It's you. Isn't it? From the airport.

JOHN   Yes. I'm sorry. I was a mess then, wasn't I? I think I
            scared your daughter.

SARAH   No. She should be apologising. Everything scares her.

JOHN   She's a little girl.

SARAH   Even smoking. That's why I have to stand out here.

            I'm Sarah.

JOHN	John.
SARAH	Hi John.
	Beat.
JOHN	Is this your house?
SARAH	It's the property of the US government. My husband. I think it's a prison. What are you up to?
JOHN	I'm going to the park. Every day I go, I speak for a while, then we sit and talk about things.
SARAH	Who's we?
JOHN	Anyone who's around.
SARAH	That sounds nice.
JOHN	You should come. We start at one o'clock.
SARAH	I'm not supposed to leave the house on my own. We're high security. If I want to go shopping I make a phone call and they send these men round. All dressed in black. They look after us.
JOHN	Maybe you could sneak away? Come with me.
SARAH	Maybe.
	Beat.
JOHN	Last time, you weren't sleeping.
SARAH	The dreams.
JOHN	How are they now?
	She looks at him.
SARAH	Do you believe in God John?
JOHN	I believe there's something, yes.
SARAH	Do you think sometimes, you have to go with your instinct, sometimes if you know something is right, you have to do it, even if everyone around you thinks you're mad?
JOHN	Sometimes you have to do what you believe to be right.

SARAH	Yes.
JOHN	If it's important.
	She looks at him for a second. Offers him a cigarette.
SARAH	Do you want one of these?
JOHN	No thank you. I should go.
SARAH	You know it wasn't the smell that she had a problem with.
	I think she could tell you were good.
	A good man. And she didn't like it.
JOHN	Bye Sarah.
SARAH	Bye.

Eleven

The park. Light, green grass, blue sky. A slightly bigger crowd, sat and stood around the bucket. ZIA, SHANNON and HOLLY are there. Also in the crowd is MARTIN, on his lunchbreak. Halfway through the speech, MARK turns up to watch.

JOHN   There are things we want. We want the very best healthcare and education, free at the point of use, for all. We want to narrow the gap between rich and poor, both here, and across the world. But with these things we are told – this is just not how the world works any more. You are naive if you think any of it is possible.

So we shrug and walk away, and learn instead the comfort of the downbeat, the safety of irony and pessimism. We sleepwalk from weekend to weekend, looking forward to the simple comforts. We earn we buy, we live we die, we earn we buy, this, we are told, is enough – central heating, delivery shopping, bread and circuses, wine and HBO.

STEPHEN *walks by, notices what's going on, and stops to watch.*

Well I want you to remove the barriers and believe that these may be the facts on the ground but the ground can be changed – to work out what you want and go for it with all your conviction and don't care if you seem outrageous or stupid. Believe in God, believe in each other, in progress or science or whatever you want but through believing in the impossible you might just make it happen. All that's needed, in the end, is belief.

JOHN *steps off the bucket.* STEPHEN *approaches* JOHN.

STEPHEN   So.

JOHN   Stephen.

STEPHEN   I live in Notting Hill, I walk into town, I attend my meeting, then on ambling back I see this group of people gathered together, reminding me of the political rallies of my youth, I go to investigate and... oh look!

A resurrection.

Of sorts.

Where have you been John?

It did you no good. Disappearing like that. Made you look guilty. And your friends... well.

JOHN   Do you think it's going to rain?

STEPHEN   It was a selfish thing to do. Don't you think? I mean I personally, I would call it a number of things far worse than that, but at the very least it was selfish, to abandon everyone. Don't you agree?

As STEPHEN *carries on,* JOHN *puts his hand out – no rain...*

Is this what you're up to? Since you've come back. Preaching.

JOHN   Your eyes are red.

STEPHEN   It happens at my age. What are you here to talk about? God?

JOHN

STEPHEN   Does Ruth know? That you're back. Have you told her?

No. Of course you haven't.

HOLLY *comes over with a clipboard.*

HOLLY   Hello.

JOHN   Holly, this is Stephen Crossley he used to be my
             lecturer at university, taught me a lot. Stephen
             famously doesn't believe in God, in fact he thinks
             belief is dangerous, not just organised religion but
             belief itself. He goes around claiming that there
             'probably isn't a God' which considering almost any
             definition of a divine being is a weirdly unintellectual
             and totally unprovable statement to make, and if
             there's one thing Stephen objects to it's things you
             can't prove. But he's a good man. And he can drink a
             lot. Holly's collecting email addresses, she's started a
             website, and she has sex for money.

HOLLY   What? Shut up.

JOHN   You said you're fine with it.

HOLLY   Yeah I am.

JOHN   Well then.

             JOHN *puts his hand out. Still no rain.* ZIA*'s in the
             background.*

STEPHEN   John, let me give you her number.

             SHANNON *interrupts as* STEPHEN *writes on a piece
             of paper.*

SHANNON   Hi.

STEPHEN   Let me give you her number.

SHANNON   Sorry, to interrupt – oops – I'm Shannon, I've been
             watching the other speeches – thought I'd come down
             and see for myself.

JOHN   Hi

SHANNON   I just wanted to say... they're really... I've quit my
             job! I think you're right. We have to do something
             important.

STEPHEN   You've quit your job?

SHANNON   I hated my boss.

STEPHEN   How do you do it John?

SHANNON   I beg your pardon?

STEPHEN   These people – she quit her job? The way things are at
           the moment – who does that?

SHANNON   I am here.

STEPHEN   What is all this? The park. The speeches. Your little
           friends. What are you up to?

JOHN   Have you had bad dreams?

STEPHEN   …

           JOHN *looks at him.*

JOHN   Oh.

           Hang on…

           *Thunder and it starts to rain. Everyone gets umbrellas
           and coats out.*

           STEPHEN, *unimpressed, writes a number down.*

STEPHEN   This is her personal number – you'll get straight
           through.

           Call her.

           He walks away. JOHN *leaves with* ZIA *and*
           SHANNON, *as* HOLLY *puts her hood up and tries to
           sort out her phone.*

           MARK *is there.*

MARK   You haven't answered my calls. You're here every day.
           I see you on my lunchbreak. Going round with your…
           clipboard.

           Why didn't you get back to me?

HOLLY   I don't…

MARK   You don't… what?

HOLLY   What we do. I don't like it.

MARK   What? – You don't like it – Then why didn't you say?

HOLLY   I was scared.

MARK   Of what?

HOLLY	Of you.
MARK	…

JOHN *comes over with an umbrella.*

Oh. Hello. Good. Saw your speech.

HOLLY	Mark –
MARK	Saw the website too. Funny. It is supposed to be funny right?
HOLLY	Just fuck off yeah this isn't anything to do with you.
JOHN	It's okay.
MARK	What?
JOHN	Really. Mark. It's okay.
MARK	Right. I need to get back to the office. You know. Job. Money.

Holly. Call me yeah?

He looks at JOHN. *Something unnerving, which he ignores.*

He goes off, into the rain. HOLLY *turns to* JOHN, *on the point of tears, in the rain. Just the two of them.*

Pause.

JOHN	Are you alright?

She isn't. JOHN *opens the umbrella and she hugs him underneath, and cries.*

Twelve

In RUTH's *Number 10 flat.* STEPHEN *enters.* RUTH *is getting ready.*

RUTH	This better be important. I'm late and then there's a call saying that the famous *atheist* Stephen Crossley has just turned up at Number 10. The press all saw you walk in. What's going on?
STEPHEN	I thought you'd want to know.
RUTH	What?

STEPHEN	John's come back. I saw him.
	Beat.
	I gave him your number. Said he should call you.
RUTH	What number?
STEPHEN	Your number, your personal number.
	RUTH *looks at a phone on the side.*
RUTH	I'm... I'm late.
	I'm really...
	I have to go...
	She slams the side of her dressing table, hard. Angry.
	She looks out the window. The rain pours down hard.
	Is it me, or is getting darker?

Thirteen

SARAH *is chopping vegetables in the kitchen. Tense. The rain outside.* RUBY *enters reading her Kindle.*

SARAH	It's bedtime.
RUBY	I'm reading.
SARAH	You've read enough.
RUBY	I'm nearly at the end.
SARAH	You can finish it in bed.
RUBY	I don't want to finish it in bed, once you get to bed you start to fall asleep, I want to think about this.
SARAH	....
RUBY	Mom, do you read books?
SARAH	Of course.
RUBY	I never see you. What was the last book you read?
	SARAH *chops.*
	What do you do?

SARAH	I'm your mommy.
RUBY	But what do you do for a living?
SARAH	I run a charity.
RUBY	On Thursdays.
SARAH	Yes.
RUBY	In the afternoons on Thursdays.
SARAH	…
RUBY	Between two and four-thirty.
SARAH	…
RUBY	I'm reading a book about emancipation and it seems to me that it's okay for women to go out in the world and make something of themselves, in fact it seems to me that that's a good thing and it's been fought for by generations of women in the past, but you don't do that, you stay in most of the time with me, and even when I'm at school you're still here.

SARAH *chops*.

Maybe if you read books it would take you out of yourself.

SARAH	Ruby…
RUBY	We read to know we're not alone.
SARAH	It's your bedtime.
RUBY	No.
SARAH	I've had enough.
RUBY	You should read.
SARAH	I'm not alone.
RUBY	You don't like me asking questions.
SARAH	It's time to listen to your mommy.
RUBY	I think questioning makes us who we are.
SARAH	You're not a good child, are you?
RUBY	Why don't you like me asking questions Mom?

SARAH   You're not *good*

RUBY   You always get angry when I ask questions.

SARAH *chops. Chops.*

Is it possible for a daughter to be cleverer than her mother?

SARAH *stops chopping and looks at* RUBY.

The fluorescent light above flickers. Strobes.

Mom?

The cupboard door opens in the kitchen and an emaciated figure all in black slowly emerges.

Mom!

RUBY *starts screaming as the figure grabs her. She kicks and screams as he drags her into the cupboard. The moment the door is shut again, the kitchen returns to normal.* SARAH *carries on chopping.*

Slow fade to black.

ACT THREE

One

We again hear Laurie Anderson's 'Someone Else's Dream'.

This time it's cut even shorter.

The twelve wake up again, as before, terrified and breathing.

Two

Music plays. EDITH *stares straight forward – terrified, in a trance – we're not sure…*

MARK *and* ALICE *enter.*

MARK	Edith the door was open.
	He sees her.
	Edith?
EDITH	Oh. Mark. Didn't hear you. Going a bit deaf.
MARK	They're going to drop the case.
EDITH	What?
MARK	They're going to drop the case.
EDITH	I'm a bit deaf…
MARK	They're going to drop the case!
EDITH	Is this your girlfriend?
MARK	Oh for Christ's –
ALICE	I'm Alice. Mark's assistant. We spoke on the phone.
EDITH	Do you have a girlfriend?
MARK	Look we're in a bit of a hurry.
EDITH	My granddaughter Holly, she's your age.

MARK   I know, she's the one who –

EDITH   But she's black. You might have a problem with that.

MARK   No.

EDITH   Some white guys get scared by black girls that's what she told me.

MARK   The bank have been persuaded to stop.

EDITH   What did you tell them?

MARK   They thought this was your house.

EDITH   I rent it.

MARK   I know but they thought it was yours. When I proved to them that wasn't the case, they said they'd let it go, on one condition.

EDITH   Maybe you should go out with Alice. She seems like a nice girl.

ALICE   He's not my type.

MARK   Can we concentrate?

EDITH   You know Mark, there was a time when the high street bank wouldn't sue an old woman for all she was worth.

MARK   You threw a shopping trolley through their window.

EDITH   They did far worse to me.

MARK   Yes, look –

EDITH   (*To* ALICE.) I was stood in that queue for half an hour and my legs were hurting and there were no chairs and no one was helping, and I asked for help but no one did anything, they just thought I was mad, so I left, and I was going to change to another bank but then I realised I couldn't because I've got a terrible credit rating because of the overdraft charges they made and I was walking down that road and all these young people were out protesting and rioting and I thought good for them – I thought, I've had enough so there was a trolley yes and I picked it up and put it through their window, the money they've taken off me more than makes up for it, I hate that bank. It's shit. It's a shit bank.

NatWest. It was NatWest if you want to know.

She goes to her computer.

MARK   Edith you're not allowed in any branch from now on.

EDITH   Suits me. Do you wear those shoes to work?

ALICE   Yes I do.

EDITH   Shoes say a lot about a person dear.

ALICE   Really?

EDITH   And your shoes say I'm a fucking idiot don't take me seriously whatever you do. How much are you charging me then?

MARK   We'll send you an invoice.

EDITH   I found a plate I can put on eBay, that's a start…

ALICE   Mark…

MARK   Alright, call it a favour…

EDITH   What?

MARK   Don't worry about the money.

EDITH   If only. Here we are!

         Money yes, none of that, I thought the world was going to hell in a handcart, another Thatcher making everything worse and worse but then my granddaughter showed me this. She's been making these videos.

MARK   Oh don't tell me –

EDITH   It's this man. He goes into the park and he stands there and speaks and look.

         Look how many people have been watching. Thousands. That's where she is now.

         I like him.

         His name's John.

Three

DENNIS *arrives back at the house. He has a suitcase.* SARAH *is in her dressing gown, watching something on a laptop.*

DENNIS   Hey!

SARAH   Hey.

           She closes the laptop down.

           How was the flight?

DENNIS   Aargh. Red eye.

SARAH   Toast?

DENNIS   Toast! Good.

           SARAH *starts slicing bread with a knife and puts the bread into a toaster.*

           Missed you. How's munchkin? Where is she?

SARAH   In bed. Reading. She's never off that thing you gave her.

DENNIS   She's a good kid.

SARAH   Here.

DENNIS   What?

SARAH   Coffee?

DENNIS   Oh. Thanks. Still in bed?

           Doesn't she have... what is it? *Ballet* this morning?

SARAH   She didn't want to go.

DENNIS   Really?

SARAH   Last night she said don't get me up I want to stay in bed in the morning and read.

DENNIS   She likes ballet.

SARAH   Well then you have a conversation with her Dennis, if you don't trust me, that I've done my best, why don't you go in there and ask her?

           The toast pops. SARAH *butters it.*

DENNIS   Hey.

SARAH   What?

DENNIS   …

SARAH   There.

She gives him the toast. He takes a bite.

DENNIS   Thanks.

Still the dreams?

SARAH   …

DENNIS   You should take those pills.

SARAH   They don't help.

Pause. DENNIS *eats another slice of toast. Looks at his watch.*

DENNIS   Hell. I have to go.

SARAH   How are things at work? Is everything… okay?

DENNIS   …

SARAH   …

DENNIS   I love you. We'll all catch up tonight.

He kisses her and goes with his toast. SARAH *stares for a moment. Then goes, opens the computer, and presses play on what she was watching.*

Four

The park. ZIA *and* SHANNON, *and others, wait for* JOHN.

They coyly watch each other, eventually striking up a conversation –

ZIA   Thirteen.

SHANNON   What?

ZIA   If you go through his speeches and you count the letters in the right way you get the number thirteen, again and again.

SHANNON   You've tried it?

ZIA   People have yeah, cos thirteen's unlucky in almost
               every culture. Apparently there's these insects and they
               live underground and only come out every thirteen
               years, cos thirteen's the least likely mathematically to
               coincide with other insects' breeding patterns.

SHANNON   This on the internet?

ZIA   Yeah.

SHANNON   Thought so.

               JOHN *enters with his bucket. A* HECKLER *is nearby
               and enthusiastic.*

               As JOHN*'s about to speak –*

HECKLER   Talk about Iran!

JOHN   I… what?

HECKLER   Well they're saying it's all going to kick off soon, so
               what do you think about that then?

HOLLY   No… he – let him talk –

HECKLER   Come on!

               What do you think?

               JOHN *looks at the* HECKLER. *Then steps off the
               bucket and goes.*

               What?

               Where's he going?

               HOLLY *goes after him.*

SHANNON   See ya then.

ZIA   Right.

               Do you want to… come round mine. Tonight. I've got
               a telescope.

SHANNON   I beg your pardon?

ZIA   It's new. I saved up. To look at the – you know – stars.
               So. We could.

SHANNON   Yeah.

ZIA   Do that.

SHANNON   Okay.

ZIA   If you want?

SHANNON   Yeah.

ZIA   What?

SHANNON   Yeah.

ZIA   You will?

SHANNON   Yeah.

ZIA   Shit.

            Good.

            Beat.

            Do you know anything about it?

SHANNON   What?

ZIA   Iran.

SHANNON   Not really.

Five

STEPHEN *is making a speech at the Oxford Union.*

STEPHEN   Ladies and gentlemen, the Iranian regime is, simply
          put, brutal. They have clung on to power, rigged
          elections, kidnapped, tortured, repressed, and murdered
          their own people in their thousands, and have been
          shown to actively support terrorist organisations.

          As you may imagine, the regime is deeply unpopular
          with the majority of Iranians, who are, by and large,
          young, educated and desperate to choose their own
          future. These young people know what they are
          missing, how their freedoms are curtailed. They are
          desperate to put an end to this oppression but their
          voices are silenced and their numbers reduced through
          imprisonment, torture and death. And let us not forget,
          as the mullahs have, to consider the women. The
          women here tonight, if you were Iranian, would be

possessions. If, as a woman, you cheated on your husband, you would be stoned to death. If you are interested and want to see a woman being stoned to death then I direct you to the internet where ladies and gentlemen, you will find a number of videos – but I give you a warning – it is utterly horrific and it takes her a very long time to die.

Six

A split scene – RUTH and DENNIS in her office. AMIR and RACHEL at home.

RUTH	How was the trip?
DENNIS	Good.
RUTH	You spoke to the President?
DENNIS	Yes.
AMIR	Yeah.
RUTH	What did he say?
RACHEL	Just take a minute, take a minute to breathe, cos I can't believe –
DENNIS	You've read the transcripts, I'm sure your people have spoken to you.
AMIR	I don't need a minute.
DENNIS	The feeling in Washington is that these talks were always just stalling for time.
AMIR	I know what I think.
DENNIS	The President's had enough.
AMIR	It's like everything John's been saying.
RACHEL	John? No. John's not here, let's stay on you.
DENNIS	He feels this is the moment.
AMIR	We should do it.
RACHEL	War?
RUTH	I see.

AMIR	Yes.
DENNIS	Yes.

Beat.

AMIR	This is an opportunity. You haven't been there. You're not allowed to speak your mind, the punishments the regime hands out are medieval –
RACHEL	Well if that's the criteria / there's a long list of other countries.
DENNIS	You'll talk to him yourself but the President asked me to come and speak to you tonight. To test the water.
AMIR	Government-sanctioned gangs pulling people out of cars for not dressing correctly, doctors, academics arrested for speaking out
DENNIS	He wonders how you're feeling.
RUTH	How I'm feeling?
DENNIS	That's right.
AMIR	– and there are young people like us sat in rooms like this watching TV and they'll be praying we go in and help them.
RACHEL	You've got family out there – you want them bombed?
RUTH	How I'm *feeling*?
RACHEL	You want to throw the country into civil war?
AMIR	It's exactly what John says about purpose. I've had enough of sitting back and letting them –
RACHEL	Well you would know about sitting back.
RUTH	I give an order, and then within hours, people are dead.
AMIR	I thought you believed in the rights of women.
RACHEL	Of course –
AMIR	But only in this country –
RACHEL	I'm not sure a genocidal war will benefit women in any country particularly, but seeing as you know so much about women and their rights –

RUTH   I don't want to go to war, Dennis, but if it's
            necessary –

AMIR   When did you start talking to me like this?

RUTH   I absolutely will.

AMIR   When did you entirely lose respect?

RUTH   So how am I *feeling*?

RACHEL   I don't know.

RUTH   Ambivalent.

DENNIS   Right.

AMIR   Right.

RACHEL   But... since you ask, it's probably to do with what
            you're advocating, John wouldn't want this, no one we
            know would want this – massive invasion and
            occupation of a country that hasn't attacked us,
            hundreds of thousands dead,

AMIR   The people I know over there are ready for sacrifice –

RACHEL   But this isn't them fighting this is us, with troops and
            planes that flatten blocks and villages – Amir I don't
            even know where / to start if you're stupid or naive or
            right-wing, we went on the *anti-war march* remember
            you shouting all the way –

AMIR   No, no, you can't shut up you're talking and being
            clever and sneering all the fucking time but you never
            think really *think* about anything – you wonder why I
            wake up in the night screaming it's nothing to do with
            what's going on there, it's probably being next to you
            all night, this stuff in your head, all your *problems*.

DENNIS   Ruth.

RUTH   I'm sorry?

DENNIS   Can I call you Ruth?

AMIR   John was right.

RACHEL   What?

DENNIS   May I speak freely?

AMIR   You talk and shout and tell people what to do but you
            never listen really, you never – just – stop.

RACHEL   I...

RUTH   Yes?

DENNIS   Do you have anyone?

RUTH   What?

DENNIS   Anyone you can talk to, about how you feel, because
            from what I see... can I say this? From what I see,
            you're on your own, and under a lot of pressure.

            Everyone knows you've been through a lot. And these
            people you're surrounded by, your advisors, I don't
            know how much they understand... If you needed
            someone to... To talk to...

RACHEL   Alright then.

AMIR   What?

DENNIS   I think we get on.

            RUTH *stares at him*.

AMIR   What?

            MARTIN *enters*.

MARTIN   Mr Harrison. There's a call for you.

            Your wife.

            Apparently it's urgent.

DENNIS   I'm sorry. Prime Minister, we could talk about the
            options.

RACHEL   Yes. Let's stop. You and me. Tonight.

RUTH   Dennis. Thank you for the offer and you're right, I'm
            under a lot of pressure, but I think I'm coping with it
            all quite well considering my emotional state and the
            fact I'm a woman and everything.

AMIR   That's not what I...

DENNIS   That's not what I meant.

RUTH   When the time comes, I'll make my decision.

I know what you meant.

Talk to your wife.

DENNIS *turns and enters the kitchen where* SARAH *is sat, smoking.*

RUTH *stays for a while, then leaves.*

AMIR   Rachel –

RACHEL   Yes.

             Yes.

             Let's put an end to it.

Seven

DENNIS*'s house.* SARAH *is sat smoking at the kitchen table.* DENNIS *enters. Slowly. Devastated.*

DENNIS   They say there's been no forced entry to the house.

SARAH   So where's she gone? Why would she do this to us? We look after her. I'm frightened –

DENNIS   If she had any sense of anything it was responsibility, she understood that what we do affects other people. She wouldn't run away.

SARAH   We should call her friends.

DENNIS   They don't know anything.

SARAH   Oh God oh God. Shouldn't you be at work?

DENNIS   Honey, our daughter –

SARAH   But it's important.

DENNIS   Our daughter has gone. I'm not doing anything else until we find her.

SARAH   Why?

DENNIS   What?

SARAH   Why has this happened? To us. Didn't I treat her right?

             DENNIS *looks at* SARAH, *without an answer.*

             Pray.

DENNIS   She'll be okay.

SARAH   Pray with me.

            SARAH *puts her cigarette out and shuts her eyes.*
            DENNIS *looks at her then does the same.*

            Please... God.

Eight

It's getting later now. Night. Stars.

A choral singer starts. Baroque.

As SARAH *prays we see* MARK *coming back to his flat with some
booze and cigarettes, and* ALICE, *who's a bit drunk. He lights
cigarettes, pours drink, ignores* ALICE.

SARAH   God, save us, save us from darkness, save us from
            damnation.

            EDITH *puts on her iPod and goes out running.*

            Save us from evil, from the end, from death and pain...

            ZIA *and* SHANNON *are out with a telescope looking
            at the stars.* SHANNON *smokes.* HOLLY, *with an
            iPod, calls* EDITH.

            JOHN *appears, walking through all of them.*

SHANNON   That one...

SARAH   From the end.

SHANNON   It looks like a hand, reaching out.

SARAH   Save us from what we fear, guide us to salvation,

ZIA   You ever wonder what's at the edge?

SARAH   ...show us how to live.

SHANNON   The edge of what?

SARAH   ...show us the light.

ZIA   The universe.

EDITH   Hello?

HOLLY	Gran? He's gone.
EDITH	Who? Who's gone?
ZIA	You know it's actually quite likely that there are an infinite number of parallel universes where each possibility that could ever happen is played out. Every possibility.
SHANNON	You say this stuff to all the girls?
ZIA	Er... yeah. I do actually.
MARK	Come on then.
SHANNON	I think that's where you go wrong.
	The phone is ringing. RUTH *looks at it. Then answers it.*
RUTH	Hello?
	Yes.
	I...
	JOHN *enters.*
	I can't –
	She hangs up, then unplugs the phone from the socket. Over the next page, she walks to the centre of the stage and closes her eyes. ALICE *and* MARK *start to kiss.* MARTIN *arrives with a pile of papers to sort through.*
	ROB *packs his kit bag.* STEPHEN *continues his speech from earlier...*
JOHN	Today I've read papers, watched the television.
STEPHEN	You may think I'm alarmist, that I'm exaggerating.
JOHN	I've seen the pictures we all have. Heard what's being said –
SHANNON	They all think I'm stupid.
ZIA	I don't.
JOHN	They tell us, if we do nothing, it's a risk.
STEPHEN	When I imagine what might happen in the years to come, what terrifies me the most?

MARK   Stop.

STEPHEN   A thermonuclear theocracy.

              STEPHEN *coughs.* MARK *has pushed* ALICE *off.*

JOHN   So instead, they say, we have to go in, and stop them.

ALICE   What's the problem?

HOLLY   Gran?

MARK   Go. Get out. Get out!

JOHN   The army. The airforce. Take Iran to pieces, bullets and
              bombs, just so we know, for sure.

HOLLY   Where are you?

JOHN   Just so we're safe.

              ALICE *goes.* STEPHEN *coughs again.* MARK *slowly,
              over the next, turns, kneels and prays.*

HOLLY   Gran, what are you up to?

EDITH   Late-night run. Nothing like it, and before you say
              anything, I'm an old woman, with no money, what's
              the worse that can happen?

JOHN   And we understand. We know what our leaders are
              telling us. But my question is – how do you feel?

              AMIR *and* RACHEL *are at home.*

AMIR   When you say end it? You mean…

RACHEL   I don't know, it's just nothing works, any more. Does
              it?

JOHN   Nervous?

HOLLY   Gran?…

JOHN   Sick?

HOLLY   Are you okay?…

EDITH   I'm sorry love, I was just feeling a bit… Oh.

HOLLY   Gran?

              EDITH *sees something in the ground. Goes over to it.*

JOHN   Alone?

EDITH *digs around, pulls on the object. It comes out of the ground – a child's hand.*

STEPHEN *collapses.* SARAH *shuts her eyes.* EDITH, *shocked, shuts her eyes.* MARK *praying. Shuts his eyes.* HOLLY *shuts her eyes and prays.* SHANNON, ZIA, RACHEL *and* AMIR, *the same.*

Me too.

Of all of them, only RUTH *stands – centre-stage, her eyes closed.*

So. We have to act. Together. This is the moment.

We'll meet and march, and we'll take a message to parliament that says we do not want this war. A message that says everything has to change.

This is the moment we get better.

This is the moment it happens.

Yes.

In. Our. Name.

Interval.

ACT FOUR

One

Trafalgar Square. A protest is raging. A van has been converted into a makeshift stage with a screen. Loud music. Crowds surging. Banners, chanting. Energy and conviction – passion. But good-natured.

In the daylight, JOHN *climbs up and stands on the stage, and the music fades.*

JOHN   Men and women of Britain! It's a bright day, it's a passionate day and it's time to throw things away and start again. From this day forward we will no longer simply be a country of failure, of guilt and insecurity. Instead, we will be a nation of principle, strength and peace. We will have standards. We will demand things that we have been told are out of date, things like kindness, politeness, welfare, equality. Things like *society*. And in contrast to what our generation has been told since we were born, we don't think it is foolish to believe rather than doubt, we don't think ideology is dead, we don't think it's all about compromise and pragmatism because like the best of men and women before us, we will aspire and yes, we will dream! There can be no progress without belief. Belief in the capacity of mankind, belief that we can be better, that we can be more than animals, more than selfish, more than warlike tribes, pushing each other out the way in brutal competition. The older generation, as they always do, tell us we are naive, trust us they say, we *know* that change is impossible. Well they always say that and it is up to us, with youth and hope and vision, to show them they are so, so wrong.

               We have an idea. We have a way forward for this country. And today is our first test. Today we have been moved to action. We stand here, every one of us committed to the idea that there is a future for Iran without innocent men, women and children dying in their thousands. We believe that with modern technology and old-fashioned solidarity, we can empower the Iranians to follow the example of other young people across the world, throw off their rulers and seize their country for themselves. Our generation is speaking with a clear voice, stating that one does not need violence to change the world, one needs passion, communication and conviction.

Today we say to the government that storming in with troops and taking over a country is not how we do things any more. Instead, in our names, in this time, we can communicate to people in every home in every place. In our name, in this time, we can reach out and empower them, not batter and destroy them, in our name we can demand freedom for Iran, we can encourage and support them to have a say over their future – in our name, we can all be better.

In our name!

CROWD   In our name! In our name! In our name!

JOHN walks into the crowd, as the chanting continues.

Two

In Number 10. The protest on television. RUTH and STEPHEN are watching it.

They can also hear it outside.

'In our name! In our name!'

RUTH   One year, we spent Christmas together. I'd already heard about him from Simon. This amazing best friend. He didn't have anywhere to go so Simon invited him back to ours. He arrived with a few clothes, a case of wine and a pile of books. We got on immediately, he spoke like someone much older. We talked into the night, they went for walks.

It was always about the two of them. Him and Simon. They were so... bright.

What does he want?

STEPHEN   He's got something to prove.

RUTH   Maybe. But what if it's worse.

              What if he means it?

Three

In the crowd. HOLLY's handing out leaflets. MARK with her.

MARK   Well I didn't see *this* coming. When I was a student we
              went to Trafalgar Square and got pissed, we just
              wanted a bottle of Diamond White that's as far as our
              ambition went, but you lot, you say let's go to the
              square for a party, you get what? Half a million?

HOLLY   I don't have time for this.

MARK   You said I was scary.

HOLLY   You are.

MARK   I'm helping your grandmother, for free. She doesn't
              think I'm scary when I get her off vandalism charges. I
              never made you do anything. Scary? What? Now? Am
              I *scary* now?

HOLLY   Yes.

MARK   We agreed it was a win–win situation, you were very
              empowered about it, but now you're saying that every
              time it happened and every time I paid you, you were
              in fact –

HOLLY   Stop –

MARK   Putting up with it.

HOLLY   Yes.

MARK   But you see *that* –

HOLLY   Mark –

MARK   That's a different thing – 'putting up with it' – that was
              not what we agreed. You need to be careful.

HOLLY   *Careful?*

MARK   Of when you say things, what you imply.

HOLLY   Now you're threatening me.

MARK   *No!*

He's in public. People start to look.

It's not threatening, I don't mean you need to be careful because I'll hit you –

HOLLY   Jesus Mark –

MARK   I mean you need to be *careful* of what you imply because when you say something like that to someone – like they're scary – it can go round their head, it has an effect –

HOLLY   Mark you're a bastard. You say it yourself.

MARK   Fine, but that doesn't mean I'm into *rape* or anything –

HOLLY   I'm not saying rape.

MARK   – what you're implying –

HOLLY   I'm not saying that but paying girls for sex is –

MARK   It's a deal.

HOLLY   Jesus, a *deal*? Okay.

MARK   No, no, don't do that, it is, it's a deal that we *agreed,* that you instigated in the first place – fuck's sake half the women of the world are saying you should take them seriously the other half are telling us don't listen to a word we say, 'when we *say* we're fine with it Mark, we're *obviously* not telling the truth, instead of taking us seriously you should take care of us, as women, and not believe a fucking word'. No definitely means no, but yes does not in any way apparently mean yes. Do women have a right to do what they want with their bodies?

HOLLY   You know it's wrong but you do it anyway.

MARK   The thing is, the simple thing is Holly, that you've fucked this up, this bit of your life, and you feel bad about it and that's fine, but – you – you – You have to take some *fucking* responsibility for *something*!

She looks at him. Properly. For the first time.

HOLLY   Men.

MARK   No.

A moment.

>   Anyway. I didn't come here for you.

HOLLY   Why then?

MARK   I can't sleep.

>   Where is he?

Four

Number 10. MARTIN, LIAM *and* CAROL *are there with* RUTH *and* STEPHEN.

RUTH   It's a phone call from Carol. Just testing the water.

STEPHEN   Why do it at all?

RUTH   The crowd's growing. Support in every city. Blanket television coverage. I have to do something.

STEPHEN   The people elected you, they want you to be decisive. Get the police out. You've done it before.

RUTH   They're not aggressive, they're not violent.

STEPHEN   Not yet.

RUTH   There's no harm in listening.

STEPHEN   By listening, by looking – by acknowledging his existence in any way you give him power.

>   *He coughs.* MARTIN *receives a notification on his iPad.*

MARTIN   Prime Minister

RUTH   What is it?

MARTIN   It's about Dennis. They're charging his wife.

RUTH   His – oh – God –

MARTIN   Apparently they're not looking for anyone else.

RUTH   How old was his daughter?

MARTIN   Eleven.

>   *A moment.*

RUTH   What was her name?

No one says anything.

Martin. Her name?

MARTIN   I just told you.

RUTH   What?

MARTIN   I just said Prime Minister.

Ruby.

Her name was Ruby.

RUTH   Oh.

STEPHEN   Are you alright?

RUTH   Martin. Send a message to Dennis. Anything I can do.

LIAM   I would advise that you stay very distant from the whole –

RUTH   Send the message. Keep me updated. Carol. Any word back?

CAROL   Back?

RUTH   From the square.

CAROL   Well. No. It may take some time.

RUTH   Why?

CAROL   These are young people Prime Minister. Easily distracted.

Five

In the square, JOHN, RACHEL, AMIR, HOLLY, ZIA *and*
SHANNON *discuss the call.* MARK *stands towards the back,*
waiting.

JOHN   Rachel, tell them I want to talk, just me and her, for an hour, this afternoon.

AMIR   Why just the two of you?

ZIA   We can come as well yeah?

JOHN   No. Thank you.

ZIA   But we've got this far –

RACHEL	John if she saw how many of us there are –
SHANNON	I'd tell her a thing or two –
JOHN	She's watching the television. We've shown our numbers. But now the two of us have to sit and down and talk, listen, face to face. If we do that, we can get what we all want.
	So.
	Alright to make the call Rachel?
RACHEL	Okay.
JOHN	Thank you.
	RACHEL *goes to call.*
AMIR	What are you going to talk about?
JOHN	What do you think?
AMIR	Simon?
JOHN	Why now?
AMIR	What?
JOHN	You hardly talk about it, I've been back for weeks and he's never mentioned, not really, not until now.
AMIR	Because you're seeing her for the first time so I thought –
JOHN	You miss him.
AMIR	
JOHN	So do I but these people are here for a reason. We're not going to talk about Simon, we're going to talk about a change of direction. Offering something new.
AMIR	But she might want to –
JOHN	Amir you wanted me to support the war, then when I disagree and we occupy the square, you change your mind, you stay with us. Why? What persuaded you?
AMIR	You.
JOHN	Well then. Trust me.
	They look at each other.

MARK *steps forward.*

MARK   Sorry… don't want to intrude…

JOHN   Mark.

MARK   You remember my name. Good. So the thing is every
         night I have this dream. The same one they all get. I'm
         not sleeping, I'm not working, in fact I'm not doing
         anything at the moment, and the more I thought about
         it the more strange it was that you knew, back then
         remember, you looked at me and you could tell.

JOHN   Yes.

MARK   So, anyway, my whole life is, basically, fucked, I'm
         not just talking about this month, this year, I'm talking
         about not speaking to my dad because of an argument
         and then him dying, I'm talking about the love of my
         life who I cheated on, and now she's gone away, I'm
         talking about jeopardising a promising career by
         turning up smelling of booze, and then – she – Holly –
         said I was *scary* and I've been thinking and maybe,
         yes, maybe I am – and then these dreams, and in the
         state I was in, a week ago, I prayed. I fucking. I've
         never prayed in my life, but I was a mess, so I knelt
         down and asked for help. I don't know why but I asked
         for… forgiveness, and someone answered.

         And it was you. Your voice.

         Isn't that *weird*?

         So.

         I need to know. Yes? What's going on? Cos I'm like…
         this far… from hitting the fan, from the fucking *edge*.
         Of what I can. Do. So you need to tell me, quickly,
         really – You need to tell me now.

JOHN   It's okay.

MARK   What?

JOHN   It's okay.

MARK   'Okay.' What the fuck does that… it's not, thanks for
         the words of. *What?*

         Thanks for the –

JOHN *looks at him.* MARK *starts crying. He can't help himself.*

Shit... oh... fuck...

He falls to the floor, JOHN *catches him. Holds on to him.*

JOHN   It's alright. It's alright.

RACHEL *comes back in.*

What did they say?

RACHEL   Yes. They said yes.

Six

Number 10. RUTH, *with* MARTIN, LIAM *and* CAROL.

RUTH   He's not bringing anyone else? None of his followers?

CAROL   No.

LIAM   The press are calling them his 'disciples'.

RUTH   So that makes him...

LIAM   Apparently he also does miracles.

RUTH   What miracles?

MARTIN   He knows when it's going to rain.

RUTH   That's not a miracle Martin, that's the weather forecast –

CAROL   Prime Minister. It's important for us all to convey that we think this meeting is a very bad idea, and whatever happens as a result of this meeting we can not take responsibility for it. None of us. Your political advisors, communications –

RUTH   Nothing like support.

CAROL   And the civil service.

RUTH   Really *nothing* like support

LIAM   If you come out of the meeting giving something away you lose credibility. On the other hand if you don't, people will say you are arrogant and patronising.

RUTH   I understand, I'm on my own. Can you make sure Stephen's here?

CAROL   Is he still –

RUTH   Yes. He's still in Number 10. He needed to lie down.

CAROL   Where?

RUTH   I don't know.

CAROL   Prime Minister –

RUTH   Carol

CAROL   You've invited a young man with no credentials except his ability to cause civil unrest into the heart of Number 10, somewhere around the building but we're not sure where is a highly controversial sleeping atheist, outside the window half a million people are protesting in the streets, and the Leader of the Free World might call at any moment to see if we want to go to war.

RUTH   That's right.

CAROL   Clear the room please!

They leave. MARTIN *hangs back.*

LIAM   She said clear.

MARTIN   I just...

RUTH   What is it?

LIAM *goes.*

MARTIN   If you want to know what the people think, of him, of you...

His gives her his iPad.

Tweets, the news, updating all the time. In case it's useful.

Prime Minister... I think you're right.

To listen to him. I've been out there – heard him speak –

RUTH   You've not been sleeping have you Martin?

MARTIN   I don't mean this politically, but over the last year. It
              feels like it's all falling apart. In the country. Across
              the world. Like people have gone wrong. And I...
              I think out of everything, he's...

              I think he's good.

Seven

A prison cell. DENNIS *enters.* SARAH *is sat.*

DENNIS   You know what I want to do? I mean there's people out
              there who would stop me doing this but I want to tear
              you to fucking pieces you know that? I want to rip you
              to shreds to do to you what you did to her, I told them
              you were protesting your innocence that's the only
              reason they let me see you, I told them this was a
              diplomatic matter that's why they let me in, but they'll
              find out in a few minutes you're guilty as hell.

              SARAH *stares at him.*

              Why? That's what I want to know. I'll never see you
              again I never want to, I wish they would kill you in this
              country, I don't care what happens to you. But I want
              to know why.

              Beat.

              They found her in pieces. Cut up with a knife.

              Beat.

SARAH   You believe in God.

DENNIS   Yes I do.

SARAH   I know you believe there are good things and evil
              things in this world. I know you believe that.

DENNIS   Good things and evil things.

SARAH   Good people and evil people.

DENNIS   Yes.

SARAH   And what would you do if you found out there was an
              evil person in your house if there was an evil person in
              the world that you had created, people say it about
              Hitler what would his parents do if they had known,

well I knew, I knew what she was going to grow up to
be, there was nothing good about her. This is better, I
may have taken a life Dennis, but I've saved more. I've
saved so many people from the things she would do.

DENNIS   You don't have any idea what she –

SARAH   But what if I did. What if I could?

DENNIS   You can't.

SARAH   But if I could –

DENNIS   You DON'T

SARAH   …

          She breaks down.

          Dennis. I just want you to reach out and touch me, to
          say that although you may hate me and I might be the
          most loathsome creature that ever walked, that you still
          see me as a human being, as someone who deserves at
          least, at least some compassion.

DENNIS   I should be working. I should be in there – they're going
          to invade and I was a voice holding them back but now I
          have no influence and we will go to this wrong war, and
          many people will die and it won't be because of Ruby it
          will be because of you. You're the evil one.

SARAH   Please. Touch me then you can go.

          He stands.

          There was a reason.

          There was a reason I did it.

          She looks at him. Crying now.

Eight

EDITH *plays piano as the scene gathers. She watches on the*
computer.

We see everyone outside waiting, hoping.

Number 10. From two different doors enter STEPHEN *and* JOHN.

RUTH   John.

She holds out her hand. JOHN *sees* STEPHEN.

JOHN   We said it was just going to be us.

RUTH   I thought you wouldn't mind if Stephen joined us for a while.

            We all know each other and it's been such a long time, I'd prefer to have him with us.

JOHN   Stephen. Are you alright?

STEPHEN   I'm fine,

JOHN   You're ill.

STEPHEN   A little.

JOHN   Cancer.

STEPHEN   What?

JOHN   Is it cancer?

STEPHEN   Well they haven't completed the tests yet, but we're not here to play doctors.

            Beat.

RUTH   Shall we sit? They've given us coffee, tea.

JOHN   Tea.

RUTH   No milk is it? Stephen?

STEPHEN   Coffee.

RUTH   Coffee. Lovely. Coffee for me. So.

            The tea and coffee is handed out.

            RUTH *sits down. A moment of looking at each other.*

            Where did you go?

JOHN   Away.

RUTH   Away?

JOHN   Yes.

RUTH   Where?

JOHN

RUTH   Everyone thought you were dead.

JOHN   I know.

RUTH   There were people who cared about you.

JOHN   Not that many. I don't have any family.

RUTH   What about your friends.

JOHN   I'm not here to talk about Simon.

RUTH   Alright let's talk about you instead. Where did you go?

              Pause.

              John it's okay. We've got time. I just wanted to know
              where you'd been. I don't see why it's a secret. I want
              to get a sense of who I'm talking to.

JOHN   You know me Ruth. I'm the same person, I've gone
              away, I've grown up, I've worked a few things out but
              other than that I'm exactly the same. But what about
              you? When you were younger we thought you were
              amazing, you were the radical in your party, a Tory but
              campaigning for all the right things – higher taxes for
              those that could afford it, social improvement, closing
              tax loopholes, forcing the banks and the corporations
              to pay their fair share, we hated your party but we
              loved you –

RUTH   I know.

JOHN   – but you've been in power two years and what have
              you done?

RUTH   It's not as simple as / you might think.

JOHN   I'm not saying it's simple, I know it's difficult. It's
              hard work even when you try but I've studied
              everything you've done and it's compromise. The easy
              route. Again and again. Why? And I think that's what
              this is today.

RUTH   You think war is the easy route?

JOHN   There's another way.

STEPHEN   She's doing her best.

RUTH   Stephen –

JOHN   She's old enough to speak for herself Stephen.

STEPHEN   You're right, she's old enough, she's an adult, she takes
            responsibility, she doesn't have the privilege of going
            off on some extended gap year and then coming back
            and just *complaining* she has to balance interests she has
            to find ways of maintaining the economy while also
            attempting to reduce the gap between rich and poor and
            all at the same time taking the short-termist increasingly
            fickle and small-minded electorate with her. It's not as
            simple as coming in here with a to-do list.

JOHN   It's even in the way she speaks. She's lost something.

            He looks at RUTH.

            Why can't we pay more tax?

RUTH   People don't want to.

JOHN   Make the case.

RUTH   It's been proven.

JOHN   It's not been proven. Make the case.

STEPHEN   Oh come on John.

RUTH   It's been proven that if you increase taxes – if you go
            to the electorate with that, you'll lose –

JOHN   That's not proof.

RUTH   It's what's happened.

JOHN   It's what's happened recently yes but that's different to
            proof, just because recent leaders haven't managed to
            persuade the people why have you given up?

RUTH   Oh John you're so vague it's endearing –

JOHN   If I'm a parent and I want my child to be able to go to
            university without feeling like they'll live their whole
            life in debt, if I want decent education for every child
            in the country, if I feel uncomfortable with the NHS
            falling into largely private hands, who can I vote for,
            where is my candidate?

RUTH   John.

JOHN   Where's the politicians who question the idea of
            choice? You're in pain, you need an operation as soon
            as possible, you don't want to go *shopping*, it's not your

job to choose the right person – you don't want choice you want delivery. Where are the politicians demanding all this? Where's the politicians with new ideas? Again and again, less and less, because we're not *naive* any more, because this is the only way that works.

Where are the ideas Ruth, where are the dreams? We should be electing leaders, not managers.

RUTH   John – there's something else we should talk about.

JOHN   You asked me where I've been. This is where I've been. This is what I want. Where's the politician who does all that?

RUTH   John –

JOHN   You Ruth. That's who you were, that's what you used to be like, when we sat up till two on New Year's Eve and we had drunk too much whisky and ginger, and you used to smoke a bit back then too, and you told me, you said you had *nothing to lose* – you weren't one of the boys you were going to shake things up. Well start today. Take the difficult route. Don't go to war.

RUTH   Sometimes things don't work out as you planned.

JOHN   I know.

RUTH   – things we don't intend.

JOHN   Of course.

RUTH   And sometimes life just gets in the way. Do you understand?

JOHN   *I don't want to talk about Simon.*

RUTH   I didn't mention *Simon.*

            Beat.

JOHN   Ruth… It's not too late to actually *do* something people will remember. Something that will change a generation.

STEPHEN   It is John.

JOHN   No –

STEPHEN   It is too late. You think you're suggesting something new? Almost of all of what you're saying is impossible. Higher taxes stifle economic growth that is just a fact, and the twentieth century has proved conclusively, and yes it is proof, that the introduction of a free-market capitalism into a country's system not only raises the quality of people's life, but also intrinsically leads to greater social and political freedom.

JOHN   For the rich.

STEPHEN   At first, but eventually for all.

JOHN   A big eventually, they're still waiting in Russia, South Africa, you could argue we're still waiting here. The chances of rising up the ladder in this country have sharply declined in the last thirty years, you know why –

STEPHEN   Yes, yes –

JOHN   The free market, smaller government, / less welfare, opportunity –

STEPHEN   I could debate that, there's increasing population, decreasing resources. But I thought you were here to talk about Iran?

JOHN   I'm here to talk to Ruth.

STEPHEN   Ruth's listening aren't you?

RUTH   Yes.

STEPHEN   She's fascinated by us.

RUTH   I like the perspective.

STEPHEN   Exactly. Now, John – Iran's nuclear intention is something else completely. You criticise us for saying you're naive, well that's difficult because all you out there, you sound it. You sound like *children*. Your criticism is that this *feels* wrong, well of course it does, it's *war*, people are going to die, war always *feels* wrong, it should feel wrong, but the world is nasty and the civilisation you live in, every single tiny aspect of the western civilisation is built upon the progress and protection that came at the cost of blood, that your ancestors fought for, even though it felt just as *wrong* then. No one wants this to happen, but we have to protect our interests and we have to be intelligent enough and proud enough to say we think our values are better than theirs – our values of freedom, democracy, equality.

JOHN   I'd question whether equality is currently / one of our values.

STEPHEN   And we have to be strong enough to know that those things are not givens. Good does not always win out, not under the ancient monarchies, not under Stalin, or Hitler. There's no God, no divine justice. We do not inevitability get better, unless we work, unless sometimes we *fight*.

He's unsteady, sweating, overwhelmed.

RUTH   Stephen –

STEPHEN   I'm fine. Come on! Let's say it, let's come out and proclaim it loud, our ways are better, yes, *better* than theirs.

JOHN   Whose?

STEPHEN   The Iranian –

JOHN   The Iranians'?

STEPHEN   The Iranian regime's. Our systems of power and law and the values we have enshrined are morally superior. We don't make our women hide themselves, we don't beat our children, we don't stone adulterers, homosexuality is legal, we give everyone the vote. We're happy to coexist and agree to differ but not where our moral principles and the bedrock of our culture are at stake. We cannot allow men we wouldn't trust with our sister to have access to a nuclear weapon.

JOHN   That sounds a bit racist to me.

STEPHEN   Absolutely not.

JOHN   Who are these men?

STEPHEN   What?

JOHN   Who do you imagine these men are? Uneducated stupid, Middle Eastern –

STEPHEN   No, sir, no, quite the opposite, over-privileged well-educated middle-class men, who thrive on corruption and torture, who cultivate a culture of hypocracy and fear, for their selfish desire. There have always been these men. Overgrown children of the world and they should be disciplined, but you'll let them have the bomb.

JOHN   No.

STEPHEN   Then what's your alternative?

JOHN   It's a different world now Stephen.

STEPHEN   Really?

JOHN   The world you're describing is the world of the ballot
              box. Him or her, left or right, valves and switches and
              binary choices, but to people like me, to us, that way of
              thinking is ancient. My generation isn't apathetic,
              we're voting every second of the day – pick up one of
              these –

              He grabs the iPad.

              Every second every subject, not simply yes or no, this
              or that, but millions of views, opinions, solutions, the
              true complexity of the world and all that's needed to
              pull it together and progress?

              Purpose. Conviction, Belief.

              He gives the iPad to RUTH.

STEPHEN   How does that stop Iran getting the bomb? You're
              saying we just sit back and hope –

JOHN   We sit foward. We don't raise a fist. Any government
              can ultimately not govern without consent. Modern
              technology has given people more information and
              more organisation than ever before. It is no longer
              possible for governments to lie. Therefore, armed with
              the truth, and the capacity to be heard, it won't be long
              before the people speak out. We do not need to invade.
              In Tunisia, Egypt, the people spoke together. And the
              voice of the people is the –

STEPHEN   Is the voice of God, and I don't trust either. By all
              accounts the Muslim Brotherhood are pretty tech savvy
              John, and from what I saw out my window earlier this
              year, riots seem easier to organise than ever – talk
              about a flash mob –

JOHN   What I'm saying –

STEPHEN   What are you saying?

JOHN   We have to believe in something.

STEPHEN   Why?

JOHN   Because the only message at the moment is money,
            success, power, and it's like a Big Mac, you're told to
            eat it, but afterwards you're still empty. That's why
            people are violent and lost and rioting. They've not
            been given a reason to live. I'm not saying God, but we
            have to have a motivation towards something, a *drive*.
            Those people in the square think a thousand different
            things but today there's something they share. That this
            is wrong and we can be better. I get emails, letters
            every day now from people across the country,
            soldiers, businessmen, old women all after something
            better. A new idea. They don't want this war. The
            people of Iran do not want this war.

STEPHEN   If you allow this technology to get out of control there
            will be no ideas new or old, everything John,
            everything will be destroyed. Yes. Armageddon. The
            end of reality. No light, just darkness. Am I talking
            your language now? Mystery, apocalypse? I'm told
            you think dreams have meaning. It's said, coincidence
            follows you around.

JOHN   Maybe.

STEPHEN   You said I had cancer. What made you say that?

JOHN   I saw it.

STEPHEN   Magic?

JOHN   There's things we don't know.

            Beat.

            Ruth believes in God.

            Don't you?

            Beat

RUTH   Stephen, maybe John has a point. Perhaps there are
            other things we could do.

STEPHEN   Ruth?

RUTH   You've always been a fan of charging in and kicking
            up a storm.

            Beat.

STEPHEN   If we refuse to take control of this now, our grandchildren will look back and see it as the greatest failure of our generation, far larger than climate change, potentially bigger than the two World Wars. Terrorist nuclear explosions in any place at any time. Imagine that, the constant fear of death, any place, any moment, utterly unavoidable. There would be no freedom at all in that world. True freedom is only ensured through leadership and government. We have a parliamentary democracy for a reason. The people cannot be trusted. Nothing good ever came from literally giving power to the people – civil war, atrocity, mob rule. No. Give power to –

He coughs.

RUTH   Stephen.

STEPHEN   Give power to –

He coughs again.

RUTH   Stephen go to the hospital.

She picks up the phone.

Hello.

STEPHEN   Give power to *parliament*. To the experts.

RUTH   I want a car / and a doctor, at the back door, now.

STEPHEN   The people are stupid and the people are dangerous. They can shout as loud as they want. But –

MARTIN *enters.*

RUTH   Martin will you show Stephen out?

MARTIN   Of course.

STEPHEN *coughs, then looks at her.*

STEPHEN   Keep your head. Don't be drawn.

It's an act.

RUTH   Thank you.

STEPHEN *looks at them both, then goes.*

What is it?

JOHN	Lung cancer.
RUTH	You're guessing, right?

The phone goes.

RUTH *answers it.*

RUTH   Yes?

She listens.

Yes.

Yes.

Alright.

She hangs up.

More tea?

JOHN   No.

Beat.

They look at each other.

RUTH   So I had a kind of breakdown.

You didn't ask so I thought I should tell you, when he died, everything in my life changed as I suppose you would expect, I stopped work, I started just looking into the distance, blanking out. I thought he'd come through the door any second, and reveal it had all been a horrible mistake but no he was gone forever and I knew there had to be a reason. But you told them it was an accident.

JOHN   I'm not here to talk about Simon.

RUTH   This is about Simon of course it is, of *course* it is, don't you *dare* tell me that you would be out there if it wasn't for him! You're pretending, pretending you don't have a past and that it doesn't matter. But you can't run away from this. He was so much *better* than you – you talk about belief? He had real belief he had belief in people. What happened?

JOHN   Ruth –

RUTH   What happened that night John? – you ran away.

JOHN	I had to leave.

RUTH   You felt guilty.

JOHN   There was nothing here for me.

RUTH   You never even spoke to me about it.

JOHN   You want me to tell you.

RUTH   Yes of course.

A tiny beat.

JOHN   There was drink, there was smoking.

RUTH   He didn't smoke.

JOHN   He did.

RUTH   You gave them to him.

JOHN   That night yes, but he did smoke. There was drink, there was weed, we were out Ruth and that's what students do. We were standing on the stone bridge and he said he thought he should jump in. What would it be like?

RUTH   He wouldn't have done that, he wouldn't have suggested it. It was you. That's exactly the sort of thing you would say.

JOHN   No. It was his idea.

But I didn't stop him. I could've done. I could've stopped him, but I didn't you're right I thought it would be funny, so I stood back and watched and he was there on the bridge and he jumped in just like they do on May Day in the morning just like we've all seen lots of them do before, but it was dark and he hit something and there was a scream and I didn't see him after that.

You know what happened after that.

It happened in seconds. He was washed down the river.

RUTH   You've never said sorry.

JOHN   It wasn't my fault.

Beat.

RUTH   What are you doing?

         Beat.

JOHN   He would've stopped you.

RUTH   Don't be ridiculous. You don't know what he would've
         done.

JOHN   I'm not him. I'm nothing like him I agree, but he
         should've been here, he would've talked to you, you're
         right I don't know why it happened. I don't see a plan
         in it. But I imagine a universe right now where he's
         still alive. I imagine dying and finding that all this was
         a computer game, a fantasy, a projection and he's still
         there. I think, bearing in mind how little we know, that
         there are possibilities.

         But if he is gone forever, that means every young man
         in the Iranian army you kill is gone forever, that means
         every piece of collateral damage, every woman, every
         child, is gone forever. This has to stop. He would've
         told you that. This isn't just about *feeling* this is about
         the very nature of who we are, the kind of actions that
         make life worth living. What you're doing is empire,
         it's territory. I think you know you're making a
         mistake, and Simon would know it too.

         RUTH *tries to pour a glass of water but she can't –*

RUTH   You didn't see the baby, the child, you didn't see him
         grow, he never did *anything* like that until he met you!
         And now this – you come here? What will you do if I
         say yes? If I go to war, what will you tell the people
         out there?

JOHN   I will tell the country to stop work. I will ask them to
         think of the people of Iran, and bring peace and I will
         win, Ruth. But I want to go out there and say that you
         have listened, and we will not bomb Iran, we will
         instead put all our efforts together into a completely
         different approach. A new idea. Something that
         changes this country for good.

RUTH   You're threatening me.

JOHN   It can't happen.

They look at each other.

RUTH   What did he look like, the last time you saw him?

Please. I'm his mother.

This is what I... want. You were there.

You're here now.

So.

What was the last you saw of him?

Beat.

JOHN   He stood on the wall on the top of the bridge, and behind him was the night sky. He lifted his arms out to jump, and I then suddenly, I don't know if it was the Moon, or whatever but he was lit up, bright, then he fell, there was a noise, then silence.

RUTH   ...

JOHN   But in that last moment, before he jumped, he was happy.

RUTH *looks at him.*

The phone rings.

She picks it up.

RUTH   Yes?

She picks up her iPad. Looks at it.

Alright. Yes.

Thank you.

She hangs up. Puts the iPad down.

Alright.

You know what I believe in John? The grey area. The bit between. To any difficult problem, there is never a *right* solution, there is only ever the *best* solution. Nothing on Earth is completely pure. I prefer complexity, difficulty, balance. Good and evil? No. Children's words.

Beat.

So this decision, when it's made, it will not ever be completely right, or wrong, it will instead be a matter of judgement.

Beat.

I'm the most popular Conservative leader of this country for decades which you might say is hardly an achievement, but I'm going to try to explain something I think you never understood. Why would a nice person like me be a Tory? Why on earth am I not on the left, like a normal compassionate human being? Do I not care? Am I heartless? No. Of course we have to protect the poor, we have to make sure there's equal opportunity, we have to have compassion and *feeling* and *emotion* but it's not those things that have created everything you see around you. Every piece of clothing, every building, every technology, every free democratic principal and institution has been made possible and paid for not by taxes, in the end, but by the market. How did you get that crowd together. Facebook. Twitter. Profit-making companies. It's the most basic function of Western civilisation. You go out and you're free to make your way, and if you do well, you're rewarded. That's what makes us happy, and productive and it's my solution to a nasty world. Hard work, opportunity, and in the end, yes, self-interest, looking after your own.

The golden rule.

Look after your own first. Because if you don't do that you can't help anyone. And that's what I intend to do in this case. As the elected representative of this government, it is my first duty to protect the people of this country and allowing Iran to get nuclear weapons is totally unacceptable. I absolutely believe in progress, and that's what this will be, stopping generations of destruction, death and pain. This isn't about ideology, it's not about Islam or God or right or left, it's about complicated, impure *reality* and protecting the future. Simple as that. In five minutes, I'll call the President and say we're in. Tonight, we begin. And that's it.

JOHN   This doesn't make it better. Simon would still –

RUTH   Absolutely. He would disagree completely. But you're
          right. It isn't anything to do with Simon. This is me.
          Doing my job.

          Beat.

JOHN   You're going to make the call in five minutes.

RUTH   Five minutes yes.

JOHN   Then who was that on the phone?

RUTH   You're not going to start a general strike, you're not
          going to go out there and do anything. Look.

          RUTH *gives him the iPad. As he watches, we see*
          SARAH *onstage in an interrogation room.*

SARAH   I saw him first at the airport, then later, there he was,
          outside my house. Why was he outside my house? He
          said sometimes you have to listen to your instinct even
          when it doesn't seem right, when everyone is telling
          you the opposite. He knew what I was struggling with,
          and he said sometimes you have to do what you
          believe to be right. He told me to watch him speaking.
          He knew me. He could *see.*

          I did the right thing.

          John knows.

          I did what was right.

          RUTH *switches it off.*

RUTH   She killed her daughter with a knife. Cut her to shreds.
          Her husband works for the US Embassy and while
          there's absolutely no way legally that footage should
          be released to the public, he's very keen. He thinks
          people should know. So I have a feeling it will be out
          there in about twenty minutes.

JOHN   Ruth, if you believe in what you're doing you don't
          need to –

RUTH   I'm also going to tell my head of communications to
          circulate everything about Simon – our involvement, the
          fact you were there, the personal reason for this protest.
          It will all come out at five o'clock. To be involved in
          one death might be a mistake but to be involved in both
          is too much of a coincidence, even for you.

From outside there begins a faint singing. The crowd outside. Beautiful, choral.

She was eleven. Her name was Ruby. She liked reading and ballet.

JOHN   I had nothing to do with it.

RUTH   I think you make people do stupid things. I think you encourage them to take the brakes off, yes, I think you had something to do with my son's death and I think you had something to do with that little girl's death. You lecture me about compromise, well compromise is safe, compromise is discussion and *thought*. Compromise is experience and making the best possible decision, not the most *exciting*.

This country should have a manager. Look where our leaders took us in the past. It's not about glory and ideologies it's about finding the solution to our problem, and you don't need belief for that you need *graft*.

The singing's louder now. They hear it.

In twenty minutes your friends will find out. They'll see what she has to say and they'll all have the same thought.

They'll realise they've been conned.

And the singing will get quieter.

JOHN   They're stronger than that.

RUTH   The singing will get quieter.

And the singing will stop and become individual voices again. Half a million different opinions. They'll all go back, and get on with their lives.

I have to make a call.

Beat.

JOHN   A lot of people are going to die tonight.

RUTH   I know.

Beat.

JOHN   You had the dream too.

RUTH   What dream?

JOHN   The explosion. The monsters. Every night.

RUTH   Of course. It's all I've been thinking about. Of course I
              dreamt of things like that.

              We dream of things that don't exist all the time.

              A long pause. They look at each other.

              The singing stops.

              Eighteen minutes.

              Now. If you'll excuse me. I need to call the President.

              RUTH *goes, leaving* JOHN… *he turns… into…*

Nine

Five o'clock – dusk. Trafalgar Square. The sound of the crowd.
RACHEL, AMIR, SHANNON, ZIA, MARK *and* HOLLY *wait, fired
up. The singing changes back to chanting.*

'In Our Name! In Our Name!'

JOHN *is led on by two police officers – he looks around. The group
expect him to come to them, but instead he goes to where he made the
speech before.*

It's getting darker now. The crowd sounds fade as they see him.

He steps forward to the microphone.

JOHN   It's two minutes to five.

              He pauses.

              She listened to everything I had to say. But… she told
              me she's… The bombing will begin overnight.

              There's a silence. He checks his watch again.

              At five o'clock you're going to receive a message,
              linking you to a video, and some information. When
              you watch it, when you read what they have to say, it
              will make you angry. But before that happens, before
              you take out your phone and you see what's happened,
              remember how you feel right now because it's not the

object of belief that is important but belief itself. Don't
give up. Today we failed, yes, but there will always be
failure, and there is so much to do, the terror goes on,
the nightmares continue, and men and women and
children will die in Iran tonight...

...

This can happen again, because it's about you, not me,
it's all about your conviction and the numbers and the
passion and –

*It's dark by now. Big Ben chimes. As it does, everyone
onstage receives a message – in fact the entire crowd
receives a message. And we see them in unison take out
their smartphones.*

Ten

Thousands of lights illuminating thousands of faces in the dark.

Chaos, shouting, cars being set on fire, violence, rioting and flames.

Fade...

The sound of the cello... taking us into...

ACT FIVE

The cello plays – the twelve stand.

The music finishes and they open their eyes.

RACHEL, AMIR, SHANNON, ZIA, MARK, HOLLY, STEPHEN, RUTH, EDITH, ROB, MARTIN, SARAH.

RACHEL   We got a cab home. I don't know what happened to him.

HOLLY   I walked round the streets, my hood up cos otherwise –

SHANNON   I went home. Watched it on the TV. The Sky coverage was better cos they had more people out. The BBC was like a phone-in.

AMIR   They said Trafalgar Square was like a war zone. I thought bearing in mind what's happening tonight, that's an unfortunate way to put it.

RUTH   For me, that night was strangely quiet.

            Once the order was given, I was updated hour to hour, but the way it works – they just get on with it.

STEPHEN   In these final weeks of my life, as I face death, I've thought about whether I would have been prepared to die for others, in war? Would I have made that sacrifice? And the answer is yes, absolutely – to protect the country I love? My way of life? I'm certain. Death is not the worst thing.

EDITH   I don't know what's happening to me. Parts of who I am drifting away. I remember something happened recently, when I was outside, something in the ground but... You see the thing is I can't even practise the piano properly, because I can't remember what I've already learnt. I could just be playing the same tune over and over again. The world's a bitch. And that man...

MARK   I got a cab, couldn't face going back to my flat, so instead, weirdly I went *home*.

EDITH   Best to put an end to it. I've ordered the pills on the internet and it seems quite straightforward. I don't want anyone to worry.

RUTH   History will judge, that's what I'm saying, in interviews, again and again. But it won't. Was it worth the loss of life? Is the world better now?

EDITH   The strange thing is, I've believed in Heaven my whole life. But now I'm facing it, and with the dreams. Well

RUTH   I don't know.

EDITH   I'm not so sure.

          Beat.

ZIA   It took me two days to call her, I was scared cos she's not my usual type I mean I normally go for the pretty ones not that this girl isn't pretty but she doesn't get bored of me which is good she's interested so that's we do Stephen Hawking impressions together? So that's… I mean… Yeah.

HOLLY   He can't have gone up to Trafalgar, people would have seen him. The same if he'd gone towards Green Park, so he must've gone down Whitehall, but even then. Maybe he got a cab or something – I called the firms but – that night was –

MARK   I'm gutted any of it had anything to do with him, but yeah…

HOLLY   I'll keep looking.

MARK   Mum was surprised to see me –

HOLLY   I'll wait –

MARK   – she cleared out the old room, didn't ask too many questions, thank God, just told me about her garden. She's growing peas, apparently.

ZIA   Her name's Shannon.

SHANNON I'm starting this course. Zia's idea.

ZIA   (*Stephen Hawking impression.*) Shannon! Huh! – She's doing this course now.

SHANNON   Open University. Physics. It's good. And you get free pens.

Beat.

SARAH   Here, my life is simple.

I'm on my own, for protection, because all the others, they know what I did. It's simple. I wake, dress, pray, read…

MARTIN   I quit. Got myself off Twitter, cleared my Facebook account.

SARAH   Of course I think of her all the time.

MARTIN   Thing was, whenever the Prime Minister talked about the tactics, I saw this look on her face. I don't think she was ever… certain. I'm going to be a teacher. I want a small life. Don't think there's anything much anyone can do, except get through it.

AMIR   We both still wake in the night, facing each other.

RUTH   At night, I think of Simon, of course.

RACHEL   We've talked about a baby but –

RUTH   What would he say?

MARK   I found this old video of me as a kid. I've got this stick and I'm digging a hole in the back garden. Dad's filming it. But anyway I watched it and I thought how did he, this kid, smiling, mucking about with a stick… how did he… become… this…

AMIR   If we have a kid, he could have the dreams too.

MARK   What happened?

AMIR   And we wouldn't know. Cos, well, kids scream anyway.

SARAH   No. I don't sleep well. How could I?

RUTH   Sometimes at night, I pick up the phone and go to call someone.

SHANNON   It's on the news every night.

RUTH   I always hang up in the end. Go back to bed.

SHANNON   Every time I see it, the war, I think was there
something we could've done? Something better –

AMIR   It's different when you know people out there, who are
in the houses, with the lights out at night, hiding under
the table. I don't know what I was thinking.

SHANNON   And the dreams –

AMIR   It was wrong. Of course. Rachel's still out every day,
campaigning.

RACHEL   Problem is you start to think what it's all going to look
like, in twenty years? How does this ever stop? We
need something...

RUTH   I lie awake, scared of what I'll see when I close my
eyes. Dennis was right.

SHANNON   I think the dreams are something to do with –

RUTH   I do need someone. I do.

Beat.

ROB   I thought I'd know. And I thought he'd help. Cos I'd
worked out it was going to be important to know and
that's what got me listening to him in the first place. I
thought he'd help me especially with these fucking
dreams. I thought it was nerves. Going out there for the
first time. Made sense.

So I followed him on the TV. On the internet. The
protest. The speeches. The riot. And then...

Then obviously. Decision made. We were sent in. And.
It was. Well. What you saw.

And then pretty soon, we're in charge, security you
know, all lessons learned from Iraq, while they're
training the police force up, sorting out the interim
government and I'm on this road block, and I'll tell
you I've got this far and I haven't had to actually shoot
at anyone. Covering fire but not actually at, anyone,
and I'm on this road block and suddenly there's this
woman and she's coming towards me, and she's
wearing this massive fucking black thing, and her eyes
are – are – anyway I'm under orders to not let anyone
near this cos they might be you know suicide bombers

all that, so I shout to her stay back, and she's a good
way off but she's still coming towards me. She's
running now and I've got the gun up and I'm gesturing
and shouting, like get back but she's coming towards
me faster and faster and by now I can see her eyes, and
this is the moment yeah I thought this is what the
dreams are about and everything that he was saying.
Cos I'm looking at her eyes, in fact that's pretty much
all I can fucking see – her eyes, and I can't tell… and I
can't tell if her eyes are scared, and she's running
away, towards us, for help and she's good, maybe she's
a mother with children and these are just the eyes of a
loving woman. Or if no – they're angry and she's
running at us, to kill us and she's well trained and she's
fucking… evil. I… I don't know. But I've got to make
a decision *now* and the training is just fucking do it,
and I'm doing all what you're supposed to but in the
end we can't risk it so I open fire and shoot her across
the chest and one goes in her head and she's down,
quickly. Lots of blood.

You know what's… what I can't deal with?

I still don't know.

Turned out she didn't have a bomb. She did have a
knife, but they didn't know if that was self-defence, or
to do some proper damage.

So in the end we can't tell. If she was good, or evil.

Why she was running.

And that was it. That's what I wanted to know. From
him.

I'm ready to fight. To protect the people I love. My
way of life.

But I needed to know what the enemy looked like.

But… now he's gone.

And he's just…

Left us all to – work it out for ourselves.

End.

MEDEA

after Euripides

This version of *Medea* was first co-produced by Headlong, Glasgow Citizens Theatre and Watford Palace Theatre, in association with Warwick Arts Centre, at the Citizens Theatre, Glasgow, on 27 September 2012, before touring. The cast was as follows:

WORKMAN	Paul Brendan
SARAH	Lu Corfield
CARTER	Christopher Ettridge
JASON	Adam Levy
PAM	Amelia Lowdell
ANDREW	Paul Shelley
MEDEA	Rachael Stirling

The character of TOM *was performed by local boys at each touring venue.*

Director	Mike Bartlett
Designer	Ruari Murchison
Lighting Designer	Johanna Town
Composer and Sound Designer	Tom Mills

Characters

MEDEA
PAM
SARAH
WORKMAN
CARTER
JASON
ANDREW
TOM (*non-speaking*)

Note on the Text

(/) means the next speech begins at that point.

(–) means the next line interrupts.

(…) at the end of a speech means it trails off. On its own it indicates a pressure, expectation or desire to speak.

A line with no full stop at the end indicates that the next speech follows on immediately.

A speech with no written dialogue indicates a character deliberately remaining silent.

ACT ONE

Scene One

The afternoon. A street on a new-build estate. Medea's house –
number 36. Her house is a reasonable four-bed. White door, double
glazing. Built around 1996. The curtains are drawn.

A lazy autumn day. Weak sunlight. A window is opened on the house
on the left.

A WORKMAN *is building a wall.*

A small tinny radio plays a song in the current top five.

PAM *arrives, speaking on the phone, using a Bluetooth headset. She*
finishes her phone conversation outside the front of the house.

PAM   Yeah I never really liked the name Jason, it's always
             made me think of Jason Donovan or that one from
             Take That. *Bearded*, yeah. What?

             No I know he hasn't actually got a beard but it's the
             same *feeling* you know, you knew I was at school with
             him?

             Yeah well I was, so I feel torn cos obviously recently
             I've been closer to her.

             Yeah I come and see her every week, that's what I'm
             saying, that's where I am now. She gave me a key.

             Least I can do.

             What?

             The radio's distracting her. She looks round accusingly.

             No not good, no, she doesn't go out, she keeps the
             curtains closed. It's the wedding tomorrow so maybe
             once that's out the way. Look I'm here so –

             Her name, is Kate, I don't know where he met her,
             she's the daughter of their landlord so maybe it was –

             Twenty-one.

Yeah, and it's just – embarrassing, that it's someone like that, that he runs off with, you know, it's embarrassing that he left her for a girl like that. And she doesn't really trust anyone, only me I think, I suppose it's different, we've all got old friends haven't we, we've all lived here for ages but she –

She reaches into her pocket, pulls out a key.

I better go in, I'm here now.

Yeah. Yeah I will, if she asks.

Yeah I will. Bye.

Bye.

PAM opens the front door and goes inside. As she does – there's the sound of scraping from inside.

As the door closes, the WORKMAN watches her. He switches the radio back on as –

TOM enters – he walks across and looks at the WORKMAN.

WORKMAN Hello.

TOM moves closer to the wall, interested.

A moment.

SARAH enters, finding the key to MEDEA's house.

SARAH   Come on Tom. Tom! Don't bother the man, he's busy.

TOM glances at the WORKMAN then turns and takes SARAH's hand, as together they go inside MEDEA's house.

As they do – a scraping sound.

Scene Two

The front room.

The door opens into an open-plan hall, front room. It's perfectly furnished in high-end Ikea/Habitat furniture and fittings. A single lamp on. There's cornflakes scattered all over the surface – the box turned on its side.

PAM *is filling up the kettle.*

PAM   Oh – hello.

SARAH   Hi.

           Upstairs, we hear footsteps. A kind of prowling.

           You must be –

PAM   I'm Pam.

SARAH   Right. Yes.

           A scraping of a piece of furniture across the floor.
           SARAH *looks up.*

           PAM *puts the kettle on.*

PAM   I just stopped in to see how she was.

SARAH   That's nice of you.

PAM   Hello Tom! How are you?

           TOM *just stares at her.*

           How was school?

           He pulls out a games console, jumps on to the sofa and starts playing it.

           Okay.

           You must be Susan.

SARAH   Sarah.

PAM   Sarah, she mentioned you, described you –

SARAH   Described me?

PAM   You live next door?

SARAH	Next door that's right –
PAM	That way? Because I *love* that house.
SARAH	That way.
PAM	Oh. Well that's a nice house too.
SARAH	They're all the same.
PAM	Built the same yes –
SARAH	Exactly identical.
PAM	Built identical that's right but it's amazing what people *do* with them. Isn't it?
SARAH	What do you mean?
PAM	I mean the one that way, the other way from yours, they've got ivy on the front. A little path. Now they're building a wall, I suppose what I mean is you can tell whoever lives in that house, they've got taste.
SARAH	They've got money.
PAM	Not a huge amount or they wouldn't be living here.
SARAH	I don't like it.
PAM	Do you not Susan?
SARAH	Sarah.
PAM	You don't like that house then Sarah?
SARAH	No.
	No I don't.
	A scratching from upstairs, they both look up.
PAM	But anyway, you're helping her out, that's kind.
SARAH	I see Tom home from school every afternoon while she's –
PAM	Every afternoon?
SARAH	Just while she's –
PAM	Right.
SARAH	Yeah.

PAM	You take time off work then?
SARAH	I only work mornings so –
PAM	Just mornings. You're part-time?
SARAH	Job share.
PAM	I'd love to be able just to work mornings.
SARAH	Well I'm very lucky.
PAM	Yes.
SARAH	You're not at work now?
PAM	As her colleague they didn't mind if I leave a little early to pay her a visit, it's a compassionate company they care about their employees, they don't mind at all if I stop by sometimes.
SARAH	You've spoken to her then?
PAM	What?
SARAH	You said she described me to you.
PAM	A couple of days ago yes.
SARAH	I haven't seen her in weeks.
PAM	We often catch up – you haven't seen her?
SARAH	Whenever I come in she's upstairs.
PAM	Really? Whenever you come in.

Well.

Beat.

SARAH	When she described me, what did she say?
PAM	I'm sorry?
SARAH	When she described me – you said she described me?
PAM	Just… what you looked like –
SARAH	Which was?
PAM	She mentioned your hair.
SARAH	What?

PAM   That it was... brown. Nice...

SARAH   Anything else?

PAM   She used the word spiky.

SARAH   My hair's not –

PAM   That wasn't about your hair.

SARAH   Oh. Right.

PAM   Yeah.

SARAH   Well.

PAM   She said you took offence easily.

SARAH   What did she mean by that?

PAM   She didn't mean it in a bad way I'm sure.

SARAH   She's not herself I know but I don't think I'm –

PAM   She's in a state at the moment and it's up to us, if we
             can, if at all possible, to suck it up and not complain
             and just be there for her after everything that's
             happened.

SARAH   I know that.

PAM   She needs support.

SARAH   Exactly, that's why I pick up Tom.

PAM   I'm sure you understand that when she says these
             things about you, it's just transferring her anger.

SARAH   These things? What else?

PAM   Hmm?

SARAH   What else does she say about me?

PAM   Oh it doesn't matter.

SARAH   What?

PAM   Just... ridiculous –

SARAH   What?

PAM   I mean you're not *short*, look at you, that's the sort of
             thing I mean she called you *short* but you're really not.

SARAH   You're a friend from work.

PAM   Old friend yes, I've known Jason since school, then
        ended up working with Medea, so we've seen a lot of
        each other over the years.

SARAH   Good friend.

PAM   We've become good friends, yes, yes we have,
        particularly in recent weeks.

SARAH   She said she didn't have anyone.

PAM   I'm sorry?

        A scratching from upstairs.

SARAH   When I offered to take Tom to school and pick him up
        she said that would be good because none of the
        friends she thought she had from years ago or from
        work, none of them were real friends and she didn't
        have anyone she could trust.

PAM   Oh.

SARAH   But as you say –

PAM   I mean I work hard all day so –

SARAH   She says these things.

PAM   Maybe I'm not around as much as I'd like to be –

SARAH   I'm sure she doesn't mean it.

        Just transferring her anger.

        The most important thing is that we understand.

PAM   …

SARAH

        SARAH *smiles.*

        So how did she look? When you saw her. When I drop
        Tom off I call for her but I never get an answer. I mean
        I can hear she's up there but…

        Then Tom runs off to play, so I don't…

        I don't…

I just slip out, mostly.

I don't want to intrude.

I don't like the name Jason, it makes me think of hair gel.

This girl he's gone off with, she's only nineteen.

PAM   Twenty-one.

SARAH   I heard she was nineteen.

PAM   Twenty-one I believe.

SARAH   Well that's bad enough anyway isn't it? I mean whether it's twenty-one or nineteen.

PAM   It's twenty-one –

SARAH   – doesn't make much difference she's still young, still a child in many ways –

PAM   Not really –

SARAH   – in the ways that matter, I mean she's pretty of course she is, you can see why he's attracted to her, she's a good-looking young woman, but why she'd go for him I don't know. Surely she could find someone her own age?

PAM   She doesn't want someone her own age. Boys are boys. She likes the power of a man I expect. When I was twenty-one there was a bloke, took me out in his Saab.

             I'm going to the wedding.

             Got a invite so.

SARAH   You –

PAM   I haven't told her. No need.

             Beat.

SARAH   She's got good legs.

PAM   Medea?

SARAH   This girl.

PAM   Kate. That's her name – the new girl –

SARAH   She's in the paper today, won some dancing thing –
wearing her costume like on *Strictly* and you could see
she's got really good legs.

Three loud bangs.

I'm never sure about leaving her with...

She means TOM.

I'm never sure about leaving them on their own.

PAM   What do you mean?

SARAH

PAM   He fends for himself. There's pizzas in the freezer, he's
got his games, and he does his homework, he's all
right.

SARAH   I don't know.

PAM   She still loves him, still cuddles him I think –

SARAH   Yes but he seems different.

PAM   They're very close –

SARAH   He never...

PAM   Tom?

Tom?

Your mum still cuddles you doesn't she?

TOM *gets up and goes upstairs. We hear the door
slam.*

SARAH   Does he still visit? Jason. Does he come and see his son?

PAM   I don't think so.

*A smash from upstairs – then music plays – we mainly
hear the bass frequencies. And there's a banging
movement. Somehow backwards and forward.*

SARAH   What's that?

PAM   She rolls around in bed. I don't think she's doing
herself too much damage but there's this expensive
wallpaper she's scratching off the walls. I caught a
glimpse last time I was here. And the music – I hate

this music normally but it seems to calm her down. Music means more when you're in trouble doesn't it?

The noise.

I'd call the hospital but they might take him away –

SARAH The hospital? You think she's –

PAM They might put her in somewhere and I don't want that on my...

SARAH But if you really think she's got to that point –

PAM I don't want anyone blaming me.

Maybe we should just leave them for the night.

Let her calm down.

I don't mind if you want to leave me to it.

I don't mind Susan.

SARAH Sarah.

PAM I don't mind if you want to leave me to it.

Not being funny but.

Perhaps she's waiting till you've gone?

The noise continues.

SARAH Medea?

The banging stops.

Medea?

SARAH *ventures closer to the stairs.*

It's Sarah.

I'm going to come up and see how you are. Yes?

The door opens upstairs and the music is suddenly louder.

All right?

I'm coming upstairs.

The music stops. This makes SARAH *wait, halfway up the stairs. A moment, then the door upstairs closes.*

SARAH *backs off, and down the stairs comes*
MEDEA. *She's in her thirties, pale, but much more
normal-looking than we might have expected. She's
obviously been crying, but has somehow pulled herself
together very quickly.*

MEDEA   Sarah. Pam. Thanks for bringing Tom back has he gone
up to his room already? It's that game, he sits in his
bed and plays it all night, I don't know what it is I can
only hear the noises, it's all guns and girls I think,
shooting, violence, but that's what boys like isn't it?
Always has been. Do either of you want a cup of tea? I
was going to make one.

Yes? Tea?

PAM   I put the kettle on.

MEDEA   You put the kettle on?

PAM   Yes.

MEDEA   Why?

PAM   I tried to call. I thought you might want tea so I…

MEDEA *goes into the kitchen area and puts the kettle
on again.*

MEDEA   I expect they're all saying things, I keep the curtains
shut because a few days ago, I was in here, sat there,
and I wasn't very happy, I mean you wouldn't expect
me to be would you? I was watching a film, one of
those Richard Curtis ones, and it got to the bit where –
it was *Four Weddings* and it got to the bit where he
reads the poem out well it's the funeral, clearly, and I
was crying – I'm a bit emotional at the moment and
anyway I looked up and across the road this woman is
just openly staring at me, through the window. And I
know her. It's Teresa, used to work with me, you
remember her. Pam? You remember her? Do you?

PAM   Teresa?

MEDEA   Yeah. Blonde.

PAM   Blonde?

MEDEA   Big hands.

PAM   Oh. Tall.

MEDEA   Tall with big hands that's it –

PAM   Thought she moved to Croatia?

MEDEA   But anyway, she hasn't come to the door to see me,
           she's just looking in the window, she doesn't even live
           round here, don't know what she's – anyway so I
           closed the curtains, and never opened them again, it's
           the only thing about this house, it looks right on to the
           street not so good when you're having a breakdown.
           Milk Pam isn't it?

PAM   You're not having a breakdown.

MEDEA   Milk?

PAM   You're getting better, slowly but surely.

MEDEA   Pam do you want some fucking milk or not?

PAM   Yes please.

MEDEA   Sarah?

SARAH   Thank you Medea yes please.

MEDEA   And no sugar for either of you.

PAM   No.

SARAH   No sugar that's right.

MEDEA   Yeah so I expect you've all been saying I'm mad. I
           expect you're chatting, saying I've gone mental. But
           what am I supposed to do? If I went back to work and
           just got on with things, you'd say I wasn't dealing with
           it properly, if I stay in, you think I'm a recluse. Men
           don't have this problem they can do what they want
           but women, *women* – whatever we do it's irrational.
           Emotional. Boo hoo.

SARAH   No one's talking about you actually Medea we all
           just –

MEDEA   And the fact I'm not from round here, that doesn't
           help, I know you thought I never played my part in the
           community, but I tried. Even though I was working
           long hours, and didn't have much support from Jason, I
           did my best, but even so you saw me as an outsider,

because you lot when you were kids you went to
school together didn't you? Or Guides or tennis club or
something you know something like that you all went
to *parties* and *got off*, you all know each other from
forever ago. There. Tea. Help yourself.

*She drops the mugs of tea heavily on the counter in
front of the women. They take them.*

SARAH   Actually we've only just met –

MEDEA   You're not better than me. None of you.

SARAH   We don't think we –

MEDEA   I don't judge you, I honestly don't.

SARAH   Of course you don't judge –

MEDEA   But you've always thought I was stuck-up, the way
those mothers stared at me when I brought that buggy
into playgroup.

SARAH   That must've been years ago –

MEDEA   Or the dress I wore to the Christmas party, you
remember, Jacqui didn't just stare like you did, after
enough gin she said it up front, told me no one liked
me cos I was a 'posh bitch wearing a fuck-me dress'.

PAM   Jacqui's difficult.

MEDEA   I could've torn her face off right there and then –
Anyway, bearing in mind all that and what's happened,
why should I give a shit about anything any more? Bet
they're all loving it, what happened to me. She's in the
paper, that girl. Did you see?

Hello – *question*. Did you see?

PAM   Sarah did.

SARAH   Yes I did.

MEDEA   Her hair. Teeth. Her fucking… sequins.

So why should I bother with any of it any more?

It's shit being a woman. Sorry but it is.

*She cleans the surface in the kitchen, occasionally
stopping to drink tea.*

I'm supposed to rise above it. I know. Be strong. A
modern woman. Hey sister go sister all the single
fucking ladies – I know that's what I'm supposed to be
but –

*She gives up and drops the cloth and the detergent on
the ground.*

I'd rather be a man. Any man. I'd rather be a man in
the worst possible situation, a man who gets sent to
war, is shot at, and starved and raped and maimed, than
be a woman. I know I'm not supposed to say that – it's
probably offensive but fuck it. How's the tea?

SARAH   Good.

PAM   Perfect.

SARAH   You make a fantastic cup of tea.

MEDEA   Yeah I do I know I do.

PAM   Medea, you need to get outside a bit, some fresh air
           would do you good –

MEDEA   I'd be good in a war. They should put me in one right
           now. The way I feel at this moment, put me on a
           battlefield and I'd massacre the lot of them. Shred
           them to pieces with my nails and teeth like some kind
           of carnivore.

SARAH   Medea –

           MEDEA *growls at them. They look worried, then she
           laughs.*

MEDEA   I can say stuff like that I can say what I like, if you
           don't like it, you can go.

           Actually yes, do, can you go please I've had enough.
           Sorry. But. Sorry.

PAM   Medea we're here to help you.

MEDEA   No come on. Tea's over. I'll show you out. I'll even do
           that. Come on.

           Beat.

PAM   All right.

PAM *and* SARAH *leave the house.* MEDEA *follows them and stands on the doorstep.*

MEDEA   Thanks for stopping by.

PAM   Not a problem, I'll see you next week.

MEDEA   All right. Bye then –

SARAH   Medea.

MEDEA   …

SARAH   I understand.

MEDEA   What?

SARAH   If what happened to you had happened to me. I'd feel exactly the same.

MEDEA   Right.

SARAH   Yeah.

          MEDEA *sees* CARTER *approaching.*

MEDEA   Oh – oh no.

SARAH   What?

Scene Three

CARTER *enters. He is a man in his fifties.*

MEDEA   You can't come in Nick go away go on piss off leave me alone.

CARTER   It's my house.

MEDEA   My home.

CARTER   Not any more.

MEDEA   For *years*.

CARTER   No, not according to anyone except you.

          Anyway I don't want to come in, I dread to think what you're getting up to in there. Are you all right?

MEDEA	What?
CARTER	Your eyes.
MEDEA	I don't know what you mean.
CARTER	Your skin. You should call someone.
PAM	There's nothing wrong –
CARTER	I'm serious, red skin like that doesn't mean good things you're drinking too much probably blotches like that.
SARAH	Make sense if she was.
CARTER	Are you her friends?
PAM	Technically a colleague but recently –
CARTER	You should look after her.
SARAH	Sorry who are you?
CARTER	Take her out for a walk sometimes.
PAM	Nick Carter, he owns the house.
SARAH	Oh.
MEDEA	What do you want?

Beat.

CARTER	Okay. I don't like this situation of course I don't, but it is what it is and we have to move on now, all right? As you well know, you're supposed to be out.
MEDEA	I am, look, I'm out, outside for a change. Fresh air. Hmm. See? This is progress.
CARTER	I served fair notice, you had the letter the man gave it to you, you signed for it. I know you've read it, the tenancy expired a month ago and has not been renewed.
SARAH	You can't just kick her out.
CARTER	No. You're absolutely right whoever you are –
SARAH	I live next door –
CARTER	I can't *just* do anything, she's got to have a substantial period of notice to find somewhere else and I've given her that, and more. She's had two months before the

expiration, it's another month since that date passed
and yet she's still here. All the paperwork's in Jason's
name anyway. I could send round the police, and I will,
if I have to, but I thought I'd come and... speak to you
myself. Give you a chance to avoid all that.

You need to go. I've had enough. It was rented
furnished so most of it's mine anyway, it's just a case
of packing a bag. Either you leave right now, or I'll
have you evicted.

MEDEA   Right now?

CARTER   Yes.

Pause.

MEDEA   I've lived here ten years.

CARTER   Things have changed.

MEDEA   My home.

CARTER   I arranged the lease on this house with Jason. And now
he's with Kate, and we... we want it back so you need
to go.

MEDEA   They're not going to move in here?

CARTER   Well probably not, no but –

MEDEA   Don't think your daughter would want that.

CARTER   No you're right she wouldn't but that's not the point,
it's the principle, yes? It's nothing against you
personally – I don't understand what the problem is,
there's nothing special about this place, they're all the
same, all the houses, identical.

PAM   It depends what you do with them.

MEDEA   Right – the floor, the kitchen, the door handles, he says
he helped choose everything and that's true he helped
me, he helped *me*, it was my decisions in the end, not
his, my home, I've lived longer here than anywhere
before he's throwing his own son out –

CARTER   I'm surprised you don't want to leave.

MEDEA

CARTER

MEDEA   I like it.

CARTER   This isn't Jason's decision it's mine. Pack a bag, I'll
           come back in an hour and you'll be gone.

MEDEA   Why?

CARTER   What?

MEDEA   You've got other houses in town, better ones, I'm
           managing the rent just about, Jason and your daughter
           they'll get a much better house than this, if you've got
           anything to do with it, we could both live in our
           different houses, so why make me go?

CARTER   Because...

           Pause.

           Because you scare the shit out of me.

           And my daughter. You shouted at her in the street.

MEDEA

PAM   Shouted?

CARTER   This must've been when you were still venturing
           outside. It was a few weeks ago when Kate was with
           her friends. She told me, and she's a strong person and
           very responsible adult but also, she's *sensitive*.

PAM   What did you say?

CARTER   She's become frightened to go out, by herself, because
           of you. The threats you made.

MEDEA   I was angry.

PAM   What? What did she say?

CARTER   You don't want to know.

PAM   Okay but I do.

SARAH   Maybe it's none of our business.

PAM   Oh come on – What happened? Medea, we're friends –

MEDEA   It doesn't matter.

           Beat.

CARTER   The sad thing is you're educated, driven, exactly the
          sort of woman I'd employ, and would do well. You
          used to have a job, a good job, you're better than most
          people in this town, you run rings round all of them.

MEDEA   That's why I'm a threat.

CARTER   Exactly. And that's the reason I don't want you just out
          of this house, I want you a long way away. What about
          your parents? They'd take you in, surely.

MEDEA   My parents are dead.

CARTER   Or wherever it is you come from.

          Friends? No?

          Some distant family?

          You've really got no one?

MEDEA   Intelligent yes, exactly, that's the problem. No one
          likes clever women. Men feel threatened and other
          women get bitchy. Most women *hate* clever women.
          Worst thing I ever did was getting smart.

          Pam hates it.

PAM   What?

MEDEA   That I'm clever. Never liked it, and it's not jealousy,
          it's the same as you. It's that she simply doesn't trust
          clever women, underneath she's sure they're always up
          to something.

          That's what you think isn't it?

PAM   No. What?

MEDEA   That I'm always saying one thing, thinking another.

CARTER   Well are you?

MEDEA   Maybe. Don't know. Maybe. See?

SARAH   I don't mind clever women.

MEDEA   You? You don't even notice.

SARAH   …

MEDEA   But you should trust me Mr Nicholas *Nicholas* Carter,
          because you're a sporting man, you're all in favour of

'fair play', you didn't want this to happen, it's true, you're absolutely right, you've given me time to leave and I ignored it completely. I don't hold anything against you it's Jason I want to murder in a brutal and horrific way. I know you're just trying to do the right thing.

CARTER   Exactly.

MEDEA   I'm not going to do anything to you I stay in the house mostly these days I like it better inside so don't be frightened.

CARTER   What about Kate?

MEDEA   What?

CARTER   What you said. Her liver.

PAM   Her *liver*?

Beat.

MEDEA   I'm sorry. It was stupid.

He looks at her.

CARTER   I can't trust you. Especially now you've calmed down. When you were angry I knew you meant what you said. But like this...

He's trying to work her out.

She smiles.

Laughs.

No. You have to go. I'm sorry.

MEDEA   Give me a day.

CARTER   You've had three months.

MEDEA   One day more, then I'll be gone.

PAM   There's a room at mine you could have for a night if –

SARAH   No, Medea, you've got rights he can't just –

CARTER   One day? No. Tomorrow's their wedding.

MEDEA   I'm not invited.

CARTER   Of course you're not, the point is I wanted you gone long before it happens.

It's going to be a special day.

MEDEA *suddenly starts laughing. They look at her.*

MEDEA   Sorry – it's just the idea of those two?... did he ask your permission?

CARTER   Yes.

MEDEA   And you agreed?

CARTER   …

MEDEA   Why?

CARTER   She loves him.

MEDEA   I'm sure she does.

CARTER   Yeah.

Beat.

MEDEA   Tom's going to the wedding, Jason wanted that, so we can't leave until afterwards, but I promise while he's there, I'll pack our things and in the afternoon when it's all over, we'll go, both of us, for good, we'll go a long way away.

I just need to find a place. Make sure we've got a roof over our heads at least... so... just give me a day.

I'm sorry.

I'm serious.

This is me. Actually begging you.

A moment.

CARTER   If you're still here tomorrow evening, I'm calling the police.

He goes.

A moment.

MEDEA *goes to the front wall, sits, takes out a packet of cigarettes, and lights one.*

Smokes. The WORKMAN *stops and leans over.*

WORKMAN Excuse me...

She gives him a cigarette.

He pulls out a lighter. Lights it.

They share a smile.

That bloke?

MEDEA   What about him?

WORKMAN Wanker.

MEDEA   Yep.

MEDEA *smiles. The* WORKMAN *leans against his wall.* SARAH *and* PAM *aren't sure what to do.*

They come and stand near her.

PAM   Medea...

MEDEA   I'm a witch.

SARAH   What?

MEDEA   I make bad things happen. If I want to.

SARAH   Are you serious? A witch?

MEDEA   I've got a hat somewhere.

PAM   Look –

MEDEA   All right I haven't got a hat, but I'm telling you I can sit here and wish it and before long Jason will mysteriously trip coming down the stairs in his new house and fall on the Dyson and impale himself, or the two of them will be driving to some bar he's taking her to, some young place he thinks is good and the car will strangely slip on some out-of-season black ice straight into the path of a large lorry which will send pieces of metal through both of them, cutting her throat killing her instantly but piercing the side of his head just enough that he has brain damage and lives the rest of his life as a vegetable. Or maybe he'll light one of his fucking cigars in the garden and accidentally set fire to his shirt like a twat which will burn him alive and keep on burning no matter what anyone puts on to it, you see the thing is I'm magic and I can make these things happen and the world's only given me evil lately so I'm just giving it some proper evil back. I'm not just bitter, I'm twisted and I'm magic, and I don't need a hat, because I've got it in my bones.

They're going to die in some way horrible. Both of them. I can feel it.

PAM   What?

MEDEA

PAM   He's right I don't know when you're serious. What plan?

MEDEA

PAM   I should get home. Will you be all right?

            MEDEA *finishes her cigarette.*

MEDEA   Yeah. Busy now. I've got packing to do.

            A moment.

PAM   All right. Well... If you need somewhere to stay. For a night.

            Call me. Yeah?

            Bye.

            PAM *walks off.*

SARAH   Medea.

            If you want to talk, just come round, knock on the door.

            I'm sure we can sort it out.

            Just come round.

            SARAH *goes into the house next door.* MEDEA *stubs her cigarette out on the ground.*

            The WORKMAN *starts humming.*

            MEDEA *looks at him, then goes inside the house and shuts the door.*

            The WORKMAN *puts on the radio which perfectly matches his humming – 'Aladdin Sane' by David Bowie.*

Scene Four

Inside in the open-plan kitchen/living room, MEDEA *is making dinner, badly. The radio on.*

TOM *sits at the small table, waiting, watching.*

MEDEA *takes out four fish fingers from a frozen bag and puts them under the grill, on full heat.*

Then she chops up carrots carelessly, and throws them into a pot of boiling water.

Slowly smoke starts pouring out of her grill. Ignoring it, she takes peas out of the fridges, rips them open, peas go everywhere. She puts them in the boiling water.

The grill is by now really smoking.

She puts two plates on the table, one for her and one for TOM.

She takes the grill pan out. The fish fingers are charcoal, and smoking.

She takes it to the table, using a fork she puts two on TOM*'s plate and two on hers, then drops the grill on the floor.*

Goes back to the pan, takes it off the heat, brings it over to the table.

Then puts her hand into the boiling water and pulls out carrots and peas and puts them on the plate. Her hand becomes raw with the heat.

TOM *just watches her.*

She tries to get every pea and carrot out of the water.

Eventually she gives up and puts the pan on the side.

Then adjusts the lighting to a lamp, and sits with TOM.

Smiles.

TOM *doesn't.*

Outside the sun sets.

ACT TWO

Scene One

Outside the house. 9 p.m. It's dark. A fluorescent street light is on.
Television plays in the front room. Lights on in windows.

JASON *arrives and watches. He's in a suit. He waits.*

MEDEA *emerges, from the house, closing the door behind her.*

JASON   You knew I was here.

MEDEA   I could smell you.

JASON   I'm told you got angry today –

MEDEA   Not unusual.

JASON   – when Nick came round.

MEDEA   Yeah it was something to do with you, if only I could
            remember –

JASON   Sarcasm. Okay.

MEDEA   – did we used to be married?

JASON   You probably could've stayed living here, no one
            would've minded. It was just because of what you said
            to Kate that day in the street, I'm still not even sure
            what it was, no one wants to tell me but she was
            terrified, and after that her dad wanted you gone for
            good. What happened? You didn't need to say
            anything.

MEDEA   I didn't want to say anything.

JASON   Right –

MEDEA   I would have preferred to remain silent I really
            would –

JASON   Then why didn't you?

MEDEA   Because it was that or smashing her head through a
            shop window.

I don't think you understand the extent of my feelings Jason, what happens to me when I have to see her or even think about her.

When she was there across the road I didn't have much choice over what happened and all things considered I think it was the best outcome I think I did all right.

They look at each other.

What do you want?

JASON   I'll pay you, something, every month. After you've gone. I'll still do that. I wanted you to know. For both of you.

MEDEA   I don't need it.

JASON   Yes.

MEDEA   I'll work.

JASON   Not at the moment look at you.

MEDEA   What's that, fifteen seconds before it *starts* – 'look at me' *what*?

JASON   I'm not starting that was *concern*.

MEDEA   Ha!

JASON   I'm saying you don't look well.

MEDEA   I'm fine.

JASON   No.

MEDEA   Actually I'm fine.

JASON   Who's looking after you?

MEDEA   *Friends.* I'm really good, yoga, this fitness video, I might not leave the house but I've got everything I need in there, *Wii Sports* on the Nintendo, I'm better than ever, telling you.

JASON   What happened to your hand?

She covers it.

Let me have a look.

MEDEA   Get off. I realised a couple of days ago I've run out of things to call you, I've been through everything, vomit,

shit, twat, puss-filled dark hole sordid fucking wank
stain man –

JASON   Okay –

MEDEA   I mean literally every word, every combination, I made
a project of it, wrote them down.

JASON   Very good.

MEDEA   You think it's clever, you think it's *on*, to fuck me over
like that, to walk out on your son, to rip us up and then
come back to *visit*. You're not seeing him, Tom, if
that's why you're here –

JASON   No I'm not here to see him –

MEDEA   – and actually yeah I've changed my mind, he's not
coming to the wedding tomorrow you can do it without
him.

JASON   I'm here to see you.

MEDEA   Why?

JASON

MEDEA   I saved your life, in that sea, when you were drowning,
I swam out, you were going to die, you had seaweed,
in your lungs, and I dragged you to the shore, pulled
the weed out, and breathed life back into you. If it
hadn't been for me you'd have been dead in a Cretan
sea years ago.

JASON   Well not really –

MEDEA   I wish I'd left you. I wish I'd pretended but actually
swum out and laughed as you choked in the water. I'm
vindictive like that sometimes as you know, as you've
pointed out quite often. Anyway after I save your life,
and you recover, and it bonds us together, we have a
relationship, I give you a son, move here where you
want me to, with all your friends, this little town, not a
place I thought I'd end up –

JASON   Beneath you is it?

MEDEA   Yes, a bit, a bit, yes, but I wanted to be happy so I
moved here for you, I go part-time, I do everything
you want and what do I get back?

JASON   That's not how it works.

MEDEA   Apparently it is.

JASON   It's not a deal.

MEDEA   It's a contract, it's called a marriage *contract* Jason you made promises you broke.

JASON   It was all me?

MEDEA   We've talked about this.

JASON   You had nothing to do with it?

MEDEA   Only that I'm bright and educated and I speak my mind. And I got old.

JASON   You completely lost respect for me.

MEDEA   For good reason seeing as all you wanted was some little girl who'd be pretty and shut up.

JASON   You gave up on me long before that and anyway I didn't mean to find Kate but she had an appeal because she doesn't ignore me, she's interested in what I have to say –

MEDEA   Ooohhhh –

JASON   She doesn't turn up at my work *shouting* –

MEDEA   Yeah arrghh the sound of your voice even that tone, it makes my teeth go inside out, I can't even hear the sound, let alone the words.

JASON   That's exactly why I left, things like that, what are you talking about? *Your teeth?*

MEDEA   Oh – Getting angry, you want to pick up something and throw it? I could go and get that plate, the same one, I got the pieces and glued it back together I don't know why but I spent two hours with some superglue –

JASON   I'm sorry how it happened, I'm not proud, but actually it's better, better it's all out –

MEDEA   What about your son?

JASON   He'll be all right.

MEDEA   You think?

JASON   A lot of parents separate now, my parents split up when
         I was his age, it's not ideal but it won't cause any
         lasting damage –

MEDEA   He's not saying a huge amount I don't know if you've
         noticed.

JASON   He'll grow out of that it's just –

MEDEA   You don't want him.

JASON   Don't *want* him, *of course* I want him –

MEDEA   You don't know him, not like I do, he came out of me,
         he *is* me, I *am* him, you feel you should be interested
         but if you never saw him again you wouldn't mind that
         much, you'd probably forget –

JASON   I'll just wait till you're done – *of course I'd mind* –

MEDEA   you're happy to give him up give us both up for a
         younger tighter fuck –

JASON   Nice.

MEDEA   Sorry but let's call it what it is – shouldn't there be
         something to strike you down, a moral force, you
         should be put in prison, there should be social
         exclusion, disapproval at least, but everyone just says
         it's a shame but that it happens all the time.

JASON   Well it does.

MEDEA   Your mate Steve, he came to get your bike from the
         garage, spoke to me, we had a bit of a thing –

JASON   A thing?

MEDEA   Not a sex thing – god no –

JASON   No?

MEDEA   This is *Steve* – no we had a shouting thing and when he
         got going he seemed proud of you, said you'd done all
         right with the new one.

JASON   I'm sorry about that.

MEDEA   *Upgraded.*

         Beat.

JASON   That's what he said?

MEDEA   Yeah.

          Beat.

JASON   Steve's an idiot.

MEDEA   He's a dick.

JASON   Yeah a dick completely yes he is.

          He shouldn't have said anything like that.

          Beat.

          But look –

          Not that it's the point but actually it does happen all the time. Sometimes relationships stop working.

MEDEA   How grown up of you to help me through this Jason, how adult of you to be so mature in this difficult time.

JASON   No problem, that was often my role as I seem to remember.

MEDEA   No don't do that, you liked me being mad, you thrived on me being unpredictable, you used to say every day was different with me that it made you feel alive.

JASON   Yeah well that was true at the time.

MEDEA   Get that with the new one do you, she does a similar thing.

JASON   No.

MEDEA   This hand. You used to hold it. And my legs. You liked my legs.

JASON   Yeah I did. Good legs.

          They look at each other.

          You know I haven't got anywhere to go. My parents are dead, I've got no old friends any more because you didn't like the ones I had before so I binned them, never spoke to them, I did that for you, but now there's no one, nowhere to go.

JASON   I never asked you to do anything with your friends.

MEDEA	The women at work, they used to say I was lucky. Good-looking, great dad, solid upright guy. Remember the way you used to touch the back of my neck? I miss that.
JASON	There's things I miss too.
MEDEA	Yeah?
JASON	Yes.
MEDEA	What?
JASON	…
MEDEA	Actually no, don't answer, I… I can't…

She looks at him.

Are those new shoes?

JASON	Yes.
MEDEA	Okay.
JASON	What?
MEDEA	Nothing.
JASON	You don't like them.
MEDEA	Not really.
JASON	Right.
MEDEA	Have you been drinking?
JASON	Not yet.
MEDEA	I have.
JASON	Yeah.
MEDEA	Loads.
JASON	You should sort yourself out, and I'm not saying this out of anything but consideration but you really need to *wash*, at least – this is too much – things are bad but…

He looks at her – genuinely doesn't understand what's happened to her.

I knew it would be difficult, but it was nine months ago. It's time to –

MEDEA   Just nine months? Feels like...

          Like –

          Don't pretend that this isn't ultimately a selfish thing to
          do and also don't pretend that this whole thing isn't
          really down to sex. You got bored of me, it's basically
          that, I don't look like the picture on the box any more.
          I'm wearing out so you want a new one.

          Beat.

JASON   Let me put a few things straight – firstly, as usual,
          you're exaggerating. You didn't save my life. Yes I got
          into trouble, but there were lots of other people ready
          to help, and you didn't give me the kiss of life after we
          got to the beach, you tried but I was fine by then and I
          had to push you off –

MEDEA   Okay so you're making things up now, that's
          interesting –

JASON   And there weren't that many sacrifices.

MEDEA   You weren't breathing when I got there, you'd *died*.

JASON   You didn't give up your friends when you moved
          here –

MEDEA   Er –

JASON   You didn't give up your friends.

MEDEA   I did.

JASON   You didn't give up your friends in London because you
          didn't have any friends in London.

          Did you?

MEDEA   What?

JASON   You didn't have any friends in London.

MEDEA   ...Some.

JASON   You had two and you didn't like either of them. And
          you know as well as I do for a long time it worked.
          Our life. For a long time. When you first came here,
          you loved it, you made friends, you loved the house.
          And then something –

MEDEA   appeared.

JASON   broke.

MEDEA   It was when you met her –

JASON   No it was long before that.

MEDEA   Since she started sitting on your lap or whatever it is she does, only since she got her legs out in your direction that there's been a problem.

JASON   It was long before that.

MEDEA   She's the cause. Little fucking –

JASON   She's the symptom, it had been going on for years, it was how you treated me, we'd be at a party, I'd tell a story, and it didn't matter which story if it was interesting or funny or not, but if I started, you'd roll your eyes behind me, and everyone would laugh.

MEDEA   Your stories are boring.

JASON   You never used to think that.

MEDEA   Well, ooh, actually, sorry, but –

JASON   You got tired of me.

MEDEA   – I did?

JASON   It was... it started when... Tom was small and we'd go to friends', and you'd never let me hold him.

MEDEA   You weren't good with him. He'd cry, whenever you touched him.

JASON   I hardly had a chance.

MEDEA   He knew, he could smell the sort of dad you'd be probably and wanted nothing to do with it.

JASON   Ever since he was born something went wrong. Ever since that moment when he was in your arms, in the hospital bed, and I looked at the two of you, and I stood there for ages, I stood there for a long time, there by the door near the bed watching, waiting for you to look up –

MEDEA   What are you talking about?

JASON   I stood there waiting and you weren't looking at me you were looking at him.

MEDEA   I just didn't know you were there.

JASON   No after that almost from the beginning you were playing games.

MEDEA   Games.

JASON   You didn't seem comfortable, happy, any more. I don't know I don't know what it was maybe you're right and it was me –

MEDEA   Yeah it was.

JASON   Maybe it was me yes, or maybe it was *you*, but something didn't work, between us, from when we became parents and I think it's to our credit, I actually think we should be pleased at how long we tried, for Tom's –

MEDEA   I wasn't *trying* I was happy, I thought we were okay.

JASON   You knew of course you did but you ignored it.

MEDEA   Then why didn't we ever talk about it if it was so obvious and if you were just trying to do the right thing why didn't we sit down –

JASON   I wish we had.

MEDEA   Too late because you didn't ever have a conversation with me, instead you just decided to start having sex with someone else –

JASON   No.

MEDEA   You cut me out entirely.

JASON   Yeah.

MEDEA   Why did you hide it?

JASON   I don't –

MEDEA   Why didn't you tell me?

JASON   It wasn't sex at first, we were friends, and I tried to stop –

MEDEA   Poor you –

JASON   I tried but in the end, yes we slept together but even
          then –

MEDEA   Even then –

JASON   *Stop it!* Even then I thought maybe it was what I
          needed and that maybe it would end and we could
          carry on because I still loved you I still want this to –

MEDEA   You were scared of me. That's why you hid it.

          JASON *laughs.*

JASON   Of course. Everyone's scared of you Medea you're
          fucking terrifying. Of course that's why I didn't tell
          you. And anyway I'm pleased it worked out as it did,
          because it turns out Kate and I love each other, we do,
          and I know you think it's because she's younger and
          better-looking or whatever –

MEDEA   Cos it is.

JASON   But it's not that –

MEDEA   Yes it is.

JASON   – it's not, actually, it's –

MEDEA   It is.

JASON   She's kinder.

MEDEA   More stupid.

JASON   She's just nicer.

MEDEA   Nicer?

JASON   Yes and Medea you're many things many good things
          but even you would have to admit that being nice isn't
          one of them. But I like it. She's generous, and caring
          and I don't expect you to accept it, I'm aware there's
          absolutely no way you can understand it and I don't
          ask you to.

          Yes I miss things, I miss Tom and I miss the life we
          had but at least in the end we're honest. And we're
          here and we're talking. So please, please, I just want
          you to –

          She spits on him. He sighs, bored of this.

This reaction has become predictable and dull. It's going on too long. You had everyone's sympathy at first. You really did. They hated me, and were completely on your side. But now, they can't see why you haven't put it behind you. Why you're still stuck here. All this, they're starting to find it indulgent. That's what they're saying.

You've got complete freedom to move on.

To do whatever you want.

You don't need to live here. You should start again. Get some dignity back, you should at least try and have some of that.

Look at you.

God.

MEDEA

JASON   Sometimes I think. There's no one else here, so I'll say this.

But sometimes I fucking hate women.

Mostly I don't. Mostly I love them, and adore them and want them. But sometimes, I just fucking hate the high voice, the crying, you know I think maybe we'd be better off without them, if we all could have kids without the hips and the tears and all that, we'd probably be happier.

MEDEA *just looks at him.*

MEDEA   I divide men into three groups – wankers, dads, and rapists.

Wankers need a mum, dads treat us like children, and rapists want to fuck us whether we like it or not. That's why it's difficult to find a man. We have to decide. To look after someone, to be patronised all the time, or alternatively, to be constantly screwed around with until we're too old and they *move on.*

JASON   I'm not a rapist.

MEDEA   It's a metaphor Jason.

JASON   Yeah I got that.

MEDEA   Well you're certainly not a *dad*. So that just leaves…

          Pause. MEDEA *cries. Stops herself.*

          Cries again.

          Stops herself.

JASON   Okay.

          If you need anything, call me, I'll send some money over.

MEDEA   I don't want money.

JASON   Or somewhere to stay, I could find a place.

MEDEA   Not with your friends. I hate your friends. They're fat. All of them, really big. Because they're greedy. Get back to your girl. It's past her bedtime and I'm sure you want to get one in before the wedding.

JASON   I want you to find a way to be happy.

MEDEA   Go on. Go. Get married.

          It'll be a disaster.

          He looks at her, then goes.

          MEDEA *stands for a moment. She nearly cries. Then pulls herself together.*

          Another wave of tears – she stops herself. Grabs hold of a bush and rips a handful of leaves out.

          SARAH *appears from next door with a large glass of white wine, slightly drunk.*

          Behind her the sound of the TV plays a Bernard Herrmann soundtrack.

          SARAH *staggers towards* MEDEA, *half-smiling.*

          MEDEA *looks at her.*

SARAH   Do you want some wine? We've got one on the go. We're watching a movie. It's scary. You'd like it. There's blood.

          She laughs. MEDEA *goes back inside the house.*

What are you doing?

SARAH *watches her, laughs, then goes back inside.*
The sound of the TV continues.

Scene Two

TOM*'s bedroom.*

TOM *is in bed, with the bedside lamp on playing his game.*

MEDEA *comes into the room and stands watching him.*

The sound of the TV next door plays a Bernard Herrmann
soundtrack. It's moving, and epic, becoming terrifying.

MEDEA *moves forward and sits on the bed near* TOM.

She takes the game off him and puts it on the side.

Strokes his head.

Then tucks him in, and switches off the light.

She goes, leaving the room.

TOM *switches back on the light, picks up his game.*

A moment.

MEDEA *comes back into the room.*

She takes the game off TOM, *puts it on the floor and smashes it with*
a chair.

She hits it and hits it – it splinters into little bits. A bit goes in her leg.

She stops for a moment. Then keeps going.

Then she switches off the light and leaves.

The music soars – huge – as she comes down the stairs to the living
room, and leans against a wall, staring out the window.

Meanwhile, TOM *switches the lamp back on, goes to a drawer, pulls*
out another computer game, and starts playing.

Scene Three

The front garden. 12.30 a.m. Moonlight.

MEDEA *still stares out the window.*

ANDREW *enters. He's fifty-seven, suited, middle-class, with a suitcase on wheels. He's about to go inside, when he thinks better of it. Puts the case by the door, then goes and sits on his front wall, gets out some cigarettes.*

MEDEA *comes out.*

MEDEA	Hi.

He turns and sees her.

ANDREW	You. Look at you!

She goes to him, kisses him on the cheek. Then they hug.

How are you?

MEDEA	Been better.
ANDREW	I heard.
MEDEA	Maggie told you.
ANDREW	She emailed. Kept me updated. When's the wedding?
MEDEA	Tomorrow.
ANDREW	I'm sorry. But you weren't happy were you? With him.
MEDEA	Yes.
ANDREW	You never looked it.
MEDEA	We were.
ANDREW	Perhaps you're better off.
MEDEA	You don't smoke.
ANDREW	I'm allowed to smoke when I'm away on business that's my rule. But not at home. So this is the last one. When I cross the border, that's it.
MEDEA	You've been gone ages.
ANDREW	Morocco for eight weeks.

MEDEA   Morocco?

ANDREW   It's an emerging market, we're setting up systems –
           you don't care –

MEDEA   No.

ANDREW   Anyway then on the way back I stopped off at the
           house in Spain. We're having a pool done. It's my
           latest go to tempt Maggie out there. Spend all this
           money on a holiday home then she never wants to go.
           Says she'll get a disease.

MEDEA   What disease? It's Spain.

ANDREW   Spanish flu?

           She's anxious, and not sleeping. It's mainly the
           business that keeps her here. It's taken off and she says
           she can't leave it. An obsession. So she never goes out
           there.

MEDEA   You'd like her to.

ANDREW   That was the whole idea – we were driving through the
           countryside and we saw it, with a sign outside and we
           said do you think it might be possible so we parked up,
           knocked on the door and they let us in, gave us a drink,
           showed us round, and it's beautiful, everything you
           could want and the two of us, we dreamed about owning
           it. Six months later it all went through, but by that point
           – I don't know – she said she was pleased but –

           She never talked about it really. Never shows much
           interest.

           I don't mind really. Gives me a place to get away, on
           my own. Every man needs that…

           I like the trees. The trees there at night, they rustle in
           the air, you can sit out all night.

           And think.

MEDEA   Sounds good.

           ANDREW *gets out his iPhone. Finds the pictures.
           Hands it to* MEDEA.

ANDREW   There.

She takes it and looks at the pictures.

The pool's going round the side, there, so you still have the view.

It's not a big house but it's...

She flicks through a few pictures.

How's Tom taking it all?

MEDEA   He doesn't talk to me. I don't talk to him.

She gives him back the phone.

Can I have one of those?

ANDREW   You don't.

MEDEA   I've started.

ANDREW   Not good for you.

MEDEA   Gets me out of the house.

He gives her one.

Nick Carter says I have to leave by tomorrow.

ANDREW   Could've seen that coming too. Where are you going to go?

MEDEA   ...

ANDREW

MEDEA   You want children don't you?

ANDREW   What?

MEDEA   You always have.

ANDREW   How do you – I never told anyone – I never –

MEDEA   How old is she –

ANDREW   Maggie? Forty-one this year –

MEDEA   The clock's ticking.

ANDREW   Yes

MEDEA   But she's not keen.

ANDREW   ...

MEDEA   And you're desperate for a little one. As you get
           older –

ANDREW   How do you –

MEDEA   I know things.

           Beat.

ANDREW   She doesn't want to discuss it but – We've tried. We
           used to anyway. Now she's too busy. Maybe she knows
           she can't and – There was... we had tests. They said it
           was her and they went over things that could be done,
           things she could do but she didn't...

           She's not maternal I don't think.

           She used to be. But something must've happened, and
           she lost all the desire for it.

           Yes. I think of having a son. Or a daughter.

           What it would be like.

MEDEA

ANDREW   It must be wonderful. It must make up for everything
           that's going on, to know that you've got that
           astonishing little boy.

           Pause.

MEDEA   I hurt my leg.

           She lifts it up to show him.

           I smashed up Tom's game and a bit of it went in. It was
           bleeding for ages.

ANDREW   You should put something on it.

MEDEA   Don't have anything.

ANDREW   We've got a bandage I'm sure, inside.

MEDEA   No your wife'll come out. I'd rather bleed to death.

ANDREW   She's not that bad.

MEDEA   She hates me.

ANDREW   She doesn't.

MEDEA   She's having a wall built.

ANDREW   That's not to do with you.

MEDEA   I tore up her flowers, it's all to do with me.

         He looks at her. Then reaches out and touches her leg.

ANDREW   Ouch.

MEDEA   Ouch.

         Pause.

         What am I to you?

ANDREW   To you? What are you? You mean...

         You're...

         You're our neighbour.

MEDEA   Am I like a daughter to you is that what you think I am?

ANDREW   What?

MEDEA   Because there's only, what, a few years between us, fifteen years?

ANDREW   Not a daughter no I don't think of you like that. You're a friend.

MEDEA   You do think of me though. Don't you?

ANDREW   I was worried about you when Maggie told me what was happening.

MEDEA   That's not what I mean.

ANDREW   What do you mean?

MEDEA   I've seen how you smile at me in the mornings I remember when you used to go to work I knew what that meant.

ANDREW   It didn't mean anything.

MEDEA   Yeah come on you know.

ANDREW   Friendly.

MEDEA   Yeah right friendly exactly, friendly not like friends though is it?

         She touches his face.

         Friendly like – oh shit –

ANDREW   Look –

MEDEA   I'm not very good at this.

ANDREW   It's late, you're going through a lot, shall we call it a
           night?

MEDEA   No, okay, stop, here's the deal you want a son, I need
           somewhere to go how about I live in your house in
           Spain, your wife she doesn't need to know she never
           goes there, so Tom and I that's where we go, and he
           goes to school there and starts talking again and
           becomes bilingual a major bonus in today's globalised
           world, particularly Spanish a fast-growing tongue,
           speaking of which whenever you visit we can have sex
           and I give you a child. You won't have a problem with
           me, I'm Mrs Fertile, I make babies like most women
           buy shoes, I've had abortions, three, one before Tom,
           two afterwards, I'm telling you, it's like a factory in
           there, they keep on coming, so assuming the problem
           isn't you he'll be born in a matter of months and grow
           up there with a brother and a mother, and if your wife
           ever finds out about me, she certainly doesn't ever
           need to know about who his father is. It's a win-win.
           Guilt-free. Everything you're not getting from her you
           get from me and I get the sun.

           And far away from here.

ANDREW   Medea –

MEDEA   It would work.

ANDREW   Did you just think of all that?

MEDEA   Yeah – Forget what I was saying before we don't need
           to feel anything, I know it sounds exploitative but I'm
           a modern woman exercising my options and making a
           choice.

           What do you think?

ANDREW   …

MEDEA   What do you think?

           We get on.

           It could work.

           I'm serious.

ANDREW   Are you?

MEDEA   Yes.

          But I need to know now. I have to be gone by
          tomorrow evening. I need an answer.

ANDREW   We can't. Medea. I don't even know you.

          Not really.

MEDEA   I could go there at least I could go there for now while
          you think about it.

          I know we don't know each other that well, but actually
          I don't know anyone that well any more. You're the best
          I've got.

          Please.

          You've just come back from the house. You've got the
          key in your pocket.

          ANDREW *smiles. Puts out his cigarette. Reaches into
          his pocket, gets out his keys and unwinds the right one.*

ANDREW   There's only the front door lock. That's all you need.

          I'll email you the details.

MEDEA   Yeah. Good.

ANDREW   Can't believe I'm doing this.

          Beat.

MEDEA   When's the pool finished?

ANDREW   Two months.

          They smile at each other.

          *He leans over, kisses her on the cheek, turns and goes
          inside.*

          MEDEA *sits.*

          Time passes.

          MEDEA *texts someone.*

          Time passes.

          Then SARAH *emerges with a glass of wine, quite drunk.*

SARAH   Did he just kiss you?

          MEDEA *puts her hand out for the glass.* SARAH
          smiles, confused, and gives it to her.

          She drinks.

MEDEA   You know what I'm doing?

SARAH   No.

MEDEA   I'm witching. It's like bitching but weirder. It's
          scheming, it's conjuring and voodoo and telling the
          future. He's going to die. Jason's going to come to a
          very bad end.

SARAH   You always say that.

MEDEA   He's going to turn up for his wedding day and find his
          bride stuck like a pig in her dress going round and
          round, with the guests held at gunpoint forced to eat
          burgers made from her thighs.

          No – I'll make her have sex with her father while Jason
          watches. Or I'll make him have sex with her father
          while she watches.

          No –

SARAH   Shut up.

MEDEA   You don't like it go away I'm on my land. Okay, I'll
          kill Tom and send him in pieces to the wedding.
          Individually wrapped.

          I'll make presents for her that she'll – Okay.

          Yeah.

          Yeah.

SARAH   What?

MEDEA   No you wanted me to shut up I'm shutting up that's
          what I'm doing. You don't want to know, goodbye
          goodbye.

          SARAH *goes back to her house.*

Scene Four

MEDEA *checks her stars on her phone.*

She waits.

Time passes.

Scene Five

2.30 a.m.

MEDEA *looks up at the stars.*

JASON *appears.*

JASON   Forgiven?

MEDEA   You know the stars.

JASON   Yeah I've seen them –

MEDEA   I mean astrology. It's rubbish I know but every day
             recently I check online for my prediction and it's
             always bad. Awful. It says today's going to contain a
             sadness, a friend betrays you, a difficult decision
             awaits. I look at the others and they're positive and
             negative in equal measure, but Aries, for the last six
             months, Aries is bad every single time. I started to
             think you were fixing it somehow, just to get at me, but
             I know that's stupid.

             You ever think it's all pre-prepared? No, preordained.

             You believe in fate?

JASON   No.

MEDEA   That this was always going to happen.

JASON   No.

MEDEA   No. Anyway, I couldn't sleep so I checked my stars,
             and this time it said 'a change for the better', 'the past
             is left behind' and that's the most positive prediction

I've had for a long time, and then I realised, it was all finished. At last, I'd let it go.

Yes. I forgive you.

JASON   And to celebrate you invite me over.

MEDEA   How's the bride?

JASON   At home. It's the night before the wedding.

MEDEA   You always liked tradition.

JASON   I never wanted to hurt you.

MEDEA   I believe that.

JASON   Really?

MEDEA

Beat.

JASON   I still don't know –

MEDEA   What?

JASON   When you're honest.

MEDEA   Doesn't matter now does it? That's the best thing for you, about all this, isn't it? You never need to worry about me ever again.

JASON   Of course I'll worry about you.

MEDEA   I mean in the future you'll never need to trust me.

          When you were standing there earlier you looked good – especially when you got annoyed, I mean come on the more we went at it, the more there was something – zzzzt zzzzt *electric* going on between us, even after everything, something chemical I thought so – anyway, I wondered if you wanted to say goodbye.

JASON   What?

MEDEA   Yeah.

JASON   Medea.

MEDEA   We've got nothing to lose either of us, at the moment you're still technically single, so am I, there's no reason not to, we're both adults and it'll be good. It always was.

JASON   Is this a game of yours? Are you going to wait until
             I've got my clothes off and then point and laugh?

MEDEA   No.

JASON   Like you did before.

MEDEA   Yeah okay I admit that was a low point, no I'm not
             going to laugh.

             This is what I need.

             I think we'll both feel better.

             Beat.

JASON   Some female spiders eat their male counterparts after
             copulation.

MEDEA   That's exactly what I had in mind.

JASON   Yes.

MEDEA   Yes. I'm going to eat you. Take your shirt off.

JASON   Here?

MEDEA   Yeah.

             He does. She goes and touches him. Kisses him.

             I was lying.

             I still hate you.

JASON   I know.

             She leads him into the house.

             As they climb the stairs, TOM *wakes up, stands in the
             middle of the room and listens.*

             MEDEA *and* JASON *go into her bedroom.*

MEDEA   Wait.

             She puts on some music, quietly.

             They fall on the bed, and kiss.

             Fade.

ACT THREE

Scene One

The curtains are open – in contrast to before, the whole place has a bright sunny feeling.

JASON *is sat anxiously in the front room waiting.*

Upstairs, TOM *is sat playing on another loud computer game, wearing a suit, as* SARAH *brushes his hair. She's also dressed for the wedding – and is hungover. The game is driving her mad.*

Meanwhile, MEDEA *is putting the presents into larger bags.*

SARAH   Tom?

Tom?

Tom do you mind turning that down?

It's just I'm not feeling that well this morning.

Got a headache.

He doesn't respond.

Tom?

She's annoyed now.

Can I just…

She takes it –

How do you turn down the…?

She switches a button. The whole thing stops suddenly.

Oh. Well… There.

She gives it back to him.

That's better isn't it?

TOM *puts the game down.* SARAH *brushes his hair.*

MEDEA *enters with the bags.*

MEDEA   All right? What do you think of his suit? Pam got it for me last week, I like the little waistcoat.

SARAH   Are you sure you want him to go?

MEDEA   Absolutely.

SARAH   You said you didn't.

MEDEA   I can't live like this forever, and Jason's his father.

SARAH   Just the ceremony.

MEDEA   Yes let him see it, you go to the reception he gives them the presents and then says his goodbyes. We've got to be packed up and gone by the end of the day.

SARAH   Where are you going?

MEDEA   Don't let him drink alcohol.

SARAH   Of course not.

MEDEA   Or eat too much.

SARAH   He doesn't eat enough if you ask me. Medea. Where are you going?

MEDEA   What?

SARAH   Where are you going?

MEDEA   Doesn't matter.

Beat.

Come on. You'll be late. Tom, put your coat on.

SARAH *stays and helps* TOM *with his coat.* MEDEA *leaves and goes down the stairs.*

Sorry to keep you waiting – thanks for coming to pick him up, it's right that he should go there with you, as you can see I've taken your advice, opened the curtains, moved on, *flowers*, you were completely right. It was indulgent. Of course he should go to his father's wedding and it's time for me to move out as well, so you'll be pleased to hear that by the evening I'll be off. I wanted you to see, to be reassured. It worked.

SARAH   What worked?

TOM *and* SARAH *come down the stairs,* TOM *now wearing the coat.*

JASON   Hi Sarah.

SARAH   Hi.

JASON   How are you?

SARAH   Yeah. Fine. You know. It's all right. Is it? If I look after Tom at the wedding.

JASON   Of course. I'm pleased he's going to be there.

           (*To* TOM.) Hi.

           TOM *looks at him.*

SARAH   He's missed you.

           TOM *looks at him.*

           A moment.

MEDEA   Tom. Hug your father.

           TOM *looks at* MEDEA.

           Go on. We like him now. It's okay. We're friends.

           TOM *goes and hugs* JASON. JASON *has missed him.*

JASON   You all right? You been all right?

           He holds him out – looks at him.

           I like the suit. You like mine?

           TOM *doesn't reply.*

MEDEA   Oh!

           MEDEA *cries.*

JASON   What? Oh what now? I thought everything was –

MEDEA   Sorry. I'm still not. It's…

           Sorry.

           I had a thought. Tom have you been to the toilet?

           TOM *doesn't reply.*

           Go to the toilet. Go on. Upstairs.

           He does.

SARAH   Should I…

MEDEA   Do you need the toilet?

SARAH   No.

MEDEA   Right then.

SARAH   – but maybe you want some time –

MEDEA   No. Stay there. You can watch. Jason, I want Tom to
live with you. You're going to have a family, I'm sure
she wants children which means Tom could have
brothers to play with and everything you can give him.
I'm leaving, going a long way away, I don't know how
things are going to be, you know what it's like you're
in a much better position, so I thought possibly, he
could live with you two. I think he'd be happier.

JASON   Kate wants a new start, I don't know if I can ask –

MEDEA   They'd get on I'm sure, and once I'm out of the house
and forgotten she'll be fine. It's me she's got the
problem with.

It would give him a family again.

Beat.

JASON   I'll ask.

MEDEA   You'd like it.

JASON   Of course.

MEDEA   You'll ask?

JASON   After the wedding yes.

MEDEA   How is she? Kate. How's she feeling?

JASON   She's worried you'll turn up I think she's nervous
you'll do something.

MEDEA   Like what?

JASON   …

MEDEA   No. I'll be too busy getting ready here. Don't worry I
won't be anywhere near your marriage. Tell her it's all
my problem, not hers, she's done nothing wrong. I've
got some presents for her. I'll give them to Tom, and
he can give them to her, afterwards. Sorry I didn't get
anything off the list but –

JASON   Of course –

MEDEA   It's your mother's evening gown, and the tiara. The
           ones she gave me.

JASON   Medea –

MEDEA   Your mum said she wanted them for your wife, so I
           thought I should pass them on and if we're honest I
           never fitted in the dress and the tiara looked stupid, but
           I've seen pictures of your Kate and she's exactly the
           right size. I thought she could wear them at the
           reception. You know the ones I'm talking about?

JASON   Of course.

MEDEA   I thought it would be nice if Tom gave them to her, a
           gesture. I mean he's never even met her before has he?
           But I wanted to check with you that you didn't think it
           was weird.

JASON   No. Not weird.

MEDEA   Good.

JASON   Thank you.

MEDEA   …

           TOM *comes down the stairs.*

           All right then. Off you all go!

           MEDEA *opens the door.*

           Have a nice time.

JASON   Wait.

MEDEA   What?

           JASON *still doesn't quite trust her. But he turns and
           they all go outside.*

           As they do –

           Tom. Here. Take these.

           *She gives him the two present bags and he goes off
           with* JASON, *leaving* SARAH.

SARAH   You'll be all right, on your own today?

MEDEA   Fine. I might give Pam a call.

SARAH   Pam?

MEDEA   Yeah. She's normally up for a chat at the weekend.

SARAH   Pam's going to the wedding.

MEDEA   What?

SARAH   He invited her. She said she was friends to you both.

MEDEA   She was my friend.

SARAH   I thought she would've told you.

MEDEA   No. But none of my business. Fine. Okay. Fine. Anyway.
          Have a good time. I've got stuff to do. Got to pack.

          Go on. Go. You'll be late. Go.

          SARAH *walks off and* MEDEA *waves.*

          Once they've gone, she stops for a moment. The
          WORKMAN *is next door.*

          They stare at each other for a long time. Then –

WORKMAN Don't.

          They look at each other.

          MEDEA *goes back inside.*

Scene Two

MEDEA*'s bedroom.*

MEDEA *puts a suitcase out on the bed. Opens it. Goes to her
wardrobe –*

Looks at it all.

Shuts the door again.

Zips the bag up and puts it away. Walks downstairs.

In the living room.

She gets the remote and switches on the television. Watches.

ACT FOUR

Scene One

Outside the house.

As SARAH *and* TOM *arrive,* MEDEA *comes out of the house.*

MEDEA   Hello! How was it?

SARAH   Oh – amazing! I mean it was a big thing, church wedding, very traditional then on to this hotel, Cranbrook, do you know it –

MEDEA   The house.

SARAH   Cranbrook House that's it.

MEDEA   We used to go for tea there sometimes.

SARAH   Well that's where it was and I mean they'd really gone to town. Sorry you probably don't want to hear this.

MEDEA   It's fine.

SARAH   Well it was very nice anyway, but as you wanted we gave Kate the presents didn't we – I think Jason had told her to expect something, so as soon as she arrived at Cranbrook, we gave them to her and he explained what they were.

MEDEA   She liked them?

SARAH   She was very touched. I don't think she – well. She's still not your biggest fan as you can imagine, but – then Jason asked her – you know – about…

MEDEA   Tom go inside please, play your game.

He does.

SARAH   Jason asked about Tom staying with them, and she loved the idea. She said she thought he was a sweet boy. And that perhaps you were better off on your own. Making a new start. That for whatever reason this place was bringing you down, and maybe Tom and

Jason and her were all part of that and it would be
better for everyone but particularly you, if you could
leave free of all of it, and start again. Not have the
stigma of being a single mum.

MEDEA   Thoughtful.

SARAH   She doesn't know what she's talking about really and
she was flush with all of it of course, but the point is,
he can live with them. And that's what you wanted
isn't it?

That is what you asked him for, in the end. I heard you.

MEDEA *is crying. From inside, the faint sound of a
computer game.*

What?

MEDEA   It's really good of you to take him along.

SARAH   It was a pleasure.

MEDEA   I need to get on now.

SARAH   Do you want a hand?

MEDEA   We have to leave by six.

SARAH   Are you dropping Tom off?

MEDEA   What?

SARAH   At Jason's?

MEDEA   Oh.

SARAH   You could leave him with me if that's –

MEDEA   Yes.

SARAH   If that's easier?

MEDEA   Yes. Yes. I'll do that. Thank you. Can you go now?

MEDEA *opens the door.*

SARAH   Right. Well. We'll see you in a couple of hours then.

MEDEA   Yes. Bye.

SARAH *leaves and* MEDEA *quickly shuts the door.*

Scene Two

TOM*'s bedroom.*

TOM *sits on the bed, with the duvet up round him.*

MEDEA *enters.*

Pause.

MEDEA   When did you stop talking? I can't remember.

Was it that night when your dad and me shouted at
each other, when I held that knife up and he was
swearing then we saw you watching on the stairs? Or
was it when he left?

Perhaps you never spoke. All children sound the same
really don't they? I can't remember the sound of your
voice. I remember the things you said. 'What's that?'
'Mummy.' 'Please don't say mummy and daddy I'm
grown up now.' You were always polite. I like that.

I do love you Tom. I know you don't think I do but –

Maybe I –

Look at me. Look at me sweetheart.

He does. She hugs him.

Come here. Come here. I know it's been difficult.
You're so small. You look to us, I know you look to us
for guidance to know how to be in the world, but it's
probably important to say that we don't know, adults
don't know what they're doing at all, they never have,
and the only thing you learn as you get older is how
short life is, and how you've already messed up more
of it than you've got left.

She lets him go.

You look a bit like him. Don't you. You've got his hair.

She touches his face.

Anyway, there's some news. You're not going to be
living with me any more. I don't know if this is a good
thing to you, because I haven't got a clue what you

think about anything these days, but we're going to move out of the house and you're going to move in with Daddy, sorry, Dad, and Kate. In their big new house. Would you like that? Because that's what's going to happen. And maybe they'll have another child, a brother or a sister, like you always wanted, and they're going to get richer and richer over the next ten years so you're going to have everything you could want. And you won't see your mum again.

What do you think about that?

I'd be really sad if my mum said that to me.

I wouldn't want her to go.

Tom.

I don't think you're going to have a good life. With your father, I think you're going to be brought up in a terrible way, in a way that places emphasis on success, and winning and money and nothing else. In a really stupid way that puts power over intelligence. What would you rather be now? Powerful or clever?

At least you're not a woman.

Pause.

You're not going to be happy with him are you?

You want to stay with your mummy.

She stands up.

Moves away.

All right. We'll stick together. You and me.

We're better off without him, aren't we?

TOM *gets off the bed, and hugs* MEDEA, *tightly.*

She has a moment. Then hugs him back.

Outside – PAM *arrives – screaming –*

PAM   Medea! *Medea!*

MEDEA *leaves.*

Scene Three

The front garden.

PAM *is there. She's come from the car, dressed for a wedding. She's fraught.*

MEDEA *opens the door and comes out. Over the next,* SARAH *emerges from next door.*

PAM   It was you, wasn't it? You always said you could do things I thought it was your thing your joke.

SARAH   What's going on?

MEDEA   What happened?

PAM   You know what happened! What happened was exactly what you planned, the presents, Tom gave them to her, as soon as they arrived at the reception, it was beautifully choreographed by Jason. Tom went up to her, gave them the boxes and kissed her on the cheek, and Jason explained they were his mother's from her wedding day and they had been given by you and all was good. Kate smiled and opened the boxes and the tiara had the diamonds and the dress was beautiful, so much more beautiful than the one she was wearing, and everyone said 'Put it on, put it on' so she giggled, really pleased, and off she went, and everyone waited with anticipation, it was then that Sarah took Tom off, so she doesn't know what happened next.

SARAH   No. No I don't –

PAM   Kate appeared at the top of the stairs, in this dress this beautiful, like, *gown* it must have been from the fifties, and wearing a tiara that *gleamed* properly sparkled and they had plaited her hair around it and the dress fitted perfectly, tightly to her figure and she's got a good figure and I'll tell you when she was there at the top of the stairs in that moment every woman watching thought, 'I give up, I have never looked that beautiful, I will never look that beautiful,' and she walked down the stairs to Jason and they started to play music, and none of this was in the plan but the two of them started to dance, to this jazz music played live – all the music was live of course – but after a while, she started to seem, uncomfortable, and she asked to stop, we could see, I was close to her and we could see she was sweating, and itching… then her legs gave way, and she fell back into a chair, and she was completely, like, white now? White as the dress. Someone shouted for a doctor. People tried to get to her to help but stood back when they saw this white foam, froth, coming out of her mouth, her eyes rolling back in the sockets, her arms starting to like punch out, stopping anyone getting too close, and then we all saw that the tiara, that you gave her, it was making red marks in her head, she scratched at herself to get it off, but it was burning, into her head. A bridesmaid tried to take it off her but it was so tightly plaited, and then Kate lurched forward, vomiting all over the dance floor, then fell over and screamed, screamed like you've never heard anyone before, more than childbirth, more than anything I've heard, crying screeching for help, the dress itself was eating away at her, underneath, and the tiara was pressing into her forehead, blood rolling down her face which was all swollen up, so you couldn't recognise her. People didn't know what to do – Jason stood back, shocked, he didn't touch her but then her dad, who'd been outside, he ran in, and went straight to his daughter, he knelt down and hugged her on the ground saying 'What's happened?', and she was still crying, sort of moaning, and then he – her father – he tried to get up to get help, but he found the dress was stuck to him, and he couldn't move away, and she was holding on to him, the dress burning him now, he tried to get up, but the dress was tearing his skin off and he tried and tried to get up but both of them got tired, from wrestling on the floor and then they both stopped moving, not breathing any more, they were both dead.

Beat.

SARAH   You're making it up. This is something you'd agreed with Jason you don't think she'll leave and –

PAM *gets out her phone, finds the file.*

– you want to *scare* her into going, I thought you were her friend.

PAM *presses play and gives it to* SARAH.

We hear jazz music, a happy crowd. Then heavy breathing, panic, and then just screaming, coming out of the tiny speakers – SARAH *watches.*

PAM   I ran out of there, to my car, and I came here, because I know it was you –

The video finishes.

– you did something to that dress and the tiara and the police are going to get you and you'll be locked away forever like you should be but I wanted to say that nothing that happened to you justifies that nothing.

She slaps MEDEA.

You're not mad are you?

MEDEA   No.

PAM   You're not ill, or deranged or depressed.

MEDEA   No.

PAM

MEDEA

PAM   Are you going to run away? They'll be here in seconds.

SARAH   Medea…

MEDEA *turns and goes back inside the house, locking the door.*

A moment.

Then –

Where's Tom?

In there?

PAM   Not our problem. I'm calling the police.

She does.

ACT FIVE

Scene One

TOM *is in bed.*

MEDEA *takes a knife from the kitchen and goes upstairs.*

TOM *hears her coming and stands.*

MEDEA *enters the bedroom, sees* TOM, *turns, and walks out again, back down to the kitchen.*

She panics.

Is nearly sick.

TOM *follows her and watches her from the bottom of the stairs. Then runs back up to his room.*

MEDEA *follows with the knife.*

Scene Two

Outside. The front garden.

The WORKMAN *is making a noise trying to get in the door.*

SARAH *is standing.* PAM *is on the phone.*

PAM   Thank you, yes, yes –

           Yeah.

           Yeah.

           Thank you. Bye.

           They're on their way.

           A moment. They wait.

           JASON *arrives, his clothes with blood on them.*

PAM   Oh.

JASON	Where is she? In there?
PAM	Jason. I'm so sorry.

He stops and cries. Can't go on for a moment.

PAM goes to him. Wants to hug him, but it's awkward.

She reaches out and puts an arm round him.

Suddenly JASON turns on SARAH.

JASON	Did you know? Did you know what was going to happen?
SARAH	No.
JASON	You took the presents – you carried the bags –
SARAH	I didn't –
JASON	You let her put on the dress, you let her dance, and then –
SARAH	I'm sorry.
JASON	Then she…

She…

JASON stands and screams up at the house.

Medea!

Pause.

Medea!

SARAH	Tom's in there.
JASON	He…
SARAH	He went inside, and she's double-locked the door.

A moment.

JASON	What did she say to you? What else did she say before they went inside?

But there's a hacking sound – a crashing and a breaking.

What?

*Tiles and rubble seem to fall – smoke and dust pouring
down the stairs – and then –*

*The roof tiles fly off from the top of the house. Breaking
through is* MEDEA, *with an axe. She has a stereo with
her playing music.*

Oh God! Oh…

*She climbs through and pushes on to the roof. Then she
reaches down, and pulls* TOM *up to lie next to her.
Puts the stereo at her feet.*

MEDEA   This was my dad's axe. Only thing I've got left of his.
He travelled a lot but when he came home he liked
nothing more than chopping animals to bits. For fun. I
don't think you ever knew that.

Tom's dead.

JASON *flings himself at the house.*

You can't get in and if you could it's too late anyway,
you wanted to help you should have shown him you
cared.

JASON   This had nothing to do with me, I love my son. I
wanted him to live with us. / I hated being away from
him –

MEDEA   No! You didn't want him, you threw everything of his
away, his happiness, his voice, his home, his trust. You
made life mean nothing. We put everything in you and
you walked out on us.

JASON   I can't… I can't!… no…

MEDEA   Shut up.

JASON, *utterly distraught, sits on the ground.*

I loved coming home and we'd all worked hard all
three of us, at the end of a long day and we'd be here
in the house we wanted, this house, the house you'd
found and I'd got an apron that you'd wear whenever
you'd cook and we'd open the back door to let the
evening air in, and we'd sit round, and tell each other
about our days and he learned what a good father he
had and a hard-working mother, and he was growing

up to be something special, and life meant something. I loved him then. I loved him then.

I'm going to Spain, I'm going to Spain with him, and in the sun I'm going to bury him under a tree, and he's going to always be remembered for the maths test, for coming second in the egg-and-spoon race at playgroup, for the picture he drew of his daddy coming home in his new car, and there will be a headstone that will say his name that we gave him.

This morning I still believed in God. I thought he gave us a house and a world and happiness and life. But now I know there's nothing.

Nothing except these bricks and that road and life and death and the waiting in between.

And unless he wants to appear right now, and sort this out, I'm going to Spain.

So.

God?

God.

Now's your chance.

A long pause.

Light breaks through cloud.

Sirens.

Blackout.